STYLE AND FORM
IN AMERICAN PROSE

STYLE AND FORM
IN
American Prose

BY
GORHAM B. MUNSON

KENNIKAT PRESS, INC./PORT WASHINGTON, N. Y.

STYLE AND FORM IN AMERICAN PROSE

Copyright 1929 by Gorham B. Munson
Reissued 1969 by Kennikat Press
Published by arrangement with Doubleday & Company, Inc.

Library of Congress Catalog Card No: 68-26291
Manufactured in the United States of America

Dedicated affectionately

to

E. H. *and* S. H.

NOTE

THE *chapters I have written for this book are condensa-
tions and recastings of lectures in a course on Style and
Form in American Prose which I was privileged to give
at the New School for Social Research, New York City,
in the fall of 1927. With the exception of a few notes on
Emerson, William James, and Santayana, which appeared in* The Figure in the Carpet, *a magazine
devoted to prose and edited by members of my course, I
have not hitherto published any of the material presented.*

*To all the publishers and authors who have given permis-
sion for reprinting the illustrative passages, I offer my
thanks: my indebtedness to each is separately acknowledged at the beginning of each extract. I regret that copyright complications will not allow the reprinting of an
example of Stephen Crane's short fiction and of a portion
of William Vaughn Moody's* THE FAITH HEALER.

G. B. M.

CONTENTS

Part One

INTRODUCTORY

Part Two

THE LANGUAGE OF IDEAS

CONTENTS

Part Three

IMAGINATIVE PROSE

Part Four

OTHER FORMS OF PROSE

CONTENTS

Part Five

THE FUTURE OF AMERICAN PROSE

Part One

INTRODUCTORY

CHAPTER I

THE BASIS OF PROSE

THE SPIRIT OF THE GOOD READER

IT IS odd that Robert Louis Stevenson began his enchanting essay on "Style in Literature" with these assertions: "There is nothing more disenchanting to man than to be shown the springs and mechanism of any art. All our arts and occupations lie wholly on the surface; it is on the surface that we perceive their beauty, fitness and significance; and to pry below is to be appalled by their emptiness and shocked by the coarseness of the strings and pulleys." Odder still is a sequent statement that "many are conscious as each new disclosure of a diminution in the ardor of their pleasure."

Not that a prejudice against peering into literary masterpieces to discover how they produce their effects does not exist, for no one can deny that many readers are opposed to the analysis of literary style and form. But this is truly the protest of laziness refusing to set to work to increase the sum of pleasure to be won from literature. Inertness, however, is offset by the fact that there is something in the mind of the reader that not only asks What? but whispers How? and Why? There is in the reader a submerged curiosity that in low tones prompts him to delve not just into the springs and mechanisms of the arts but into those vaster ones of life itself. If the reader listens to that quiet questioning, if he overcomes his inertia, he will then

3

enter into a new series of delights arising from his perceptions of the author's skill; he will learn that below the surface and concealed from the passive reader there glow, in
the greater works of art, a deeper beauty, fitness, and significance; he will experience with each fresh discovery a
heightening of the ardor of his pleasure.

The reason for this is the same as that which spurs the
writer to master his craft: the love of overcoming difficulties. In that he does not appear in person before the
reader, the writer is at the outset heavily handicapped. By
the use of printed words alone he must affect the reader as
potently as he could were he free to gesture, frown, vary his
tone of voice, move about, and act in front of him. This
absence of his person is the origin of the difficulties the
writer naturally encounters. But more than that, as we
shall presently see in this book, in the degree of his excellence as a writer, he proposes and creates difficulties for
himself in his selected medium. The measure of his success is the extent to which he overcomes his encountered
and created difficulties, and the zest of his calling depends
precisely upon the effort to overcome.

"Added difficulty, added beauty," says Stevenson after
he has forgotten the excuses of lazy readers, and it is just
so, and the reader is the more pleased. The spirit of the
good reader and that of the good writer are alike. Although they are related to each other as master and subject,
as producer of effects and recipient of effects, they are both
gallant in their attitude toward difficulties. The one encounters with gusto the inherent difficulties of composition,
interposes fresh ones, and surmounts them by dint of constant effort making. The other, the good reader, accepts the
limitations of the printed medium, proposes to himself the

rôle not alone of impressionability but of comprehending the "Beautiful Means" as well as the "Blessed Meaning," and strives to attain the fullest possible understanding of the magic exerted by literary masters.

It may be that the reader also aspires to be a writer, that he too is fascinated by this art of communicating effects through a restricted medium to absent persons, and in that event he may find the tradition of magicians inspiriting. No magician ever by explication teaches his tricks to a neophyte, nor indeed to any other magician. He performs them for an audience: let who can learn to do them. The method—it is a point of honor to have no other—is simply observation of successes and then practice by oneself to duplicate them. The reader who wishes to write must do the same: study the methods and devices of the magician with words and phrases and then practice persistently by himself the secret operations he has divined. Fortunately for him, criticism has an honorable standing, and the art of writing is to some degree teachable.

But it is to the reader first of all, and to a particular kind of reader, that this book is addressed. That kind of reader is the one who, reading Emerson's essay on History, might have marked for his own pondering the statement that "the student is to read history actively and not passively; to esteem his own life the text, and books the commentary." Still it happens that in acquiring as a reader a more extended and vivid awareness of literary texts one does, by the way, disengage from one's reflections a great many practical hints for the art of writing. Writers, it has been aptly said, should write as such, and rewrite as readers, and this may easily be varied for the reader: read as a reader, but reread as a writer.

WHAT IS PROSE?

Quite casually many readers have wandered into the "Sacred Wood" of literature and discovered that it is a rich large hunting preserve for the human spirit. As it were, one dislodges birds which flutter away, or sees hares racing to safety, or hears perhaps the distant tread of elephantine creatures; or occasionally one pauses at the sight of a stray panther sniffing against the wind. The game in that Wood is plentiful and ever issues invitations to the huntsman. In plainer words, the study of literature raises numerous and various questions, and among them there is a question that may be likened to a veritable panther on the prowl, namely, What is prose? Naturally, we cannot bring down our quarry at once and so we withdraw to the edge of the forest to estimate the beast's size and powers and to equip ourselves with what arms and provisions we shall need for the hunt.

Two ways immediately suggest themselves for trapping the question and caging it within an answer. One may try to ascertain what, in terms of the medium itself, prose is; and one may try to find out what the psychological sources for prose writing are as distinguished from those human springs that well forth in poetry. For the first endeavor, very excellent help is at hand. *The History of English Prose Rhythm,* by George Saintsbury,[1] is a wonderful arsenal of ideas for those who wish to think about the nature of prose.

---

[1]This work is indispensable to the student of prose, but how little known it is! One would think that it was written like most textbooks, flat, obvious, dull affairs, the more heinous in that they—grammars, rhetorics, literary histories, and the like—do deal with highly interesting subject matter and the dullness is only in the minds of the writers of them. But Saintsbury writes with gusto, and his book is delectable.

AN ANSWER IN TERMS OF THE MEDIUM

Saintsbury begins with two seed thoughts: Aristotle's description of prose as "neither possessing metre nor destitute of rhythm," and Quintilian's remark that "we cannot even speak except in longs and shorts, the materials of feet." From these seeds Saintsbury causes a mighty tree to flourish, one that thrusts up from Anglo-Saxon through Middle English to Modern English and its two great branching traditions, the ornate polyphonic grand prose and the standard plain-style prose. The contention of Aristotle is thoroughly sustained: good prose does not fall into fixed measures of recurrent beats but it does abide by orderly though irregular rhythms. Quintilian's remark is equally fruitful: it yields a well-developed system for scanning prose rhythms.

At the close of *The History of English Prose Rhythm* Saintsbury himself lays down a formulation no whit less important than those of the two ancient critics and perhaps also destined to become a classical utterance for future ponderers on prose. "As the essence of verse-metre," he says, "is its identity (at least in equivalence) and recurrence, so the essence of prose-rhythm lies in variety and divergence." Thus we have a polarity which is explained at some length, between prosody and prose: the first adheres to the principle of Sameness and the second to the principle of Variety.

This is not a new thought. Many writers had divined, before Stevenson said it, that in prose "the one rule is to be infinitely various," but no one has been quite so diligent as Saintsbury in proving that it is so, in giving the principle the most explicit formulation possible, and in educing specific differentiations between rhythmical practices peculiar to poetry and rhythmical practices pertaining solely to prose. In the next chapter some of these differentiations will be mentioned.

Meanwhile, we shall adopt it as already proven elsewhere that the principle of Variety is the life principle of prose, but the reader who has not yet satisfied himself on this point would do best to consider the principle as a mere hypothesis to be tested by his own reading of prose. Let that reader also, if he wishes, take a provisional stand on the statement that prose is rhythmical, but not metrical, for he benefits himself most who submits authority to his personal verification.

AN ANSWER IN TERMS OF PSYCHOLOGY

If now we ask, From what part of the psychology of the human being does prose come and whence comes poetry? we shift the ground of our approach and, if we are successful, gain a psychological distinction. It happens that there is a consensus of opinion on the answers to these questions. "Prose is the language of exact thinking," wrote an English literary critic[2] very recently, and added that "where the appeal is to the judgment, there the vehicle is prose"—familiar propositions, certainly. "Prose," said another English critic,[3] "can only be great as it differs from poetry, and the greatest prose is furthest away from poetry . . . the difference is one of plane of consciousness, prose being at the highest level of the rational mind, and poetry at the highest level of the spiritual mind." And here again there is general agreement among literary critics. Of course, prose is not confined to the expression of exact thought. Otherwise only scientists, philosophers, and their intellectual kinsmen

---

[2]John Middleton Murry.

[3]A. R. Orage.

would be entitled to use it. But it is just to say that prose springs from the mind and poetry from the emotions, that prose is primarily an intellectual form, though often accompanied and set aglow by feeling, and that poetry is predominantly emotional expression, though it may be accompanied and ballasted by thought. There is no suggestion of a revolutionary view in that article, and it, like the principle of Variety, is adopted at the outset of this series of dissertations as a demonstrated truth about our subject. But again the caution is made to the amateur: Test it for yourself as we proceed through this work.

SUMMARY OF OUR STARTING POINTS

Here, briefly, are the results of our preliminary survey:

In terms of the medium, prose is apparently more lawless than verse. This appears so because prose eschews meter, but it has an obligation to be rhythmical. This permits it to strive for the excellences of Variety, though it must not, of course, be chaotic. The principle of Variety implies a unity to be varied, just as in poetry the principle of Sameness does not mean an absolute identity, though some Eighteenth Century English poets thought so, but rather the introduction into a poem of as much variousness as the principle will allow.

Likewise, when prose is considered in terms of psychology there must be a certain amount of flexibility in one's understanding of the statement that prose is the language of the rational faculties and poetry the language of the emotional faculties. Neither prose nor poetry is purely nor absolutely as described, but the first is predominantly or essentially the vehicle of the mind and the other the prime vehicle of the feelings.

CHAPTER II

THE ELEMENTS OF STYLE AND FORM

STENDHAL ON STYLE

STENDHAL has bequeathed a very good definition of style.[1] "Style is this," he wrote. "To add to a given thought all the circumstances fitted to produce the whole effect that the thought ought to produce." If the reader has the commendable habit of using the pencil when he reads he no doubt feels an inclination to underscore "ought" and "whole effect," and to put a question mark after "thought."

What did Stendhal mean by "thought"? Not the strict meaning of our day but, as we can guess from the context of his own writing and from the context of the French sensationalist psychology of the Eighteenth Century, something much broader. We are perfectly entitled to say that by "thought" Stendhal referred to perceptions, intuitions, moods, attitudes, complexes of thought and feeling, as well as thought proper—an interpretation that, of course, greatly augments the usefulness of his definition. The underlining of "whole effect" is obviously for emphasis, but just what does "ought" cover? The French verb form is *doit,* and *doit* can also be rendered as "is intended," so

---

[1] For a careful exposition of the Stendhalian formula, consult *The Problem of Style,* by John Middleton Murry. The rest of that work is often open to dispute, but a reading of it may help to bring about the frame of mind in which one can best consider the technical problems of literary style.

that an alternative and perhaps clearer reading of the last clause would be—— But why ignore the opportunity of repeating the whole of this important statement, incorporating, while doing so, the results of our brief commentary? "Style is this: to add to a given thought [read as well: perception, feeling, mood, intuition, et cetera] all the circumstances fitted to produce the *whole effect* that the thought is intended to produce."

This is a description of a process, which will be copiously exemplified in the selections included in this volume, but for the sake of a little immediate clarity, let us improvise an elementary case. If you write to a friend, "To-day I felt very gay. My spirits were high. The whole world seemed joyous to me," you have done scarcely anything to externalize your mood. Your general statements will in all likelihood evoke only a general and weak response in your friend. But now suppose that you cite the particular circumstances that attended your mood. You write: "I walked lightly to-day and could hardly restrain my feet from dancing. 'My, how cheerful your voice sounds,' said the housekeeper when I returned for lunch. In the afternoon I went rambling again, delighted by the fresh greenery of the woods, the clean, odorous exhalations of the earth, and above all by the gay leaping of the fish in the lake." You have certainly not achieved purple in this version, but you are now working in the right direction. For the writer's aim is to evoke the general in his reader by making him see and feel the vivid particular circumstance.

BUFFON'S CELEBRATED DEFINITION OF STYLE

Buffon's definition of style is much more famous than Stendhal's and, when it is rightly comprehended, more profound, carrying us directly into the fastnesses of the writer's psychology. "Style is the man himself." We have all repeated that sentence with unction, but how explicit can we make its meaning? The writer and the reader would phrase it differently, though the thought of each can be exactly translated into that of the other. The writer, eying the primary problem of his craft, would say: "Style is a substitute for the man himself, for my person is absent when I am read. Therefore in print I must compensate for my absent qualities: I must somehow make words and phrases convey what I can ordinarily convey by posture and gesture, by dress and the circumstances of a given situation, by tone of voice and facial pantomime, by actions, and, in short, by my whole living personality. Hence, I give much thought to tone and to rhythms, to preparatory scaffolding and connective tissues, to insure so far as I can that the reader shall experience me as if I were indeed present." The reader would reply: "We know people by their behavior. Writing is necessarily one form of behavior. We watch the style of that form of behaving, and thus we come to know what the author is like. In truth, style is the man himself."

STYLE IS A MEANS

The mere acceptance of these definitions implies two things. Style cannot be considered as just the ornamentation of writing, and style must be considered as a means to an end. Stendhal speaks of producing the whole effect that a "thought" on the part of the writer ought to make upon a reader: style is a means for the production of effects. Buffon defines style in terms of the man himself: style is the means employed to enable the "man himself" to act upon the distant and unknown reader. Obviously, the necessary means cannot therefore be superfluous and purely ornamental.

Yet it does happen that some writers to-day, as in the past, mistake the means for the end or perversely insist on the elaboration of the means unrelated to an object, and it does happen that there exists a widespread doctrine of art as "self-expression." These aberrations will come in for incidental treatment later. Our business now is to lay down our cards, and among them is one that signifies that in this book literature is held to be essentially an art of communication of effects.

THE ELEMENTS OF STYLE

The dicta of Buffon and Stendhal apply with equal pertinence to both poetry and prose, since style is a subject that includes both branches of literature. It is only when we consider separately the elements of style that we begin to secure findings that belong alone to prose. How does prose differ from poetry in word choice, vowel and consonantal combinations, sentence structure, rhythms, and order of thought?

1. *Vocabulary*. In general, words relate to an intellectual or an emotional or a sensational source in ourselves. There is a vocabulary for the mind, another for the feelings, and a third for the senses. The first is composed of words denoting comparison, contrast, relationship, judgment, and abstraction. When we consider prose for literary criticism and philosophy we shall comment further on the prevalence, in the purest examples, of abstract nouns. The emotional vocabulary is composed principally of the names of feelings and their shades, and the adjectives and adverbs derived from these names. The vocabulary of the senses refers to

those objects of which one or another sense makes report.

It is sometimes a matter of nicety to discriminate among these groups of our total vocabulary. "Desk," "forest," "frog," "boy," are clearly sensational terms; "irritation," "anger," "fury," "panic," are just as clearly emotional; "judgment," "velocity," "value," are at once seen to be intellectual terminology. But we have to reflect when someone asks what is the classification of a word like "danger." A deaf man may be unconcernedly walking across a track down which a locomotive is roaring, but it is we, the spectators, who *feel* the danger of his situation. Swiftly identifying ourselves with him, we wring our hands over a menace he does not know of. Thus, we can say the word "danger" belongs in the emotional vocabulary.

Another difficulty is given by the fact that many words, while basically members of one groping, have acquired associations from one or the other of the remaining groups so that they overlap in their range of suggestiveness. And again there are words that are equally mental, emotional, and sensational—words of large, well-distributed meaning that apparently spring from man as a unit. "Life" and "death" are such words.

The principle itself is simple and valid and at the moment we are not called upon to solve the difficulties of its detailed application. But it should be evident now that prose will make greater use of the mental vocabulary and poetry will be more partial to emotional words—and this is the origin of what is known as "poetic diction," the preference for words of an emotional character about which have accreted layers of rich emotional associations.

2. *Combinations of vowels and consonants.* Is there in the harmonious groupings of consonants and vowels any broad distinction between verse and prose such as we have

just observed in the different propensities toward vocabulary of the poet and the proseman? I do not believe so. The secrets that one discovers in the art of letters (I speak at this moment quite literally of letters) are common to both forms. Thus, a melancholy passage in either prose or poetry will probably show a plentiful number of open vowels and guttural consonants, and a gay passage in either form will turn out to be in many cases a dance of short vowel sounds tripping swiftly among dentals and gutturals.

The student should, of course, familiarize himself with the classification of consonants: the labials, the gutturals, the dentals, and the other varieties,[2] for it is just the failure to memorize such rudimentary categories as these that among other reasons causes so many American critics to become vague and pointless when they discuss style: they are like pseudo-physiologists who have never troubled to learn the classification of cells.

3. *Syntax*. In an accessible corner of one's mind there should be lying ready for use the grammatical distinctions of simple, complex, and compound sentences and the rhetorical distinctions of periodic and loose sentences, of balance, antithesis, and parallelism, for all these when actually employed in the analysis of style will often lead one to unexpectedly precise conclusions. Variety in style will frequently be found to depend upon variety in sentence structure—in the shiftings from short simple sentences to loose complex ones, from antithesis to parallelism, from a balance of affirmative clauses back to a simple negation.

But all these modes of building a sentence are equally available for either prose or verse harmony, and again we are balked.

---

[2] See Table of Consonants at the back of the book.

4. *Rhythm*. Here, thanks to Saintsbury's pioneering, the differentia are now seen to be very specific. For one thing, prose can accommodate the six-syllable foot or "sixer," and the grace syllable, which is unthinkable in verse, is conceivable in prose writing. This is, however, a lesser distinction and one derived principally from prose of very low tension and a disposition toward slurring. The five-syllable foot, the various forms of the dochmiac,[3] finds very little place in verse, but it is a kingly foot for prose, and certain quadrisyllabic feet, notably those termed the Ionic *a minore* and the third pæon, are all-important for the highest prose harmonies. Again, the amphibrach, a trisyllabic foot which is of doubtful utility for the versifier, is a very effective foot for his rival in prose. Another trisyllabic foot, the molossus, is impossible in verse but occasionally turns up in prose scansion. Another differentiation consists in the much greater prevalence of monosyllabic feet in English prose than in English poetry.

The aim here is not to be exhaustive but merely to set down a few of the many special characteristics of prose rhythm enumerated by Saintsbury. My purpose in skimming the subject is only the humble one of flicking the curiosity of the student to take a deeper plunge or, if I do not succeed in that, to induce him at least to credit the possibility of a musical system for prose that differs from prosody.

5. *Order of thought*. Order of thought is a pervasive element of style. It governs not alone sentence structure, which we have already touched upon, but governs, too, the linkage of sentence to sentence. In every sentence there are operative words or points of stress, and these important

---

[3] See the Table of Feet at the back of the book.

words placed in stressed positions determine the character of the sentence that is built. What is more, they decide for us by logical and mathematical laws where the points of stress shall fall in the succeeding sentence. Order of thought, then, is related to the minute musculature of sentences and paragraphs.

But there is a larger order of thought that has to do with our definition of form, a term which as yet we have not considered. Form will take us up into the general again, and since we have just discovered firm ground for an examination of prose style, let us tread over it a second time before we take another ascent.

We ask of a prose stylist such questions as these: Is his choice of words accurate, apt and brilliant? Are the words chosen to keep the idea uppermost in the writing or does the idea get drowned in sound, in very intense or incoherent feelings, or in a pictorial suggestiveness that vainly tries to do what another art, painting, is designed to accomplish? Are his rhythms proper to prose or does he unconsciously fall into meter which has every likelihood of being slipshod because it is accidental?

Furthermore, is he cunning or gross in his ear for vowels and consonants? What is his characteristic syntax? For example, what structure makes the Johnsonian sentence so recognizable? And what signs of skillful distribution of stresses does he reveal as his thought arranges itself?

FORM

Style, in short, has to do with mode of presentation, but form is concerned with the mold of the presentation. At the present time form is used in two senses, one sense being that of a type of mold, such as the five-act play, the short story, the aphorism, et cetera, and the other sense being more technical and somewhat more difficult to explain. When a painter speaks of form he does not mean the genre of the canvas, which may be still-life or portrait or "abstract," but he means the æsthetic organization of the painting as a whole. Form in the painter's sense has passed into the vocabulary of the modern literary critic[4] and is used by him to designate the total æsthetic organization of a piece of writing, the particular mold within the typical mold, so that a novel may be spoken of as poorly conceived and lacking in form though it is clearly enough a novel.

Form is what one sees and feels when one takes a whole view of the structure of a given work. Style one sees and feels concurrently with one's passage through the work. It is with such denotations as those just given that the term "form" is employed in this book.

STRUCTURE AND ITS FUNCTIONS

To be more concrete about form, let us say that form is the functioning structure of a work of art. The concept includes what Aristotle called the plot or fable and which nowadays we call design, architecture, or structure, and it includes the functions of the various parts of the plot or structure. Thus, it should be seen that to skeletonize the contents of a story is not to account for its form, but only for its anatomy. But to add to the skeleton outline the

---

[4]In the *Dial* for July, 1925, there was an excellent paper entitled "The Psychology of Form," by Kenneth Burke. It led to a conclusion that seems to me to discriminate quite unnecessarily against the value of subject matter in literature as opposed to eloquence of presentation, but the preliminary paragraphs by argument and example certainly conveyed a very full content for the word "form" when used in a technical sense.

appropriate functions, showing how the work achieved movement and climax, balance and symmetry, is to give it a physiology, to show that structurally it is alive.

The Poetics of Aristotle is the canonical treatise on form, and since form is a common property of prose and poetry, the treatise bears just as fully on the nature of form in prose as its title indicates it does on poetry. It includes precisely what we are looking for: an enumeration and definition of the principal functions of form. These are the Beginning, the Middle, and the End; or, as some modern critics would say, the Introduction, the Progression, and the Conclusion, all arranged according to a principle of crescendo. Let the reader take the Aristotelian definitions of the Beginning, Middle, and End and translate them into emotional language. As soon as he discovers that to the emotions a Beginning means the arousing of an expectation he is directly on the path to an understanding of form. For psychologically form is this: the creation in the reader of a sense of something coming, the nursing, exciting, delaying, and intensifying of this expectation, finally the gratification of the anticipation. It is as simple as that in principle, but the working out of the principle may assume very great complexity.

It should be seen from this that only in details of formal organization will form in prose differ from form in poetry. On the basis of all that has been said thus far we can now frame a leading question: Will form in prose tend to be more various and more logical than poetic form? We shall attempt to gather material for the answer as we proceed.

CHAPTER III

STYLE AND FORM AS BEHAVIOR

THE imaginary reader who explained a few pages back what Buffon's pronouncement meant to him offered us a very suggestive statement. He was apparently acquainted with the position that modern psychologists are rapidly being forced to accept, for he began by saying, "We know people by their behavior," and we can infer from the rest of his statement that he regards writing as a special form of intellectual and emotional behavior. Observe clearly the style, he seems to say, and you will know the man.

DIFFICULTY IN DEMONSTRATING BUFFON'S DEFINITION

Possibly it is by means of this approach that we may, each of us, demonstrate to our satisfaction the validity of the French naturalist's saying, for the fact is that hitherto the attempt to prove that the style is the man himself has usually been not quite successful. Lacunæ remain gaping between what is said of the style and what is said of the author: the sources—the writings on the one hand, and on the other, biographical information—stay disparate, and in consequence whatever correspondence is alleged to exist between style and the man is often inexact—even grossly inexact, as witness the case of the contemporary critic who has inhaled, too deeply and too long, the fumes of psychoanalysis and can no longer believe that things are as they are.

The causes for this failure appear easy to name. They are insufficient knowledge of style and deficient knowledge of psychology. Both the elements of style (rhythm, letters, vocabulary, syntax, and order of thought) and the elements of psychology (actions, emotions, and thought) are indistinctly seen and often utterly slighted. As it were, a lunar witchery distracts the eyes of readers and their brethren, the critics, from the object in question, which is a man writing, and instead of focusing on him and on his work they grope in the forest of their own associations. Are there, then, any spells that will be potent against this bondage to one's accidental likes and dislikes, to one's tracts of associations (again accidentally formed) with this or that theory, ethical, sociological, economic, or philosophic?

It is at this juncture that the statement of our imaginary reader is particularly suggestive. May it not be possible that just as we have been unconsciously trained to take our eyes from the object, so may we consciously train ourselves to turn them back to the work we have read? See what the style *does,* our reader says in substance, and then you will know what the man *is,* for the man is implicit in his workmanship.

THE SELF-TRAINING OF THE READER

Our first undertaking, then, must be to study the means of literary production, to appreciate technical beauties, to make ourselves at home in the writer's workshop. That will be a guarantee that our eyes are really upon the object and that the first term of Buffon's definition is acquiring amplified content for us. Our second undertaking is much larger: to become active, interrogating, observant, and serious students of life.

Experimentally, we shall decide that the writer is revealed in his style, and that therefore a complete account of stylistic behavior will tell, to one of sufficient experience and knowledge, exactly what composition of mind and emotions the author had. To one of sufficient experience and knowledge—there is the spur for us. For we shall find that we do not know our own behavior to any great extent and that there is much more to be observed about the behavior of other people—as anyone who takes a few lessons in the art of pantomime will quickly and probably with astonishment discover.

THE EXAMPLE OF PANTOMIME

In pantomime, as in literature, the aim is to manage a severely restricted medium so as to produce the least restricted effects on an audience. Through the languages of gesture, posture, carriage, movement, and facial expression the pantomimist will seek to convey emotions and ideas, to convince you of the presence of a full psychology in the body that is being manipulated before your eyes. We see, for example, a pantomimist walking with a confident step, wearing a mouth visibly ready to break into a broad smile and eyes that are lit with benevolence, the whole body appearing to expand with good feeling, and we know that here is a portrayal of a sanguine optimistic type.

How would such a type behave when writing? What words would it prefer? What character of sentences? What order of thought? The reader learned in literary technic will be able to say what the style is, but the same critic must be learned in life to build up the mental, emotional, and instinctive constitution that must have existed in order to manifest in just that way. In other words, literary criticism is ultimately psychology.

THE RELATIONSHIP OF STYLE AND FORM TO PERSONALITY AND WORLD CONCEPTION

But how to get started in the psychological divination of the writer? The suggestion is here made that each of us may be regarded as a divided person. We began by being purely biological, a sum of potentialities, and as we grew, some of these potentialities took form as actualities, crystallized or concretized into a unit which we call our personality. Many more possibilities, however, still exist in us than those that have found expression, but they are latent, not actual.

But our personalities were molded by the environment into which we happened to be born. Sociology is responsible for them, and thus there may be said to be a split between what we sociologically have become and what we basically and essentially are from a biological viewpoint.

This division is represented by two attitudes in us: one an attitude toward ourselves, generally expressible in terms of vanity, and the other an attitude toward life and the world in general, an attitude that often remains childish.

Thus we may expect that a writer, since he carries about in himself a personal attitude and a world view or conception, will manifest these in his works. Since it seems decidedly worth while to test experimentally such a thesis, throughout this volume we shall try to discover if style is related to personality. And form, about which I have said nothing else in this chapter, will also be experimentally treated as behavior. We shall try to relate it to the submerged biological base of the writer, to find it in correspondence with his world view, of which, by the way, the writer may be so unconscious that instead of busying himself with its articulation he is being continually given away by it.

Part Two

THE LANGUAGE OF IDEAS

CHAPTER IV

PROSE FOR LITERARY CRITICISM: EDGAR ALLAN POE AND T. S. ELIOT

WHATEVER else prose may take unto itself, it is past dispute the language for exact thought; it is the obligatory vehicle for the scientist, the philosopher, and the literary critic. Therefore, to begin with these communicators of ideas is best, taking the critic first and accepting the advantages of William James's versatility, when we reach him among the philosophers, by letting his prose represent both prose for philosophy and prose for science.

THE ESSENCE OF CRITICISM

About eighty-five years ago Edgar Allan Poe was writing the finest literary criticism in America, and I am not certain but that it remains still the best that our literature can show. Among our contemporary critics T. S. Eliot is in the first rank. If in some respects he is inferior to Paul Elmer More and Irving Babbitt, he is more distinguished in finesse of style than they are, and for that reason a better specimen for our purposes. But Poe and Eliot are exceptions to the principal trends of American criticism.

As a matter of fact, these trends are downward and sig-

nify the degeneracy of literary criticism in Western litera-
tures. It is even necessary now to ask: What is a critic?
He is every reader, in a sense, for no reader escapes forming a judgment of what he has read. The reader likes or
does not like a given book; he says the work was enjoyable
or tedious; he has opinions about its worth and more or
less formulated descriptions of his emotions and thoughts
while reading it; he can, more or less, summarize a book's
contents, point out what he regards as the author's mis-
takes or victories, even classify the intention; he speculates
as to what the author is like. This is what every reader
does, though nearly always in an extremely rudimentary
way. The critic is the unusual reader who wishes to discriminate *exactly* among his reactions and to formulate
precisely what his judgments are, and to sustain and justify
them to the limit of his ability; that is, the critic aspires to
be a conscious reader so far as he can and always to be
able to give an account of himself in his commerce with
books.

But the making of discriminations and judgments is a
mental process, and the decisions, though they probably
coincide with the critic's emotional preferences and antipa-
thies, are expounded, and rendered, if possible, free of
prejudices. It follows, then, that criticism is designed to
appeal to the mind of its reader: it is a case of the faculty
of judgment calling unto the reader's faculty for judging.
And it is this, the measurement of literary works by standards, the insistence upon judgment as the core of criticism,
that we shall find well exhibited in Poe and Eliot. But, as
remarked before, they are exceptions in recent criticism,
which is a decline from the making of rational judgments
to the purveying of gossip.

THE IMPRESSIONISTS AND OTHER SCHOOLS

The following schools will illustrate the falling away. The most prominent to-day are the Impressionists, who unroll before us the embellished tablets of their sensory, emotional, and mental (but chiefly sensory and emotional) associations while reading. For them—Arthur Symons is a prime example—criticism is no more than the record of a reading experience, and rests quite candidly on taste (the polite term for private preferences, however well educated). But for us, the readers of impressionistic criticism, their procedure is bound to be unsatisfying. If we have not read the author who has stimulated them we may be enticed to do so by the spectacle of their enjoyment, but when we have read him, then we have our own assemblage of associations, which naturally we prefer. If, however, we have earlier read the author we already have our impressions of his work, and again we prefer our own to other people's. Impressionism fails because it adds no new term to the judgment of literature.

The Technical critics make up a much smaller school, but they are more valuable. Saintsbury, for instance, in his studies of literary technic not only advertises his taste but improves our actual knowledge of the art of writing. The Impressionistic position is not relinquished, but the Technical critic partially abandons it when he says in substance: "I have been out in front experiencing this production. Now let me go backstage and study how certain effects were produced on me." The error into which this school often plunges is to become purely æsthetic: to say that the most that matters from literature is the pleasure it gives: and that therefore criticism limits itself to an analysis of the means for giving pleasure. The difficulty is that literature gives many pleasures perfectly, and there can be no hierarchy of perfect pleasures. To the æsthetic analyst literature is liable to divide into only three categories: good, indifferent, and poor. This may be called criticism with blinders: the focus is sharp but exceedingly limited.

In certain other schools, however, the focus is not even on literature at all, but on some dear craze such as psychoanalysis, or upon some sociological or economic or moral theory. In such cases the critic can fairly be called squinteyed, for he reads a book with his eye cocked in advance on an anterior and perhaps alien thesis, and quite naturally he cuts to this thesis. He does not, cannot, respect the integrity of the work of art, for he is strongly aware of it only when it conflicts with or confirms his *a priori* theory. Hence it succeeds that his criticism has only the value that his thesis has, and no more.

Discounting the out-and-out gossipers who peddle over again the contents of books, adding as sauce the scrapings of the author's biography, and discounting also the scholarly specialists in literary history and in comparative literature, we have remaining only the Critic Proper, represented here by Poe and Eliot. Such a critic includes necessarily the elements of the other schools, but with a difference in the use he makes of them. Thus, his impressions are not to him the end, but only raw material; his expert knowledge of technic is not a sufficiency, but a tool; his psychological and moral and sociological theories are tamed down to minor accessories of the broad understanding of human experience; and his literary scholarship remains a means and is not paramount. His aim, in fine, is to write reasonably about literature, to arrive at rational judgments of its values to the reader.

E. A. POE: HIS IDEAS ABOUT HAWTHORNE

Sequent to this chapter there is a note on Nathaniel Hawthorne which Poe, on the watch for new ability in letters, was impelled to write before *The Scarlet Letter* brought Hawthorne into the sunshine of popular appreciation. The note was in fact based on a perusal of *Twice Told Tales* and *Mosses from an Old Manse,* the latter appearing in 1846. I have taken the liberty of entitling this piece "The Idiosyncrasy of Hawthorne's Prose."

Poe introduced his subject by making one of his favorite distinctions. It happened in his day, as it does in ours, that private criticism was much more candid and independent than public criticism, and that often, for one or another reason such as personal influence in the right quarters, the figures who were praised in public were privately condemned, and, vice versa, there were privately admired but publicly unappreciated men of genius.

This calls for some remarks about Poe himself. This extraordinarily gifted man did not entirely escape provincialism of judgment. Very often he did not take a long view in point of time, and his cosmopolitan taste in letters did not wholly counterbalance his enthusiasm for local writers. He was, as we all know, betrayed into superlatives for certain soon-forgotten authors, and these superlatives seem ridiculous to us now, though our age cannot plead before posterity that it is innocent of this fault. But one thing Poe did. He fought clear of any subserviency in his opinions: he came out with the truth about a writer as he saw it, regardless of that writer's obscurity or fame. So it is in the paper here reprinted. Before Hawthorne was accepted Poe was on the ground appraising him.

The point at issue, he quickly saw, was whether Hawthorne was an original or a peculiar writer. Poe decided on second thought that Hawthorne was idiosyncratic and monotonous. For true originality implies "the continuous peculiarity—a peculiarity springing from ever-active vigor of fancy—better still if from ever-present force of imagination, giving its own hue, its own character to everything it touches, and especially, *self-impelled to touch everything.*" Whereas what Hawthorne achieved was a uniform, not continuous, peculiarity; an habitual manner which such a writer as Tieck, Poe says, sometimes employs; a monotone, novel, it is true, at first reading, but losing all effect of novelty as soon as one passes beyond the acquaintance stage.

Literature was to Poe a magical matter of producing designed effects upon a designed reader, and this view should be the standing-place of all criticism : it is the fundamental view of the fundamental relation existing between writers and readers. Therefore, originality should be judged by the effect designed, and therefore "the simple truth is that the writer who aims at impressing the people is *always* wrong when he fails in forcing that people to receive the impression." As to how far Hawthorne addressed the people at all is, Poe says, not a question for him to decide, but "his books afford strong internal evidence of having been written to himself and his particular friends alone."

The central idea of Poe's paper is a definition of true originality. First, Poe disposes of a type of novelty very much in vogue while I pen these lines, a novelty of combinations of thought, incident, words, and so on, which requires the straining of the intellect to grasp. (Some of the poetry of Ezra Pound would be a good example of this type.) Poe insists that it is "the novelty of effect alone which is worth consideration," and according to that criterion the cerebral ingenuity called for in absolutely novel combinations fails to make popular appeal. What then? Here Poe shows his knowledge of general human experience. The true originality lies in producing responses in the reader that are not his commonplace ones but of an elevated character and latent most of the time since no stimulus is applied to bring them forth. True originality then strikes at the potentialities of a reader for heightened existence.

Furthermore, there is an inferior degree of originality—reached by Hawthorne—which Poe explains very clearly, and its vehicle is the so-called "natural" style. But Hawthorne fails to vary and extend his "natural" style, most grievously of all in his strain of allegory, and once again we must speak of him as a peculiar rather than an original writer.

ANALYSIS OF POE'S STYLE AND FORM

But now let me say that these ideas of Poe are not at all our present concern. I have enumerated them only for the sake of impressing the fact that we remove from our consideration the intellectual content of a critical essay when we examine the style. So far as Poe's style matters, I have said nothing yet. So let us begin afresh.

Read the following little essay on Hawthorne, or recall your previous reading of Poe's criticism, and then try to describe the style. You will say that it is in the plain-style tradition, which means that rhetoric is here subordinate always to the sense or meaning. You will say that it is a terse style, simple, direct, pointed, precise, sharp, and so on. Adjectives all, and descriptive of the effects Poe's manner of writing makes on you. This is adjectival criticism, and it is about as far as most book reviewers ever get. But it is certainly not enough. What we seek, *after* the descriptive adjectives have come to us, is the important thing, and that is the answer to the question, How do we come to find certain adjectives appropriate and others not? What are the mechanisms in the writing that cause the effect of terseness or clarity or subtlety? Our progress should be from the adjective descriptive of an effect to the statement that sets forth a process.

For example, what statements can we make about Poe's vocabulary when he wrote criticism? Here is a passage from "Marginalia."

> "The *pure Imagination* chooses, from *either Beauty or Deformity,* only the most combinable things hitherto uncombined; the compound, as a general rule, partaking, in character, of beauty, or sublimity, in the ratio of the respective beauty or sublimity of the things combined— which are themselves still to be considered as atomic— that is to say, as previous combinations. But, as often analogously happens in physical chemistry, so not unfrequently does it occur in this chemistry of the intellect, that the admixture of two elements results in a something that has nothing of the qualities of one of them, or even nothing of the qualities of either. . . . Thus, the range of Imagination is unlimited."

The preponderating number of words is mental, as anyone can test for himself. There is scarcely a sensational word used, and only two or three emotional terms such as "sublimity." On the other hand, the mind is kept busy by such words as "compound," "qualities," "unlimited," "ratio," "atomic," "chemistry," "admixture," to mention but a few. The passage is neither sensuous nor stirring, but abstract—the appeal direct to our reason in reason's own language. The essay on Hawthorne is not so abstract as this concentrated specimen, but if the student will examine it with an eye for word choice he will find that its clean precision depends on the purity of its mind vocabulary.

The next step is to note Poe's characteristic sentence structure. He was very skilled in the use of the emendation, the afterthought, the additional clarification: and indeed one passage of his "Marginalia" is an excellent little note on the use of the dash in punctuation for just this device. His fondness for the emendation was consistent with his habit of parallelism in sentence building. Notice how in the quoted paragraph on Imagination he makes a statement, and then extends it in another parallel statement, and then advances it still further in a third parallel arrangement—all terminating in a short triumphant demonstrated conclusion. Not to so great a degree but quite noticeable is this habit in "The Idiosyncrasy of Hawthorne's Prose," while it is much more pronounced in Poe's cosmological treatise, *Eureka.*

The form of Poe's criticisms is related to his favorite sentence structure. He seldom achieves a perfectly clean form, for concessions to the journalism of his day often made his critical notes a little disjointed and scattered them at the end, where he frequently hitched on a paragraph or two descriptive of the appearance and personality of the author under his glass. But their frame was always that of the demonstration. The book in question would quickly suggest a principle to him, as it does in the case of Hawthorne's early works, and he would then proceed to demonstrate by ratiocination and evidence the truth or fallaciousness of the principle. The *quod erat demonstrandum* was always implicitly signed to his proofs.

We have now made several simple statements about the mechanics of Poe's critical prose. It is a prose that forswears the ornate rhetorical persuasive style, and therefore subordinates rhythm and metaphor to the sobrieties of reason. It gains its precision and sharpness and directness by word choice exercised among the words of the intellect. Its syntax, order of thought, and form are mathematical: all coöperate in enforcing a demonstration of critical principles. Thus, by a little analysis, we earn our right to the adjectives we felt were proper to describe his prose, and further, if we take style and form as behavior, we can now make certain statements about the constitution of Poe's mind.

One who wishes quickly to estimate the physical capacities of a person can do so by answering three simple questions: Is the person quick, agile, versatile in his movements? Is he regularly in good health? Is he strong and forceful in physique? Quickness, Health, and Strength—these are the signs of the state of what might be called his instinctive psychology.

It is very interesting that the mind can be "sized up" in a similar rough-and-ready manner. Obviously, the cast (or one might say the polarity) of Poe's intellect inclined him to the analytical and mathematical. But was his a quick-moving brain? The facts show that it was, since it applied itself with facility to a variety of intellectual problems: cryptograms, science, philosophy, prose fiction, literary criticism, and the composition of verse. Was it a healthy (that is, a really sane) mind? This would be shown by the strictness of its logic and the scope of its views, and I think that on both counts we must call Poe's mind a sane vehicle. Poe was a close reasoner and he tended always to the broad view; in fact, he adventured among the giants of broad views when he attempted to elaborate and prove a cosmology. But his intellect does not appear to have had so large a measure of force and weight and strength. Thus far, at any rate, his ideas have remained outside the larger currents of our lives. They have not, it would seem, the specific gravity to sink into us that the ideas of Francis Bacon, for one instance, have so marvelously displayed.

This is, of course, a scanty account of Poe, but by way of a beginning to interpret writing as a form of behavior it should be suggestive of the possible extent of the method.

AN ANALYSIS OF T. S. ELIOT'S STYLE AND FORM

If we now examine the prose of T. S. Eliot we shall find ourselves making discriminations. In "The Critic and the Perception of Values" Eliot signalized an important extension of his critical policy. In *The Sacred Wood* he had sought to found criticism upon the sensibility as it was affected by art and to remain unattached to an ethic. But in our age of disagreement over fundamental values that position, to a man of culture, is untenable. He is obliged to see, as Eliot remarks, that "the existence and concept of literature depends upon our answer to other problems," and hence that contemporary criticism must base itself, not on sensibility alone, but upon our whole general experience. So the essay here reprinted is a crucial one in Eliot's development, but again I remind myself that our present business is not with the critic's ideas, but with his manner and mode, and promptly turn to observing the type of vocabulary utilized in this essay. Like Poe's it is pronouncedly abstract, as anyone can verify, but the tone is more suave, more refined in its modulations. This may doubtless be attributed to the greater training Eliot has received in the "finishing schools" of literary deportment. Poe had genius, but the rough bark of a provincially trained writer was never wholly peeled from him.

This is a difference certainly ascribable to education and perhaps ascribable in part to temperament. Temperament comes out more clearly when we perceive that one of Eliot's chief graces as a stylist is a sense of balance in his sentences. He likes best the compound sentence, its parts of equal weight, the balance achieved most noticeably by varying degrees of antithesis. Here are examples of the characteristic Eliot sentence:

"One is tempted to commend, to French and Italian readers respectively, Mr. Read's observations on Diderot and Guido Calvacanti; to English readers, M. Fernandez' observations on Meredith, Newman and Conrad. But such comparisons and eulogies are likely to be made; what is not likely to be made is the contrast of two points of view, of which these two critics are important as types. . . .

"M. Fernandez has a very high, very serious, and very difficult ideal of perfection, of the development and perfection of character: this ideal is nowhere better conceived than in his essay on *'Le message de Meredith.'* We may not accept M. Fernandez' estimate of Meredith; in fact, for a contemporary Anglo-Saxon reader, it is difficult to place Meredith so high as does M. Fernandez."

There is a clue here in this matter of balance. In reading the essays of T. S. Eliot we are conscious of a respectful hushed state induced in us: there are a gravity of deportment and an air of learning and detachment that remind us of some parallel in civilized life, and then, as Eliot proceeds to cite case and precedent, to make comparison and contrast, we realize what the parallel is. We are convened in a literary court room to hear, not the disputations and special pleadings of lawyers or the fragmentary reports of witnesses or the defense testimony of the accused himself, but to hear the judicial decision handed down in dignified accents. For the form of Eliot's essays is not explanatory or analytical or demonstrative, though he has used all these processes in private, but it is the elucidation. The judicial decision has been reached, and now it is merely being elucidated. Not principles so much, though Eliot has them, but qualities are at stake. The reader is called on to perceive one discrimination after another among the various authors, and these discriminations are relevant to the particular writer under consideration and carry out the aim of letting that writer's special quality emerge.

Later certain guidance will be proffered for estimating the weight of ideas, but for the present and by way of practice it should be rewarding to ask the same questions of Eliot's mind that we applied to Poe, matching the former against the latter for quickness, saneness, and force, and observing that Eliot's differs in its general cast and activity, inasmuch as it tends so frequently to fall into the passive, receptive, balancing, judicial mold of thought.

Having made this effort, then let us ask a test question, assuming, if we can, an ignorance of the careers and ideas and tastes of the two men. What would be the attitude of each man, both Americans by birth and education, toward the traditional mind of Europe and the formative mind of America? We happen, however, to know the answers. We know that Poe fought for the autonomy of American literature, that he sought to clear the ground of rubbish so that native literature might grow, and that his main interests were in its development. And we know that Eliot has exiled himself in England, that he has assiduously trained himself to become an atom in the mind of Europe, that he wishes to write with the whole feeling of European traditions in his nerves, that he is in effect a cosmopolitan by now. This is not the entire story, of course, but is there not something correspondent between Poe's demonstrating, mathematically inclined mind and his striking out for American letters and between Eliot's precedent-loving, case-comparing mentality and his establishment of himself at the very seat of traditionalism?

THE IDIOSYNCRASY OF HAWTHORNE'S PROSE

By Edgar Allan Poe

The reputation of the author of *Twice-Told Tales* has been confined, until very lately, to literary society; and I have not been wrong, perhaps, in citing him as *the* example, *par excellence,* in this country, of the privately-admired and publicly-unappreciated man of genius. Within the last year or two, it is true, an occasional critic has been urged, by honest indignation, into very warm approval. Mr. Webber, for instance, (than whom no one has a keener relish for that kind of writing which Mr. Hawthorne has best illustrated,) gave us, in a late number of *The American Review,* a cordial and certainly a full tribute to his talents; and since the issue of the *Mosses from an Old Manse,* criticisms of similar tone have been by no means infrequent in our more authoritative journals. I can call to mind few reviews of Hawthorne published *before* the *Mosses.* One I remember in *Arcturus* (edited by Matthews and Duyckinck) for May, 1841; another in the *American Monthly* (edited by Hoffman and Herbert) for March, 1838; a third in the ninety-sixth number of the *North American Review.* These criticisms, however, seemed to have little effect on the popular taste—at least, if we are to form an idea of the popular taste by reference to its expression in the newspapers, or by the sale of the author's book. It was never the fashion (until lately) to speak of him in any summary of our best authors.

The daily critics would say, on such occasions, "Is there

not Irving and Cooper, and Bryant, and Paulding, and—
Smith?" or, "Have we not Halleck and Dana, and Longfellow, and—Thompson?" or, "Can we not point trium-
phantly to our own Sprague, Willis, Channing, Bancroft,
Prescott and—Jenkins?" but these unanswerable queries
were never wound up by the name of Hawthorne.

Beyond doubt, this inappreciation of him on the part of
the public arose chiefly from the two causes to which I have
referred—from the facts that he is neither a man of wealth
nor a quack; but these are insufficient to account for the
whole effect. No small portion of it is attributable to the
very marked idiosyncrasy of Mr. Hawthorne himself. In
one sense, and in a great measure, to be peculiar is to be
original, and than the true originality there is no higher
literary virtue. This true or commendable originality, however, implies not the uniform, but the continuous peculiarity
—a peculiarity springing from ever-active vigor of fancy
—better still if from ever-present force of imagination, giving its own hue, its own character to everything it touches,
and, especially, *self impelled to touch everything.*

It is often said, inconsiderately, that very original writers
always fail in popularity—that such and such persons are
too original to be comprehended by the mass. "Too
peculiar," should be the phrase, "too idiosyncratic." It is, in
fact, the excitable, undisciplined, and child-like popular
mind which most keenly feels the original.

The criticism of the conservatives, of the hackneys, of
the cultivated old clergymen of the *North American Review,* is precisely the criticism which condemns and alone
condemns it. "It becometh not a divine," said Lord Coke,
"to be of a fiery and salamandrine spirit." Their conscience
allowing them to move nothing themselves, these digni-
taries have a holy horror of being moved. "Give us

quietude," they say. Opening their mouths with proper caution, they sigh forth the word *"Repose."* And this is, indeed, the one thing they should be permitted to enjoy, if only upon the Christian principle of give and take.

The fact is, that if Mr. Hawthorne were really original, he could not fail of making himself felt by the public. But the fact is, he is not original in any sense. Those who speak of him as original, mean nothing more than that he differs in his manner or tone, and in his choice of subjects, from any author of their acquaintance—their acquaintance not extending to the German Tieck, whose manner, in *some* of his works, is absolutely identical with that *habitual* to Hawthorne. But it is clear that the element of the literary originality is novelty. The element of its appreciation by the reader is the reader's sense of the new. Whatever gives him a new and insomuch a pleasurable emotion, he considers original, and whoever frequently gives him such emotion, he considers an original writer. In a word, it is by the sum total of these emotions that he decides upon the writer's claim to originality. I may observe here, however, that there is clearly a point at which even novelty itself would cease to produce the legitimate originality, if we judge this originality, as we should, by the effect designed: this point is that at which *novelty becomes nothing novel;* and here the artist, *to preserve his originality,* will subside into the commonplace. No one, I think, has noticed that, merely through inattention to this matter, Moore has comparatively failed in his "Lalla Rookh." Few readers, and indeed few critics, have commended this poem for originality—and in fact, the effect, originality, is not produced by it—yet no work of equal size so abounds in the happiest originalities, individually considered. They are so excessive as, in the end, to deaden in the reader all capacity for their appreciation.

These points properly understood, it will be seen that the critic (unacquainted with Tieck) who reads a single tale or essay by Hawthorne, may be justified in thinking him original; but the tone, or manner, or choice of subject, which induces in this critic the sense of the new, will—if not in a second tale, at least in a third and all subsequent ones—not only fail of inducing it, but bring about an exactly antagonistic impression. In concluding a volume, and more especially in concluding all the volumes of the author, the critic will abandon his first design of calling him "original," and content himself with styling him "peculiar."

With the vague opinion that to be original is to be unpopular, I could, indeed, agree, were I to adopt an understanding of originality which, to my surprise, I have known adopted by many who have a right to be called critical. They have limited, in a love for mere words, the literary to the metaphysical originality. They regard as original in letters, only such combinations of thought, of incident, and so forth, as are, in fact, absolutely novel. It is clear, however, not only that it is the novelty of *effect* alone which is worth consideration, but that this effect is *best* wrought, for the end of all fictitious composition, pleasure, by shunning rather than by seeking the absolute novelty of combination. Originality, thus understood, tasks and startles the intellect, and so brings into undue action the faculties to which, in the lighter literature, we least appeal. And thus understood, it cannot fail to prove unpopular with the masses, who, seeking in this literature amusement, are positively offended by instruction. But the true originality—true in respect of its purposes—is that which, in bringing out the half-formed, the reluctant, or the unexpressed fancies of mankind, or in exciting the more delicate pulses of the heart's passion, or in giving birth to some universal sentiment or instinct in embryo, thus combines with the pleasurable effect of *apparent* novelty, a real egotistic delight. The reader, in the case first supposed, (that of the absolute novelty,) is excited, but embarrassed, disturbed, in some degree even pained at his own want of perception, at his own folly in not having himself hit upon the idea. In the second case, his pleasure is doubled. He is filled with an intrinsic and an extrinsic delight. He feels and intensely enjoys the seeming novelty of the thought, enjoys it as really novel, as absolutely original with the writer—*and* himself. They two, he fancies, have, alone of all men, thought thus. They two have, together, created this thing. Henceforward there is a bond of sympathy between them—a sympathy which irradiates every subsequent page of the book.

There is a species of writing which, with some difficulty, may be admitted as a lower degree of what I have called the true original. In its perusal we say to ourselves, not "how original this is!" nor "here is an idea which I and the author have alone entertained," but "here is a charmingly obvious fancy," or sometimes even, "here is a thought which I am not sure has ever occurred to myself, but which, of course, has occurred to all the rest of the world." This kind of composition (which still appertains to a high order) is usually designated as "the natural." It has little external resemblance, but strong internal affinity to the true original, if, indeed, as I have suggested, it is not of this latter an inferior degree. It is best exemplified, among English writers, in Addison, Irving and *Hawthorne*. The "ease" which is so often spoken of as its distinguishing feature, it has been the fashion to regard as ease in appearance alone, as a point of really difficult attainment. This idea, however, must be received with some reservation. The natural style is difficult only to those who should never intermeddle with it—to the unnatural. It is but the result of writing with the understanding, or with the instinct that the *tone,* in composition, should be that which, at any given point or upon any given topic, would be the tone of the great mass of humanity. The author who, after the manner of the North Americans, is merely at *all* times *quiet,* is, of course, upon *most* occasions, merely silly or stupid, and has no more right to be thought "easy" or "natural" than has a cockney exquisite, or the sleeping beauty in the wax-works.

"The "peculiarity," or sameness, or monotone of Hawthorne, would, in its mere character of "peculiarity," and without reference to what *is* the peculiarity, suffice to deprive him of all chance of popular appreciation. But at his failure to be appreciated, we can, *of course,* no longer wonder, when we find him monotonous at decidedly the worst of all possible points—at that point which, having the least concern with Nature, is the farthest removed from the popular intellect, from the popular sentiment, and from the popular taste. I allude to the strain of allegory which completely overwhelms the greater number of his subjects, and which in some measure interferes with the direct conduct of absolutely all.

In defence of allegory, (however, or for whatever object employed,) there is scarcely one respectable word to be said. Its best appeals are made to the fancy—that is to say, to our sense of adaptation, not of matters proper, but of matters improper for the purpose, of the real with the unreal; having never more of intelligible connexion than has something with nothing, never half so much of effective affinity as has the substance for the shadow. The deepest emotion aroused within us by the happiest allegory, *as* allegory, is a very, very imperfectly satisfied sense of the writer's ingenuity in overcoming a difficulty we should have preferred his not having attempted to overcome. The fallacy of the idea that allegory, in any of its moods, can be made to enforce a truth—that metaphor, for example, may illustrate as well as embellish an argument—could be promptly demonstrated; the converse of the supposed fact might be shown, indeed, with very little trouble—but these are topics foreign to my present purpose. One thing is clear, that if allegory ever establishes a fact, it is by dint of overturning a fiction. Where the suggested meaning runs through the obvious one in a *very* profound undercurrent, so as never to interfere with the upper one without our own volition, so as never to show itself unless *called* to the surface, there only, for the proper uses of fictitious narrative, is it available at all. Under the best circumstances, it must always interfere with that unity of effect which, to the artist, is worth all the allegory in the world. Its vital injury, however, is rendered to the most vitally important point in fiction—that of earnestness or verisimilitude. That *The Pilgrim's Progress* is a ludicrously over-rated book, owing its seeming popularity to one or two of those accidents in critical literature which by the critical are sufficiently well understood, is a matter upon which no two thinking people disagree; but the pleasure derivable from it, in any sense, will be found in the direct ratio of the reader's capacity to smother its true purposes, in the direct ratio of his ability to keep the allegory out of sight, or of his *in*ability to comprehend it. Of allegory properly handled, judiciously subdued, seen only as a shadow or by suggestive glimpses, and making its nearest approach to truth in a not obtrusive and therefore not unpleasant *appositeness,* the *Undine* of De La Motte Fouqué is the best, and undoubtedly a very remarkable specimen.

The obvious causes, however, which have prevented **Mr.**

Hawthorne's *popularity,* do not suffice to condemn him in the eyes of the few who belong properly to books, and to whom books, perhaps, do not quite so properly belong. These few estimate an author, not as do the public, altogether by what he does, but in a great measure—indeed, even in the greatest measure—by what he evinces a capability of doing. In this view, Hawthorne stands among literary people in America much in the same light as did Coleridge in England. The few, also through a certain warping of the taste, which long pondering upon books as books merely never fails to induce, are not in condition to view the errors of a scholar as errors altogether. At any time these gentlemen are prone to think the public not right rather than an educated author wrong. But the simple truth is, that the writer who aims at impressing the people, is *always* wrong when he fails in forcing that people to receive the impression. How far Mr. Hawthorne has addressed the people at all, is, of course, not a question for me to decide. His books afford strong internal evidence of having been written to himself and his particular friends alone.

There has long existed in literature a fatal and unfounded prejudice, which it will be the office of this age to overthrow—the idea that the mere bulk of a work must enter largely into our estimate of its merit. I do not suppose even the weakest of the Quarterly reviewers weak enough to maintain that in a book's size or mass, abstractly considered, there is anything which especially calls for our admiration. A mountain, simply through the sensation of physical magnitude which it conveys, does indeed, affect us with a sense of the sublime, but we cannot admit any such influence in the contemplation even of *The Columbiad.* The Quarterlies themselves will not admit it. And yet, what else are we to understand by their continual prating about "sustained effort"? Granted that this sustained effort has accomplished an epic—let us then admire the effort, (if this be a thing admirable,) but certainly not the epic on the effort's account. Common sense, in the time to come, may possibly insist upon measuring a work of art rather by the object it fulfils, by the impression it makes, than by the time it took to fulfil the object, or by the extent of "sustained effort" which became necessary to produce the impression. The fact is, that perseverance is one thing and genius quite another; nor can all the transcendentalists in Heathendom confound them.

THE CRITIC AND THE PERCEPTION OF VALUES[1]

By T. S. Eliot

The intelligent and sensitive critic who discussed Mr. Read's book in the *Times' Literary Supplement* (leading article, July 8th, 1926), begins his article by remarking that "the comparative quiescence of the creative spirit in our literature of recent years has found a certain compensation in the increased activity of the critical." This antithesis between the "creative" and "critical" periods had some validity or utility in the last century, when "literature" was still composed in accepted forms, of poetry, of prose, of the novel; when the writers of verse, prose or the novel could assume for themselves a position respectable or disreputable (it is now much the same thing) in a respectable or disreputable world (according to the way in which you looked at it); when accordingly the "critic" existed, had a position in "literature." But at the present time, when we have begun to suspect that "literature" depends for its existence, even its subsistence, upon other things the existence of which we now doubt; when one of our most conspicuous *littérateurs* can exclaim: *la littérature est impossible. Il faut*

[1]A review of *Reason and Romanticism: Essays in Literary Criticism,* by Herbert Read (Faber & Gwyer) and *Messages,* par Ramon Fernandez (1re série, Gallimard, Paris), in *The New Criterion,* October, 1926, and reprinted by permission of Mr. T. S. Eliot.

en sortir; when it appears that the existence and the concept of literature depends upon our answer to other problems, the distinction between the "critic" and the "creator" is not a very useful one. The significance of the term critic has varied indefinitely: in our time the most vigorous critical minds are philosophical minds, are, in short, creative of values.

Mr. Read and M. Fernandez provide an excellent example of this invalidation of the ancient classification. They are of the same generation, of the same order of culture; their education is as nearly the same as that of men of different race and nationality can be; and they are occupied with similar material. Both books are collections of reprinted essays: and both volumes have a unity of purpose hitherto uncommon in volumes of collected essays. Both have rewritten and improved their essays, under the impulse of this unity of purpose. Both are primarily students of literature, and animated by the desire to find a meaning and justification for literature. Mr. Read has the advantage of being European and English; M. Fernandez that of being European and American (he was born in Mexico). Both, instead of taking for granted the place and function of literature—and therefore taking for granted the whole universe—are occupied with the inquiry into the whole moral world, fundamentally, with entities and values. And they represent, finally, in my opinion, two divergent directions which the human spirit can take.

Both are occupied with what M. Fernandez calls the *problème de hiérarchie.* Let us start from the novel, in which both writers are interested, and from the particular point—a capital point for every contemporary mind—on which we find them most closely in agreement: their judgment of the work of Marcel Proust. I will take a sentence which Mr.

Read, in his book, quotes from the book of M. Fernandez, and quotes obviously with warm approval:

"Les objections que soulève l'œuvre de Proust, considérée comme analyse intégrale du cœur, comme révélatrice du fond de notre nature, peuvent être à mon avis réduites à deux essentielles: elle n'édifie point une hiérarchie des valeurs, et elle ne manifeste, de son début à sa conclusion, aucun progrès spirituel."[2]

This sentence in itself is enough to show the penetration, the seriousness, and the novelty of M. Fernandez' criticism. And as, from this point of agreement—the rejection of Proust (and by Mr. Read, of Joyce also, with whom Fernandez is not concerned) because of what M. Fernandez notifies as *l'absence de l'élément moral chez Proust*—as from this point the divergence begins, and becomes more and more manifest, we have, from these two writers, almost incorrigible testimony to the actual lack of value of Proust, or more exactly, to his value simply as a milestone, as a point of demarcation between a generation for whom the dissolution of value had in itself a positive value, and the generation for which the recognition of value is of utmost importance, a generation which is beginning to turn its attention to an athleticism, a *training,* of the soul as severe and ascetic as the training of the body of a runner.

There are two sharp distinctions to be drawn: first, that between "this generation" and the last, between the generation which accepts moral problems and that which accepted only æsthetic or economic or psychological problems—and this is the distinction which assimilates Mr. Read and M. Fernandez; and second, the distinction between two different ways of dealing with the moral problem, and this is the

---

[2]Fernandez,*op. cit.,* p. 147; Read, *op. cit.,* p. 220.

distinction which separates Mr. Read and M. Fernandez. Both are, like St. Thomas and Nietzsche, theologians and moralists: but the directions in which Mr. Read and M. Fernandez seek their solution are opposite. M. Fernandez —who is, incidentally, a critic as well qualified to pronounce upon English literature as any English critic living —finds an ensample in Meredith; Mr. Read (who, of living English critics, in that one with the best understanding of *American* literature) in Henry James. The contrast is significant.

One of the finest, the most fecund, of the essays in M. Fernandez' volume, beside the essay on Proust, which is probably the most profound that has been written on that author, is his essay on Cardinal Newman, which originally appeared in *The Criterion*. M. Fernandez is, from a certain point of view, in closer sympathy with Newman than are many of Newman's Christian or literary apologists; he is in much closer sympathy with Newman in his place and *time:* with Newman, in fact—and it is a large part—in so far as Newman was *not* Christian or Catholic. He does not understand, perhaps, that in which Newman believed or tried to believe, but he understands, better than almost anyone, the *way in which* Newman believed or tried to believe it. And this is a capital difference: a different way of facing the "moral" problem: M. Fernandez as a psychologist, Mr. Read as a metaphysician. Mr. Read is interested in St. Thomas Aquinas, because he is interested in metaphysical and logical truth; M. Fernandez is interested in Newman, because he is interested in *personality*. The difference between Read and Fernandez is a difference of focus, a difference of value: M. Fernandez is in a sense with Bergson, with the pragmatists, with those who have reached a certain degree of sophistication about "the nature of truth":

theory of reality which seems to be that of traditional psychology. The Mind seems to have for M. Fernandez a primary reality, psychology seems to take precedence over ontology. The Aristotelian commentator, Zabazella, observes:

"Dicamus quod intellectus seipsum intelligit, quatenus supra suam operationem reflectitur, dum alia intelligit, cogniscit enim se intelligere, proinde cogniscit se habere naturam talem, quae est apta fieri omnia. . . ." and on the other hand we find in Watson's *Behaviourism* the following definition of personality:

"The sum of activities that can be discovered by actual observation of behaviour over a long enough term to give reliable information. In other words, personality is but the end product of our habit systems."

The last definition is a little unsatisfactory, because one wonders what is a "long enough" term to give "reliable" information. There is, however, a certain agreement between Aristotle and Professor Watson (though Professor Watson may not think so) : they are both, I think, in disaccord (by implication) with M. Fernandez. "Personality" for both Aristotle and Professor Watson, refers to something outside.

This something outside is something for which Mr. Read is seeking, though not with complete success. Mr. Read is extremely honest, but not (it is extremely difficult) absolutely thoroughgoing. The critic of the *Times,* above mentioned, quotes the following passage from Mr. Read's book:

"The criticism of revealed religion has been operative not only on the empirical plane (which matters little) but also on the psychological plane. A religion like Christianity is built up largely on unconscious symbols : it finds its most powerful forces in subconscious processes like prayer, grace and faith. The effect of experimental science has been to destroy the unconsciousness of these symbols; it understands them and therefore equates them with conscious equivalents, which are no longer symbols and which on that account no longer compel the imagination."

The critic of the *Times* has very cleverly fastened on one of Mr. Read's weakest points, and he observes, in passing, that the word "subconscious" comes "very strangely from the pen of a Thomist." Mr. Read has here got himself into a muddle; but it is a muddle which testifies to his honesty (for we all get into a muddle somewhere, and the question is only *where*). Mr. Read stating that the empirical plane matters little (and I think he is wrong, because we cannot pass over so cavalierly the difference between "planes") and implying that the psychological plane matters much, is throwing away a trick to M. Fernandez. Why should Mr. Read take the psychological plane so seriously; and what does he mean by unconscious symbols? If we are unconscious that a symbol is a symbol, then is it a symbol at all? and the moment we become conscious that it is a symbol, is it any longer a symbol? Mr. Read is on the verge of getting involved in the problem of Transsubstantiation. M. Fernandez is in danger of being an idealist without ideals; Mr. Read of being a realist without real object. Both are struggling to find an objective truth; both are encumbered by the wipings of psychology. It is M. Fernandez who has arrived the nearest to a coherent theory: the great weakness of Mr. Read's book (if I have read these essays correctly) is that it represents a period of transition from psychology to metaphysics.

I believe myself in sympathy with both Mr. Read and M. Fernandez, and out of sympathy with the critic of the former in the *Times,* in the conception of Intelligence. The critic of the *Times* reproves in Mr. Read an "uncritical frame of mind" for which "verse that contains a maximum of explicit conceptual thought becomes superior to poetry that is mindful of its proper function and excellence— namely to pursue its rhythmic progress through an identity of image and idea." This statement, about Mr. Read, is only intelligible to me on the assumption that his critic is incapable of appreciating the verses of Guido Cavalcanti which Mr. Read quotes (p. 50) and incapable of understanding the *Vita Nuova.* To a critic with such incapacities, Mr. Read must naturally seem to have a "bias toward intellectualism." "Intellectualism" is a pejorative flung at Aristotle—and at St. Thomas—by those who have not taken the trouble to acquaint themselves with the sense of the texts. Similarly, the same critic, objecting simultaneously to Mr. Read and to St. Thomas, comments:

"To a modern mind the word 'intelligence' does not connote the faculty or act of 'simple apprehension of truth'. To a modern mind that act or faculty is 'intuition'. Whether we know as much as we ought to know about intuition may be doubted, but we shall not increase our knowledge by calling it intelligence."

To this it may be replied, that we only complicate our ignorance by calling it "intuition," and that for anyone who has devoted even a little attention to St. Thomas, or to Aristotle, the term "intelligence" is adequate. *Intelligibilia se habent ad intellectum sicut sensibilia ad sensum:* they may be, and sometimes are, grasped immediately by inspection; and to insist on another faculty "intuition" is merely to demand a more potent and thuriferous ju-ju. And I think that M. Fernandez, as well as Mr. Read, will be on the side of what we call "the intelligence."

CHAPTER V

PROSE FOR PHILOSOPHY: RALPH WALDO EMERSON

THE VEXED QUESTION OF RHETORICAL MEANS VERSUS SUBJECT MATTER

WHENEVER a speaker dwells exclusively on the stylistic elements of literature, it is certain he will be halted sooner or later by some hearer who protests against the seeming neglect of Content and pointedly accuses the speaker of narrowness and triviality. Such a person may even go so far— in my experience I have encountered several—as to argue that there is no such subject for consideration as Style. Style can, he will maintain, only be mentioned in subordinate connection with Content, and then simply as one of the aspects of the latter. In the first place, however, there is no reason why one should not be concerned with both Style and Content, and to be temporarily preoccupied with one implies no disrespect whatever for the other.

Then, secondly, the fact is, of course, that the work of art is always a unity. "Imitation of nature" is truly the principle of art, and it is *as if* an example of art had organic life. What is alive—a human being for instance—is a unit, and what is imitatively alive (*as if* alive) will also be a unit, and its aspects, features, apparent divisions, and so on will ultimately resolve into a oneness.

But we can speak at one while of the behavior of a man, and at another of his psychology. The two are at last inextricably one, but for a long time they can, for purposes of knowing the many-sidedness of this man, be kept separate. Just so with a work of literature. One can approach it curious to see how it works, to learn its technic, and otherwise one can study its content, its inner life, without much thought for its technic. But either approach when it is thoroughly pursued will lead one, by and by, into the other, and thus one finally comes to realize what is really meant by the phrase "a marriage of form and content."

A great writer is doubly great, for he is an expert in the manipulation and hypnotic treatment of the reader and he is an expert in his knowledge of life. But this is a book devoted only to the first kind of expertness. However humble and short in its accomplishment it may be, it is intended to join in that stream of literary criticism that stems from Aristotle's approach and methods in examining literature. The other great stream of literary criticism I shall call Socratic, and this deals primarily with the writer as an expert knower of life and the universe. How necessary each approach is to the other, both Aristotle and Socrates show, but Socrates makes the more thorough argument. If I say that I subscribe wholeheartedly to the latter's views of composition as spoken for in Plato's "Phædrus," I do so now in order to set some readers' minds at peace regarding our present emphasis upon literary skill. To make the kind of study of literary skill we are about to undertake with Emerson is not to forswear values. That should be plain.

WHY PROSE IS THE VEHICLE FOR PHILOSOPHY

Emerson is commonly taken as a philosopher. Between prose and philosophy as between prose and literary criticism there is the utmost congeniality. For philosophy is, of course, basically intellectual. As a usual rule, the philosopher has a complete faith in reason as the instrument for discovering truth, and though there are cases in which the philosopher has argued against intellectualism and although certainly a philosopher's motives are seldom reasonable, yet he uses reason to justify himself and his view of the world. From the philosophers we always expect an intellectual report upon life: we assign them as their highest value the discovery, if they can make it, of the *reason* for man's existence. Further, then, since this is the nature of their subject, we expect philosophers to make use of the vocabulary of the mind, to show the virtues of clarity and precision, to adopt in their writing the forms of reason: in short, we anticipate from them a consistent appeal to our own minds, and the medium for such an appeal is prose.

But does Emerson fit with these specifications? By selecting his essay on Intellect, I have done him more than justice as a philosophic writer—as should be apparent after we have analyzed his prose and read this essay together. On the whole, there is not enough rhythmical elaboration, not sufficient arabesquing of phrases and sentences, to give us warrant for classifying Emerson's prose as grand-style. Plain-style it is, but there are occasional flights into the more magnificent symphonic regions, and the dazzling character of one of those flights I have tried to follow in the rhythmical scansion at the close of this chapter.

SEVEN TRAITS OF EMERSON'S STYLE

The first thing about Emerson's style that particularly strikes me—and I intend to mention seven things in all— is the rotundity, the full-soundingness, of the vocabulary. These are words that a tongue can roll forth. You can pick him up anywhere, and the temptation will come to read aloud the polysyllabled resonant terms.

"The Supreme Critic on the errors of the past and the present, and the only prophet of that which must be, is that great nature in which we rest, as the earth lies in the soft arms of the atmosphere; that Unity, that Oversoul, within which every man's particular being is contained and made one with all other; that common heart, of which all sincere conversation is the worship, to which all right action is submission; that overpowering reality which confutes our tricks and talents, and constrains every one to pass for what he is, and to speak from his character, and not from his tongue, and which evermore tends to pass into our thought and hand, and become wisdom, and virtue, and power, and beauty."

Second, as everyone knows, Emerson was affected by the peculiar exclamatory style of Carlyle, but more indelible than that is the faint strain of Biblical phraseology in his writing. He was fond of the abrupt exclamation—and here sometimes we hear a Carlylean ring; and of the rhetorical question—and here often the King James Version governs the wording. It is dangerous to introduce archaic flavoring, but Emerson does not over-do it, and the associations he arouses in the reader are to the writer's advantage.

Third—my discontent with this formal scheme of numbered points is somewhat assuaged by the brevity won thereby—it should be of interest to the student to track down the variations in Emerson's repetitious thought. Repeat himself he does, but also, and this partially saves him from giving tedium, he shows a degree of cunning in varying and restating his ideas.

"Genius studies the casual thought, and, far back in the womb of things, sees the rays parting from one orb, that diverge ere they fall by infinite diameters. Genius watches the monad through all his masks as he performs the metempsychosis of nature. Genius detects through the fly, through the caterpillar, through the grub, through the egg, the constant individual; through countless individuals, the fixed species; through many species, the genus; through all genera, the steadfast type; through all the kingdoms of organized life, the eternal unity."

No one can escape having noticed for oneself what my fourth point refers to: the pronounced preference of Emerson for hearty affirmative sentences; but the fifth is more subtle. It is his trick of argument by metaphor, again and again resorted to. "Nature is a mutable cloud, which is always and never the same." This device in a philosopher should be watched, lest, as so often happens in Emerson, we are in actuality offered a figure of speech when we have cried for an idea. There is a proper use, beautiful and effective, for images in philosophic discourse, but discussion of that ·had better be postponed until we attempt to assay the style of Santayana.

Somewhat allied to the last point is Emerson's inclination for the short aphoristic statement and a quantity of pithy illustrations. "Trust thyself: every heart vibrates to that iron string"; and "A man Cæsar is born, and for ages after we have a Roman empire. Christ is born, and millions of minds so grow and cleave to his genius, that he is confounded with virtue and the possible of man. An institution is the lengthened shadow of one man"—these are examples of both, and of argument by metaphor as well.

But to me it seems most important to catch the seventh

point, and that has to do with the sweep of Emerson's statement. He is not an author given to qualifying and modify-
ing his affirmations. On the contrary! He loves sweep, the
sweeping word, the full sweeping generality. Take away
from his essays the words "all," "each," "every," "whole,"
and the other inclusive words, substitute for them restricted
substantives, and you have not Emerson, for then you
have not the undifferentiated expanses of thought and feeling that he expressed.

ITS FORENSIC CHARACTER

But what picture now grows before our imaginative eye?
Not that of the philosopher reflecting and writing in his
study or walking and discoursing reasonably and quietly
in the groves of the Academy. No: somehow we feel ourselves not alone in reading Emerson. We are being publicly
addressed; we are one of a crowd in a public hall and a
speaker has mounted the platform. He does not shout, but
there is a booming undertone to his words, and the roll of
his eloquence suddenly brings us up as it shortens into
rhetorical questioning, into homely aphorisms. He piles on
illustration after illustration, strews his hearty affirmations
about, subdues us with his confidence in the broadest gen-
eralities. He keeps circling about his major ideas, repeating
them over and over in new phrases. With the poetry of his
figures, he stirs us. That is it: we are stirred but not
illumined.

For the appeal of this one-time Unitarian preacher is to
our emotions. His writing is energized less by thought than
by feeling, and it is, in fact, a species of oratory. The aim
is to persuade us to share the beliefs of the orator; not to
convince us by dialectic of their truth.

Oratory and its means of persuasion, well exemplified

in the habits of Emerson's style, are perfectly legitimate in their place, but in the particular relation that is supposed to exist between the writer and the reader of philosophy, emotional declamation is an unfair substitute foisted on the reader. The style of Emerson is a bad philosophic style because it is inappropriate for the communication of philosophic thought.

WHY EMERSON'S PROSE IS WEAK IN FORM

The form of Emerson's essay confirms what we have learned from the style. There is no strictness here, such as the mind calls for, and the looseness is so great that one may without loss to the development of the essay shuffle its paragraphs in a quantity of arrangements. One can usually, for example, put any one of the first four or five paragraphs at the top of the essay, and the essay will open just as well. It is, in fact, easy to compose an essay on the Emersonian model, for its form is simply and merely the association of ideas with a given topic. One sets out to write on such a topic, one of the virtues: let it be Courage. Courage naturally suggests cowardice, and further associations are likely to be the following: overcoming difficulties, facing danger, physical and moral courage, defeat, victory, slavery and Stoicism (the last for a touch of philosophic tradition). One writes several paragraphs about each of these associated ideas, cites copious illustrations, broadens the emotional appeal, and then blocks the passages together. This is tessellated writing.[1]

---

[1] The way Emerson worked at his writing was responsible for this checkered effect. He was the industrious keeper of a Journal for his thoughts, and his Journals were carefully paged and indexed by subect. When he was asked to lecture he would then cull from his Journals all the thoughts appropriate to his topic, and string them together like beads. These made his lecture, and from

A friend of mine, an amateur of letters,[2] once took the pains of tracking Emerson's associations throughout the essay on The Poet. He found that the subject at once suggested to the "Concord Sage" an aspect of itself, and that thereafter the essay consisted merely of twenty-one associations with this aspect of the topic! As I hinted before, "Intellect," the essay that follows this chapter, is better knit than usual.

LIKE STYLE, LIKE PHILOSOPHY

Unless one has carried in mind the purport of the beginning of this chapter it is curious to find now that a description of Emerson's style and form is to a large extent a description of his philosophy, too. The prose is sanguine, expansive, and tessellated. From it one should be able to deduce what we know, namely, that the philosophy is optimistic, it is founded upon emotional assurances that man is potentially a greater being than he actually is, and it is unsystematic. The wide sweep of the style lacks refinement and precision, and it is so with the philosophy, which is inexact and lost in its general concepts of Eternal Unity

---

the lecture he would write his essay by the simple expedient of pruning and condensing what he had spoken. There was therefore no effort at careful construction and planning of an essay as a whole.

The view here advanced of Emerson's style is certainly not new, although usually it is not reached by close induction from the elements of the style but by inference from the general effect of his prose. The keynote of Emerson's style, says W. C. Brownell in *American Prose Masters*, "is that of the pulpit modified by the lyceum, and the forensic element struggles in it with the literary. Its ideal is eloquence, not exposition." Brownell believes that the styles of the orators, Phillips and Everett, were particularly influential on Emerson when he was forming his own style.

[2]Mr. Hansell Baugh of New York city.

and the Oversoul. Emerson's philosophic method, so far as he had any, was a large trust in the natural, spontaneous, irresponsible operations of the human mind and feelings, and could not this also be deduced from an accurate account of the way his style works? As the behavior, so the man.

There is a fundamental dislocation between the prose of Emerson and the demands of philosophy as a subject, and he is in truth an impure philosopher, being part moralist, part literary essayist, part sermonizer with philosophical leanings. He wrote to inspire readers to meditative reflection on the matters on which he reflected, and he sought to persuade them to agree with his general bias. But persuasion and inspiration were almost his all, while his philosophy hovered always mistily above his literary practice, a vapory mass that he was not able to precipitate into the proper downpour of ideas.

A POSTSCRIPT ON EMERSON'S BEAUTY OF RHYTHM

I am not denying, of course, that Emerson's style has its beauty, and shall even go out of the way now for the sake of an exercise in scansion of one of his purple paragraphs. It is a good specimen for illustrating the difference between the "Blessed Meaning" and the "Beautiful Means." In the final paragraph of the essay entitled "Spiritual Laws" Emerson encountered Luck and wrote above his usual eloquent strain.

"We are the | photometers, | we | the irritable | goldleaf | and tinfoil | that measure the | accumulations | of the subtle | element. | We know | the authentic | effects | of the true fire | through every one | of its million | disguises."

With complete preservation of the thought, the passage can be rewritten as follows:

"Men can be compared to photometers, the instruments that physicists employ for recording the relative intensities of light. In a spiritual sense, we are the irritable goldleaf and tinfoil that measure the accumulations of that subtle element, the great soul we have been delineating. Thus it is that through every one of the soul's million disguises we can detect the authentic effects of the true fire."

Now, why is the original passage far superior to the revision? The second is more explicit and speaks to the mind more clearly: but this gain (if it be one) is not welcomed. The fact is that all particular claims to prose harmony have been abrogated.

But by taking the delightful pains of scanning Emerson's paragraph, the rhythmic secrets of the beauty of his means are bared. They are (a) the frequency of the Ionic *a minore* and third pæon feet, which Professor Saintsbury, after very long experience in scanning English prose, asserts are practically a specific for "harmonious prose, especially of an emotional kind"; (b) the gradations in feet which end each sentence, this being in the first sentence a declension of dochmiac, third pæon, and cretic, and in the second sentence a decline from dochmiac through third pæon to amphibrach, and the charming slight variance between them produced by the cretic ("element") and the amphibrach ("disguises"); (c) the majestic tone that is contributed by the monosyllabic foot ("we") and the spondaic words ("goldleaf" and "tinfoil") in the second clause; and (d) the cunning enhancement of the pronoun "we" by each time changing slightly the stress on it instead of clumsily smiting it with an identical blow.

Let anyone who wishes to be thorough scan the rewritten passages; he will find no such finesse, no such elevation of the rhythm. Nor will he find there other glories of the Emerson original not entered upon in this postscript, such as the peculiarly felicitous combinations of vowels and consonants, the compression and tension of metaphorical language. Yet the thought—and it is a thought which has been much more accurately stated and set as corner stone in much deeper philosophies than Emerson's—is the same.

INTELLECT

By Ralph Waldo Emerson

Go, speed the stars of Thought
On to their shining goals;—
The sower scatters broad his seed,
The wheat thou strew'st be souls.

Every substance is negatively electric to that which
stands above it in the chemical tables, positively to that
which stands below it. Water dissolves wood, and iron, and
salt; air dissolves water; electric fire dissolves air, but the intellect dissolves fire, gravity, laws, method, and the subtlest
unnamed relations of nature, in its resistless menstruum.
Intellect lies behind genius, which is intellect constructive.
Intellect is the simple power anterior to all action or
construction. Gladly would I unfold in calm degrees a natural history of the intellect, but what man has yet been able
to mark the steps and boundaries of that transparent
essence? The first questions are always to be asked, and the
wisest doctor is graveled by the inquisitiveness of a child.
How can we speak of the action of the mind under any
divisions, as of its knowledge, of its ethics, of its work,
and so forth, since it melts will into perception, knowledge
into act? Each becomes the other. Itself alone is. Its vision
is not like the vision of the eye, but is union with the things
known.

Intellect and intellection signify to the common ear consideration of abstract truth. The considerations of time
and place, of you and me, of profit and hurt, tyrannize over

most men's minds. Intellect separates the fact considered from *you,* from all local and personal reference, and discerns it as if it existed for its own sake. Heraclitus looked upon the affections as dense and colored mists. In the fog of good and evil affections, it is hard for man to walk forward in a straight line. Intellect is void of affection, and sees an object as it stands in the light of science, cool and disengaged. The intellect goes out of the individual, floats over its own personality, and regards it as a fact, and not as *I* and *mine.* He who is immersed in what concerns person or place can not see the problem of existence. This the intellect always ponders. Nature shows all things formed and bound. The intellect pierces the form, overleaps the wall, detects intrinsic likeness between remote things, and reduces all things into a few principles.

The making a fact the subject of thought raises it. All that mass of mental and moral phenomena, which we do not make objects of voluntary thought, come within the power of fortune; they constitute the circumstances of daily life; they are subject to change, to fear, and hope. Every man beholds his human condition with a degree of melancholy. As a ship aground is battered by the waves, so man, imprisoned in mortal life, lies open to the mercy of coming events. But a truth, separated by the intellect, is no longer a subject of destiny. We behold it as a god upraised above care and fear. And so any fact in our life, or any record of our fancies or reflections, disentangled from the web of our unconsciousness, becomes an object impersonal and immortal. It is the past restored, but embalmed. A better art than that of Egypt has taken fear and corruption out of it. It is eviscerated of care. It is offered for science. What is addressed to us for contemplation does not threaten us, but makes us intellectual beings.

The growth of the intellect is spontaneous in every expansion. The mind that grows could not predict the times, the means, the mode of that spontaneity. God enters by a private door into every individual. Long prior to the age of reflection is the thinking of the mind. Out of darkness, it came insensibly into the marvelous light of to-day. In the period of infancy it accepted and disposed of all impressions from the surrounding creation after its own way. Whatever any mind doth or saith is after a law; and this native law remains over it after it has come to reflection or conscious thought. In the most worn, pedantic, introverted self-tormenter's life, the greatest part is incalculable by him, unforeseen, unimaginable, and must be, until he can take himself up by his own ears. What am I? What has my will done to make me that I am? Nothing. I have been floated into this thought, this hour, this connection of events, by secret currents of might and mind, and my ingenuity and willfulness have not thwarted, have not aided to an appreciable degree.

Our spontaneous action is always the best. You cannot, with your best deliberation and heed, come so close to any question as your spontaneous glance shall bring you, whilst you rise from your bed, or walk abroad in the morning after meditating the matter before sleep on the previous night. Our thinking is a pious reception. Our truth of thought is therefore vitiated as much by too violent direction given by our will, as by too great negligence. We do not determine what we will think. We only open our senses, clear away, as we can, all obstruction from the fact, and suffer the intellect to see. We have little control over our thoughts. We are the prisoners of ideas. They catch us up for moments into their heaven, and so fully engage us, that we take no thought for the morrow, gaze like children, without an effort to make them our own. By and by we fall out of that rapture, bethink us where we have been, what we have seen, and repeat, as truly as we can, what we have beheld. As far as we can recall these ecstasies, we carry away in the ineffaceable memory the result, and all men and all the ages confirm it. It is called Truth. But the moment we cease to report, and attempt to correct and contrive, it is not truth.

If we consider what persons have stimulated and profited us, we shall perceive the superiority of the spontaneous or intuitive principle over the arithmetical or logical. The first contains the second, but virtual and latent. We want, in every man, a long logic; we cannot pardon the absence of it, but it must not be spoken. Logic is the procession or proportionate unfolding of the intuition; but its virtue is as silent method; the moment it would appear as propositions, and have a separate value, it is worthless.

In every man's mind, some images, words, and facts remain, without effort on his part to imprint them, which others forget, and afterwards these illustrate to him important laws. All our progress is an unfolding, like the vegetable bud. You have first an instinct, then an opinion, then a knowledge, as the plant has root, bud, and fruit. Trust the instinct to the end, though you can render no reason. It is vain to hurry it. By trusting it to the end, it shall ripen into truth and you shall know why you believe.

Each mind has its own method. A true man never acquires after college rules. What you have aggregated in a natural manner surprises and delights when it is produced. For we cannot oversee each other's secret. And hence the differences between men in natural endowment are insignificant in comparison with their common wealth. Do you think the porter and the cook have no anecdotes, no experiences, no wonders for you? Everybody knows as much as a savant. The walls of rude minds are scrawled all over with facts, with thoughts. They shall one day bring a lantern and read the inscriptions. Every man, in the degree in which he has wit and culture, finds his curiosity inflamed concerning the modes of living and thinking of other men, and especially of those classes whose minds have not been subdued by the drill of school education.

This instinctive action never ceases in a healthy mind, but becomes richer and more frequent in its informations through all states of culture. At last comes the era of reflection, when we not only observe, but take pains to observe; when we of set purpose sit down to consider an abstract truth; when we keep the mind's eye open, whilst we converse, whilst we read, whilst we act, intent to learn the secret law of some class of facts.

What is the hardest task in the world? To think. I would put myself in the attitude to look in the eye an abstract truth, and I cannot. I blench and withdraw on this side and on that. I seem to know what he meant who said, No man can see God face to face and live. For example, a man explores the basis of civil government. Let him intend his mind without respite, without rest, in one direction. His best heed long time avails him nothing. Yet thoughts are flitting before him. We all but apprehend, we dimly forebode the truth. We say, I will walk abroad, and the truth will take form and clearness to me. We go forth, but cannot find it. It seems as if we needed only the stillness and composed attitude of the library to seize the thought. But we come in, and are as far from it as at first. Then, in a moment, and unannounced, the truth appears. A certain, wandering light appears, and is the distinction, the principle, we wanted. But the oracle comes, because we had pre-

viously laid siege to the shrine. It seems as if the law of
the intellect resembled that law of nature by which we
now inspire, now expire the breath; by which the heart now
draws in, then hurls out the blood,—the law of undulation.
So now you must labor with your brains, and now you must
forbear your activity, and see what the great Soul showeth.

The immortality of man is as legitimately preached
from the intellections as from the moral volitions. Every intellection is mainly prospective. Its present value is its least.
Inspect what delights you in Plutarch, in Shakspeare, in
Cervantes. Each truth that a writer acquires is a lantern,
which he turns full on what facts and thoughts lay already
in his mind, and behold, all the mats and rubbish which had
littered his garret become precious. Every trivial fact in
his private biography becomes an illustration of this new
principle, revisits the day, and delights all men by its
piquancy and new charm. Men say, Where did he get this?
and think there was something divine in his life. But no;
they have myriads of facts just as good, would they only get
a lamp to ransack their attics withal.

We are all wise. The difference between persons is not in
wisdom but in art. I knew, in an academical club, a person
who always deferred to me, who, seeing my whim for writing, fancied that my experiences had somewhat superior; whilst I saw that his experiences were as good as mine.
Give them to me, and I would make the same use of them.
He held the old; he holds the new; I had the habit of tack-
ing together the old and the new, which he did not use to
exercise. This may hold in the great examples. Perhaps if
we should meet Shakspeare, we would not be conscious of
any steep inferiority; no: but of a great equality,—only
that he possessed a strange skill of using, of classifying, his
facts, which we lacked. For, notwithstanding our utter in-

capacity to produce any thing like Hamlet and Othello, see the perfect reception this wit, and immense knowledge of life, and liquid eloquence find in us all.

If you gather apples in the sunshine, or make hay, or hoe corn, and then retire within doors, and shut your eyes, and press them with your hand, you shall still see apples hanging in the bright light, with boughs and leaves thereto, or the tasseled grass, or the cornflags, and this for five or six hours afterwards. There lie the impressions on the retentive organ, though you knew it not. So lies the whole series of natural images with which your life has made you acquainted in your memory, though you know it not, and a thrill of passion flashes light on their dark chamber, and the active power seizes instantly the fit image, as the word of its momentary thought.

It is long ere we discover how rich we are. Our history, we are sure, is quite tame: we have nothing to write, nothing to infer. But our wiser years still run back to the despised recollections of childhood, and always we are fishing up some wonderful article out of that pond; until, by and by, we begin to suspect that the biography of the one foolish person we know is, in reality, nothing less than the miniature paraphrase of the hundred volumes of the Universal History.

In the intellect constructive, which we popularly designate by the word Genius, we observe the same balance of two elements as in intellect receptive. The constructive intellect produces thoughts, sentences, poems, plans, designs, systems. It is the generation of the mind, the marriage of thought with nature. To genius must always go two gifts, the thought and the publication. The first is revelation, always a miracle, which no frequency of occurrence or incessant study can ever familiarize, but which must always leave the inquirer stupid with wonder. It is the advent of truth into the world, a form of thought now, for the first time, bursting into the universe, a child of the old eternal soul, a piece of genuine and immeasurable greatness. It seems, for the time, to inherit all that has yet existed, and to dictate to the unborn. It affects every thought of man, and goes to fashion every institution. But to make it available, it needs a vehicle or art by which it is conveyed to men. To be communicable, it must become picture or sensible object. We must learn the language of facts. The most wonderful inspirations die with their subject, if he has no hand to paint them to the senses. The ray of light passes invisible through space, and only when it falls on an object is it seen. When the spiritual energy is directed on something outward, then it is a thought. The relation between it and you first makes you, the value of you, apparent to me. The rich, inventive genius of the painter must be smothered and lost for want of the power of drawing, and in our happy hours we should be inexhaustible poets, if once we could break through the silence into adequate rhyme. As all men have some access to primary truth, so all have some art or power of communication in their head, but only in the artist does it descend into the hand. There is an inequality, whose laws we do not yet know, between two men and between two moments of the same man, in respect to this faculty. In common hours, we have the same facts as in the uncommon or inspired, but they do not sit for their portraits; they are not detached, but lie in a web. The thought of genius is spontaneous; but the power of picture or expression, in the most enriched and flowing nature, implies a mixture of will, a certain control over the spontaneous states, without which no production is possible. It is a conversion of all nature into the rhetoric of thought, under the eye of judgment, with a strenuous exercise of choice. And yet the imaginative vocabulary seems to be spontaneous also. It does not flow from experience only or mainly, but from a richer source. Not by any conscious imitation of particular forms are the grand strokes of the painter executed, but by repairing to the fountain-head of all forms in his mind. Who is the first drawing master? Without instruction we know very well the ideal of the human form. A child knows if an arm or a leg be distorted in a picture, if the attitude be natural or grand, or mean, though he has never received any instruction in drawing, or heard any conversation on the subject, nor can himself draw with correctness a single feature. A good form strikes all eyes pleasantly, long before they have any science on the subject, and a beautiful face sets twenty hearts in palpitation, prior to all consideration of the mechanical proportions of the features and head. We may owe to dreams some light on the fountain of this skill; for, as soon as we let our will go, and let the unconscious states ensue, see what cunning draughtsmen we are! We entertain ourselves with wonderful forms of men, of women, of animals, of gardens, of woods, and of monsters, and the mystic pencil wherewith we then draw has no awkwardness or inexperience, no meagerness or poverty; it can design well, and group well; its composition is full of art, its colors are well laid on, and the whole canvas which it paints is lifelike, and apt to touch us with terror, with tenderness, with desire, and with grief. Neither are the artist's copies from experience ever mere copies, but always touched and softened by tints from this ideal domain.

The conditions essential to a constructive mind do not appear to be so often combined but that a good sentence or verse remains fresh and memorable for a long time. Yet when we write with ease, and come out into the free air of thought, we seem to be assured that nothing is easier than to continue this communication at pleasure. Up, down, around, the kingdom of thought has no inclosures, but the Muse makes us free of her city. Well, the world has a million writers. One would think, then, that good thought would be as familiar as air and water, and the gifts of each new hour would exclude the last. Yet we can count all our good books; nay, I remember any beautiful verse for twenty years. It is true that the discerning intellect of the world is always much in advance of the creative, so that there are many competent judges of the best book, and few writers of the best books. But some of the conditions of intellectual construction are of rare occurrence. The intellect is a whole, and demands integrity in every work. This is resisted equally by man's devotion to a single thought, and by his ambition to combine too many.

Truth is our element of life, yet if a man fasten his attention on a single aspect of truth, and apply himself to that alone for a long time, the truth becomes distorted and not itself, but falsehood; herein resembling the air, which is our natural element, and the breath of our nostrils, but if a stream of the same be directed on the body for a time, it causes cold, fever, and even death. How wearisome the grammarian, the phrenologist, the political or religious fanatic, or indeed any possessed mortal whose balance is lost by the exaggeration of a single topic. It is incipient insanity. Every thought is a prison also. I cannot see what you see because I am caught up by a strong wind, and blown so far in one direction that I am out of the hoop of your horizon.

Is it any better, if the student, to avoid this offense, and to liberalize himself, aims to make a mechanical whole of history, or science, or philosophy, by a numerical addition of all the facts that fall within his vision? The world refuses to be analyzed by addition and subtraction. When we are young, we spend much time and pains in filling our notebooks with all definitions of Religion, Love, Poetry, Politics, Art, in the hope that, in the course of a few years, we shall have condensed into our encyclopædia the net value of all the theories at which the world has yet arrived. But year after year our tables get no completeness, and at last we discover that our curve is a parabola, whose arcs will never meet.

Neither by detachment, neither by aggregation, is the integrity of the intellect transmitted to its works, but by a vigilance which brings the intellect in its greatness and best state to operate every moment. It must have the same wholeness which nature has. Although no diligence can rebuild the universe in a model, by the best accumulation or disposition of details, yet does the world reappear in miniature in every event, so that all the laws of nature may be read in the smallest fact. The intellect must have the like perfection in its apprehension and in its works. For this reason, an index or mercury of intellectual proficiency is the perception of identity. We talk with accomplished persons who appear to be strangers in nature. The cloud, the tree, the turf, the bird are not theirs, have nothing of them: the world is only their lodging and table. But the poet, whose verses are to be spheral and complete, is one whom Nature cannot deceive, whatsoever face of strangeness she may put on. He feels a strict consanguinity, and detects more likeness than variety in all her changes. We are stung by the desire for new thought; but when we receive a new thought, it is only the old thought with a new face, and though we make it our own, we instantly crave another; we are not really enriched. For the truth was in us before it was reflected to us from natural objects; and the profound genius will cast the likeness of all creatures into every product of his wit.

But if the constructive powers are rare, and it is given to few men to be poets, yet every man is a receiver of this descending holy ghost, and may well study the laws of its influx. Exactly parallel is the whole rule of intellectual duty to the rule of moral duty. A self-denial, no less austere than the saint's, is demanded of the scholar. He must worship truth, and forego all things for that, and choose defeat and pain, so that his treasure in thought is thereby augmented.

God offers to every mind its choice between truth and repose. Take which you please,—you can never have both. Between these, as a pendulum, man oscillates. He in whom the love of repose predominates will accept the first creed, the first philosophy, the first political party he meets,— most likely his father's. He gets rest, commodity, and reputation; but he shuts the door of truth. He in whom the love of truth predominates will keep himself aloof from all moorings, and afloat. He will abstain from dogmatism and recognize all the opposite negations, between which, as walls, his being is swung. He submits to the inconvenience of suspense and imperfect opinion, but he is a candidate for truth, as the other is not, and respects the highest law of his being.

The circle of the green earth he must measure with his shoes, to find the man who can yield him truth. He shall then know that there is somewhat more blessed and great in hearing than in speaking. Happy is the hearing man; unhappy is the speaking man. As long as I hear truth, I am bathed by a beautiful element, and am not conscious of any limits to my nature. The suggestions are thousandfold that

I hear and see. The waters of the great deep have ingress and egress to the soul. But if I speak, I define, I confine, and am less. When Socrates speaks, Lysis and Menexenus are afflicted by no shame that they do not speak. They also are good. He likewise defers to them, loves them, whilst he speaks. Because a true and natural man contains and is the same truth which an eloquent man articulates : but in the eloquent man, because he can articulate it, it seems something the less to reside, and he turns to these silent beautiful with the more inclination and respect. The ancient sentence said, Let us be silent, for so are the gods. Silence is a solvent that destroys personality, and gives us leave to be great and universal. Every man's progress is through a succession of teachers, each of whom seems at the time to have a superlative influence, but it at last gives place to a new. Frankly let him accept it all. Jesus says, Leave father, mother, house and lands, and follow me. Who leaves all, receives more. This is as true intellectually as morally. Each new mind we approach seems to require an abdication of all our past and present possessions. A new doctrine seems, at first, a subversion of all our opinions, tastes, and manner of living. Such has Swedenborg, such has Kant, such has Coleridge, such has Hegel or his interpreter Cousin, seemed to many young men in this country. Take thankfully and heartily all they can give. Exhaust them, wrestle with them, let them not go until their blessing be won, and, after a short season, the dismay will be overpast, the excess of influence withdrawn, and they will be no longer an alarming meteor, but one more bright star shining serenely in your heaven, and blending its light with all your day.

But whilst he gives himself up unreservedly to that which draws him, because that is his own, he is to refuse himself to that which draws him not, whatsoever fame and authority may attend it, because it is not his own. Entire self-reliance belongs to the intellect. One soul is a counterpoise of all souls, as a capillary column of water is a balance for the sea. It must treat things, and books, and sovereign genius, as itself also a sovereign. If Æschylus be that man he is taken for, he has not yet done his office, when he has educated the learned of Europe for a thousand years. He is now to approve himself a master of delight to me also. If he cannot do that, all his fame shall avail him nothing with me. I were a fool not to sacrifice a thousand Æschyluses to my intellectual integrity. Especially take the same ground in regard to abstract truth, the science of the mind. The Bacon, the Spinoza, the Hume, Schelling, Kant, or whosoever propounds to you a philosophy of the mind, is only a more or less awkward translator of things in your consciousness, which you have also your way of seeing, perhaps of denominating. Say, then, instead of too timidly poring into his obscure sense, that he has not succeeded in rendering back to you your consciousness. He has not succeeded; now let another try. If Plato cannot, perhaps Spinoza will. If Spinoza cannot, then perhaps Kant. Anyhow, when at last it is done, you will find it is no recondite, but a simple, natural common state, which the writer restores to you.

But let us end these didactics. I will not, though the subject might provoke it, speak to the open question between Truth and Love. I shall not presume to interfere in the old politics of the skies;—"The cherubim know most; the seraphim love most." The gods shall settle their own quarrels. But I cannot recite, even thus rudely, laws of the intellect, without remembering that lofty and sequestered class who have been its prophets and oracles, the high-priesthood of the pure reason, the *Trismegisti*, the expounders of the principles of thought from age to age. When, at long intervals, we turn over their abstruse pages, wonderful seems the calm and grand air of these few, these great spiritual lords, who have walked in the world,—these of the old religion,—dwelling in a worship which makes the sanctities of Christianity look *parvenues* and popular; for "persuasion is in soul, but necessity is in intellect." This band of grandees, Hermes, Heraclitus, Empedocles, Plato, Plotinus, Olympiodorus, Proclus, Synesius, and the rest, have somewhat so vast in their logic, so primary in their thinking, that it seems antecedent to all the ordinary distinctions of rhetoric and literature, and to be at once poetry, and music, and dancing, and astronomy, and mathematics. I am present at the sowing of the seed of the world. With a geometry of sunbeams, the soul lays the foundations of nature. The truth and grandeur of their thought is proved by its scope and applicability, for it commands the entire schedule and inventory of things for its illustration. But what marks its elevation, and has even a comic look to us, is the innocent serenity with which these babe-like Jupiters sit in their clouds, and from age to age prattle to each other, and to no contemporary. Well assured that their speech is intelligible, and the most natural thing in the world, they add thesis to thesis, without a moment's heed of the universal astonishment of the human race below, who do not comprehend their plainest argument: nor do they ever relent so much as to insert a popular or explaining sentence; nor testify the least displeasure or petulance at the dullness of their amazed auditory. The angels are so enamored of the language that is spoken in heaven, that they will not distort their lips with the hissing and unmusical dialects of men, but speak their own, whether there be any who understand it or not.

CHAPTER VI

PROSE FOR PHILOSOPHY: WILLIAM JAMES

THE SIMPLE RHYTHMIC LIFE OF JAMES'S PROSE

EMERSON has, as we have seen, some rhythmic interest, but who would dream of scanning the rhythms of William James's prose? It is even straining matters to subject a characteristic passage of the latter to what Saintsbury calls "block scansion," a method of reading he reserves for simple prose of relatively low rhythmic tension. Of course, we can try it—as follows:

(a) "But whether we take it abstractly or concretely, our considering the spiritual self at all is a reflective process, is the result of our abandoning the outward-looking point of view, and of our having become able to think of subjectivity as such, *to think ourselves as thinkers.*"

(b) "But whether we take it abstractly or concretely,
our considering the spiritual self at all
is a reflective process,
is the result
of our abandoning the outward-looking point of view,
and of our having become able to think
of subjectivity as such,
to think ourselves as thinkers."

But I fail to see that in this instance our pains are in any way rewarded. That there is something in "block scansion" is incontestable after Saintsbury's application of it to the prose of Adam Smith, but the writing of William James is not subtle enough in its breathing and pulsing to have anything hidden which can be extracted by this form of analysis.

It is better to observe that he displays a modicum of skill in the distribution of points of stress in his sentences, that what might be called his operative words stand boldly out. Every well-built sentence has at least one, sometimes two or three, points of greatest emphasis which are often determined by the points of stress in the preceding sentence and which in turn influence the placing of such points in the following sentence. In general, James throws his center of gravity far back in the sentence. He is fond, that is to say, of the periodic sentence with the full definite stop, and it is this that gives, in spite of a vivacious vocabulary, a certain mild monotony to his style. The reader's attention is always being picked up, carried along, and then landed at the close of a sentence with a bump. On this matter it is more than well to refer to Saintsbury again. "Such superior importance as belongs to the ends is one rather of connection with other ends, clause- or sentence-, in regard to the total rhythm of the sentence or paragraph, than intrinsic or peculiar. These ends may be abrupt, complete, or dying, emphatic or gliding off. In some cases there appears to be something in them corresponding to *catalexis* in verse— the following pause supplying what is wanted. But Variety, in the composition of the feet which compose these ends, is of special and paramount importance." But James is not the writer to exemplify these subtleties.

By way of an exercise in understanding what is meant by

distribution of points of stress, take the following quotation from *Essays in Radical Empiricism* and rearrange the order of clauses and phrases in each sentence. You will then see that when you have shifted the center of gravity in one of them it necessitates a new order and a shifting of emphasis in the next sentence.

"In this continuing and corroborating, taken in no transcendental sense, but denoting definitely felt transitions, *lies all that the knowing of a percept by an idea can possibly contain or signify.* Wherever such transitions are felt, the first experience *knows* the last one. Where they do not, or where even as possible they cannot, intervene, there can be no pretense of knowing. In this latter case the extremes will be connected, if connected at all, by inferior relations—bare likeness or succession, or by 'withness' alone."

A PROSE FOR SCIENCE

These minutiæ lead us to the general descriptive statement that William James had a plain, simple, serviceable, expository style. Furthermore, whereas Emerson, as I have just contended, had an inappropriate style for philosophy, James had a fitting style for his philosophy and for science, too. The scientist, like the philosopher, is preëminently a man of ideas: his account of life and the world is equally an intellectual report. In general, the philosopher attempts to answer the question, Why?, with a system of ideas and to argue for his system. The scientist often is unconcerned with the Why of things, but all-absorbed in answering the questions, What? and How? His answers are intellectual in form and incarnate themselves in expository prose, sometimes of a fine quality, as in Thomas Huxley's essays. A hostile thinker could point out that William

James was a sort of straddler of science and philosophy. He was not satisfied with the margin at which science usually halts, but on the other hand he could not soar into the higher, more rare, regions of philosophic speculation. It was natural, therefore, that his prose instrument was just as handy for an exposition of pragmatism as it was for explaining the principles of psychology. The selection from *The Varieties of Religious Experience* which follows this chapter is chosen because in it the scientific and philosophic outlooks of William James are very well blended.

In the case of Emerson we ascertained first the character of his style and then, by referring to the philosophic content, found that style-characteristics corresponded to the latter's character with the same mysterious parallelism that a man's behavior matches his interior being. Now I propose to work the other way with James: to set forth first the character of his philosophy and then see if the character of the style duplicates it.

THE CHARACTER OF PRAGMATISM

Pragmatism loves concrete facts most of all and it loves them the more because they are plural; these numerous, multiplying, diverse, ordered, and unordered facts are simply a collection with only the unity of a collection. It says (at least its founder said) : "There is no such superstition as the idolatry of the Whole." In James's own words, the pragmatist may be said to be one who "lays the explanatory stress upon the part, the element, the individual, and treats the whole as a collection and the universal as an abstraction." He has "essentially a mosaic philosophy, a philosophy of plural facts," and so we can sum all this up by saying that pragmatism is distinguished by its vivid concrete factual character. Side by side with this, remember that James wrote: "To be radical, an empiricism must neither admit into its constructions any element that is not directly experienced, nor exclude from them any element that is directly experienced." He tried to live up to that, and hence pragmatism has a strong experiential character: so far as possible James sought to make his philosophy come out of his actual experience and possess when formulated a direct personal application for those who studied it. And his philosophy must be, above all, he wished, a workable doctrine. The aim was not to make a perfect system of abstraction, but to provide hypotheses and schemes for *doing*. A practical theory—that was what he wanted, and not a chance-proof system. For life, as he viewed it, is constantly producing novelties along with recurrences: accidents are plentiful; chance and variety are too much for determinism to explain.

THE CHARACTER OF JAMES'S STYLE AND FORM

In other words, there is a certain quantity of improvisation in the world going on all the time, and it is certainly striking that there is an air of improvisation about James's style. Emerson made us feel ourselves seated on the pews of a Unitarian church. James puts us into the classroom of a gifted university professor who is doing part of his thinking out loud and on the spur of the occasion. If chance was exciting and in the end good in life, it was equally good in lecturing or writing. One mustn't be too formal, too prepared in one's discourses, James seems to have reasoned. The style has of course working virtues: it is clear, adapted to the comprehension of a fairly intelligent audience, active in mood, an instrument shaped for the routine business of communication. What gave it life was the vocabulary, which was as little technical as possible. Whenever James, without detriment to his ideas, could stir up his style by introducing his own lively sympathies and excitements, his own quick responses to sensory stimuli, he did so. The style comes from a man vibrating in his sensations and emotions, and it is not purely a mental manifestation. An experiencing style! But do not search in it for the grander elaborations, for complex harmony, for perfection of pattern. The line-for-line texture is good enough, but there is no Whole to admire, however superstitiously.

These remarks are not vitiated but strongly confirmed by the form of James's papers. The favorite was the discussion. The opening proposes a question, then various opinions as to the answer are assembled and discussed, and then he concludes by advancing his own opinion of the matter. It will be seen that the discussion is not a stringent form.

A SPECULATIVE INQUIRY

In the end, not a great deal can be said about the technical side of William James's writings. But one can remark on the influence which his spirited semi-popular manner has exerted on American journalism of the better class. Examine the leading editorials and articles of our liberal weeklies and you will perceive that the style of William James has strongly appealed to the writers. In fact, this author does raise an exciting question when he writes like this: "This world *may,* in the last resort, be a block-universe; but on the other hand, it *may* be a universe only strung-along, not rounded in and closed."

What he raises I shall call the question of an American Prose Style, and in order to develop this thought I invite you to read the following extract. With the exception of the word *facts,* the italics are mine, and I have used them, not to underline the argument but to draw attention to something already mentioned, namely, that what distinctiveness James has is due to his choice of words.

"To no one type of mind is it given to discern the totality of truth. Something escapes the best of us,—not accidentally, but systematically, and because we have a *twist.* The scientific-academic mind and the feminine-mystical mind shy from each other's facts, just as they fly from each other's temper and spirit. Facts are there only for those who have a mental affinity with them. When once they are indisputably ascertained and admitted, the academic and critical minds are by far the best fitted ones to interpret and discuss them,—for surely to pass from mystical to scientific speculations is like passing from lunacy to sanity; but on the other hand if there is anything which human history demonstrates it is the extreme slowness with which the ordinary academic and critical mind acknowledges facts to exist which present themselves as *wild* facts, *with no stall or pigeon-hole,* or as facts which threaten to break up the accepted system. In psychology, physiology, and medicine, wherever a debate between the mystics and the *scientifics* has been once for all decided, it is the mystics who have usually proved to be right about the *facts,* while the scientifics had the better of it in respect to the theories."

With some haste and more dubiety, this style may now be called the "American standard style" for the expression of ideas, philosophic, scientific, or critical, in such fields as politics and letters. Unfortunately, it is a contraction when compared with such a style as Southey's, which is a model for English standard prose. William James had less rhythmical sense, less capacity for variation of sentence structure, and, as we have noticed, only one way of ending the sentence. Whereas English standard prose has its subdued beauties, "American standard style" as fathered by James is only a working style, only serviceable. But why, for what other reason than that James was born in New York and has influenced a number of our editors and authors, do I speak even guardedly of his style as American?

Chiefly because of the tendency in word selection illustrated above. The movement in his exposition is always from the technical statement to the popular one, from the orthodox abstruseness of vocabulary to freer non-technical terms. This is a general trait of American exposition, and when carried out on a relatively high plane, as in the case of James, it brings about simplifications that are often as true as the technicalities. But more often there is infidelity to the difficult technical statement, and the latter is odiously vulgarized.[1] This by the way, however, for the point here is that it is in the selection of the words for a popular phrasing of his ideas that James's style acquires whatever individuality it has.

"We have a twist . . . wild facts, with no stall or pigeon-hole . . . scientifics"—the American reader likes the improvised air of these; he responds to the energy of "twist" and "wild," the slight sense of words being

---

[1] Thanks to our leniency with such crimes, we have in America a luxuriant crop of vulgarizations—do I need to mention those of Messrs. Slosson and Durant?—and we look wide and far in our country for just one well-trained observer and critic of the sciences of the caliber of C. K. Ogden or J. W. N. Sullivan in England. Leo Stein seems to be qualified, but he writes of science only incidentally.

"speeded up" that is produced when James, as he does elsewhere, uses "swerve" instead of saying "deviate"; he is gratified that the writer impinges on the same area of word-associations that the more striking language of the advertiser, the journalist, and his friend in the street have planted.

Admitted that the foundation is scant for my contention that William James is the father of the "American standard" expository prose—or, to speak more strictly, the American variation of English standard. Yet one has a total feeling about James's writing that it really is different from a corresponding grade of writing in London or Oxford, and this feeling seems to arise from a mere sprinkling of unquiet words.

The matter cannot be intelligently disposed of until we obtain more results from the following speculations: (1) that the psychological center of gravity of America is radically other than that of England, (2) that the word associations of American readers vary considerably and characteristically from the word associations of the English reader, and (3) that the possibilities of whatever American style may be in the making are of kind and number sufficient to forge both a broad and a subtle instrument. H. L. Mencken's prose will hardly do as a fund of possibilities.

THE COMMON CONTENT OF ALL RELIGIONS[2]

By William James

First, is there, under all the discrepancies of the creeds, a common nucleus to which they bear their testimony unanimously?

And second, ought we to consider the testimony true?

I will take up the first question first, and answer it immediately in the affirmative. The warring gods and formulas of the various religions do indeed cancel each other, but there is a certain uniform deliverance in which religions all appear to meet. It consists of two parts:

1. An uneasiness; and
2. Its solution.

1. The uneasiness, reduced to its simplest terms, is a sense that there is *something wrong about us* as we naturally stand.

2. The solution is a sense that *we are saved from the wrongness* by making proper connection with the higher powers.

In those more developed minds which alone we are studying, the wrongness takes a moral character, and the salvation takes a mystical tinge. I think we shall keep well within the limits of what is common to all such minds if we formu-

---

[2]From *The Varieties of Religious Experience,* by William James, and reprinted by permission of Longmans, Green & Co., Publishers.

late the essence of their religious experience in terms like
these:

The individual, so far as he suffers from his wrongness
and criticizes it, is to that extent consciously beyond it, and
in at least possible touch with something higher, if anything
higher exist. Along with the wrong part there is thus a better part of him, even though it may be but a most helpless
germ. With which part he should identify his real being is
by no means obvious at this stage; but when stage 2 (the
stage of solution or salvation) arrives[3], the man identifies
his real being with the germinal higher part of himself;
and does so in the following way: *He becomes conscious
that this higher part is conterminous and continuous with a
MORE of the same quality, which is operative in the universe
outside of him, and which he can keep in working touch
with, and in a fashion get on board of and save himself
when all his lower being has gone to pieces in the wreck.*

It seems to me that all the phenomena are accurately de-
scribable in these very simple general terms. They allow
for the divided self and the struggle; they involve the change
of personal center and the surrender of the lower self; they
express the appearance of exteriority of the helping power
and yet account for our sense of union with it; and they
fully justify our feelings of security and joy. There is
probably no autobiographic document, among all those
which I have quoted, to which the description will not well
apply. One need only add such specific details as will adapt
it to various theologies and various personal temperaments,
and one will then have the various experiences reconstructed
in their individual forms.

---

[3]Remember that for some men it arrives suddenly, for others
gradually, whilst others again practically enjoy it all their life.

So far, however, as this analysis goes, the experiences are only psychological phenomena. They possess, it is true, enormous biological worth. Spiritual strength really increases in the subject when he has them, a new life opens for him, and they seem to him a place of conflux where the forces of two universes meet; and yet this may be nothing but his subjective way of feeling things, a mood of his own fancy, in spite of the effects produced. I now turn to my second question: What is the objective "truth" of their content?

The part of the content concerning which the question of truth most pertinently arises is that "MORE of the same quality" with which our own higher self appears in the experience to come into harmonious working relation. Is such a "more" merely our own notion, or does it really exist? If so, in what shape does it exist? Does it act, as well as exist? And in what form should we conceive of that "union" with it of which religious geniuses are so convinced?

It is in answering these questions that the various theologies perform their theoretic work, and that their divergencies most come to light. They all agree that the "more" really exists; though some of them hold it to exist in the shape of a personal god or gods, while others are satisfied to conceive it as a stream of ideal tendency embedded in the eternal structure of the world. They all agree, moreover, that it acts as well as exists, and that something really is effected for the better when you throw your life into its hands. It is when they treat of the experience of "union" with it that their speculative differences appear most clearly. Over this point pantheism and theism, nature and second birth, works and grace and karma, immortality and reincarnation, rationalism and mysticism, carry on inveterate disputes. . . .

The "more," as we call it, and the meaning of our "union" with it, form the nucleus of our inquiry. Into what definite description can these words be translated, and for what definite facts do they stand? . . .

The *subconscious self* is nowadays a well-accredited psychological entity: and I believe that in it we have exactly the mediating term required. Apart from all religious considerations, there is actually and literally more life in our total soul than we are at any time aware of. . . .

Much of the content of this larger background against which our conscious being stands out in relief is insignificant. Imperfect memories, silly jingles, inhibitive timidities, "dissolutive" phenomena of various sorts, as Myers calls them, enter into it for a large part. But in it many of the performances of genius seem also to have their origin; and in our study of conversion, of mystical experiences, and of prayer, we have seen how striking a part invasions from this region play in the religious life.

Let me then propose, as an hypothesis, that whatever it may be on its *farther* side, the "more" with which in religious experience we feel ourselves connected is on its *hither* side the subconscious continuation of our conscious life. Starting thus with a recognized psychological fact as our basis, we seem to preserve a contact with "science" which the ordinary theologian lacks. At the same time the theologian's contention that the religious man is moved by an external power is vindicated, for it is one of the peculiarities of invasions from the subconscious region to take on objective appearances, and to suggest to the Subject an external control. In the religious life the control is felt as "higher"; but since on our hypothesis it is primarily the higher faculties of our own hidden mind which are controlling, the sense of union with the power beyond us is a sense of something, not merely apparently, but literally true.

This doorway into the subject seems to me the best one for a science of religions, for it mediates between a number of different points of view. Yet it is only a doorway, and difficulties present themselves as soon as we step through it, and ask how far our transmarginal consciousness carries us if we follow it on its remoter side. Here the over-beliefs begin: here mysticism and the conversion-rapture and Vedantism and transcendental idealism bring in their monistic interpretations and tell us that the finite self rejoins the absolute self, for it was always one with God and identical with the soul of the world. Here the prophets of all the different religions come with their visions, voices, raptures, and other openings, supposed by each to authenticate his own peculiar faith. . . .

Disregarding the over-beliefs, and confining ourselves to what is common and generic, we have in *the fact that the conscious person is continuous with a wider self through which saving experiences come,* a positive content of religious experience which, it seems to me, *is literally and objectively true as far as it goes.* If I now proceed to state my own hypothesis about the farther limits of this extension of our personality, I shall be offering my own over-belief— though I know it will appear a sorry under-belief to some of you—for which I can only bespeak the same indulgence which in a converse case I should accord to yours.

The further limits of our being plunge, it seems to me, into an altogether other dimension of existence from the sensible and merely "understandable" world. Name it the mystical region, or the supernatural region, whichever you choose. So far as our ideal impulses originate in this region (and most of them do originate in it, for we find them possessing us in a way for which we cannot articulately account), we belong to it in a more intimate sense than that in which we belong to the visible world, for we belong in the most intimate sense wherever our ideals belong. Yet the unseen region in question is not merely ideal, for it produces effects in this world. When we commune with it work is actually done upon our finite personality, for we are turned into new men, and consequences in the way of conduct follow in the natural world upon our regenerative change. But that which produces effects within another reality must be termed a reality itself, so I feel as if we had no philosophic excuse for calling the unseen or mystical world unreal. . . .

What the more characteristically divine facts are, apart from the actual inflow of energy in the faith-state and the prayer-state, I know not. But the over-belief on which I am ready to make my personal venture is that they exist. The whole drift of my education goes to persuade me that the world of our present consciousness is only one out of many worlds of consciousneses that exist, and that those other worlds must contain experiences which have a meaning for our life also; and that although in the main their experiences and those of this world keep discrete, yet the two become continuous at certain points, and higher energies filter in.

CHAPTER VII

PROSE FOR PHILOSOPHY: GEORGE SANTAYANA

WARNING AGAINST BOOKS AS DRUGS

THE Twentieth Century has filched a clause from Francis Bacon's essay on How to Read, and it has degraded the clause into a slogan for the walls and bulletins of the public library. "Reading maketh a full man" is the catch-clause we mutter as we try so hurriedly to become "well read." But it is high time now to speak against quantity of reading, and to say that what only matters is to read well, to read for the satisfaction of one's organic needs, to read with the object of enhancing the quality of one's intercourse with authors.

The sad fact is that if we think we shall gain fullness by merely reading a great number of works, we shall awake one day with a surfeit, not of experience, but of dreams: we shall find that we have not so much profited by books as we have been exhausted by their constant strong stimulation. "Books," said the disillusioned Anatole France, "are the opium of the Occident. They devour us." But Bacon in a famous aphorism implied that the best reader is not a substance for books to exploit, but rather he himself is the active masticator of literature. "Some books are to be tasted, others to be swallowed, and some few to be chewed and digested."

We require to become masterly toward our literary experiences, and *one* of the means for such mastership is the
exercise of our awareness of the phenomena of style and
form. We are then (some of us) to read in a new way with
a double attention: in addition to responding to the
author's emotion and comprehending his ideas, we are to
be alert for winning insight into his manner, alert for knowing, so to speak, the functioning of the vocabularian body
into which his thought and feeling have dipped themselves
and become fused with the words.

MARGINALIA ON SANTAYANA

Perhaps the practice of making notes in the margin will
hasten the birth of this habit of double reading. One reads
in the usual way to absorb what the author is saying, but
one makes the resolution to jot down beside the text whatever observations can be made as to how the writer delivers
his message. To illustrate the procedure and the results possible to be attained by studying one's marginalia, I shall give
in order the notes I made on the first chapter of George
Santayana's *Character and Opinion in the United States.*

This is the first sentence of that book: "About the middle of the nineteenth century, in the quiet sunshine of provincial prosperity, New England had an Indian summer of
the mind; and an agreeable reflective literature showed how
brilliant that russet and yellow season could be." Now it is
almost impossible to exaggerate the importance of opening
sentences, for they set the tone of the writing. Of tone I
shall have something to say in later chapters, especially in
the study of Stephen Crane, but for the present think of
people's actual tones of voice. So, after reading the very
first sentence of Santayana, pause and ask, what is his tone?

I find that I wrote in the margin of my copy: "The tone is polite, suave, even courtly."

I turn over to page 3 of *Character and Opinion in the United States* and discover this notation: "The second point lacks clarity." This happens not to be quite so. Santayana has been saying that *belles lettres* in America have had two points of contact with the "great national experiment": the first has been oratory, and second, one learns on close rereading, has been reflective enjoyment of the activities of the nation. But Santayana began talking about reflection while still on the topic of oratory and before the reader notices it he has sinuously glided into his second point—with no clear demarcation that is apparent at once. So down went my pencil to record my protest.

On page 6 I underscored a number of s's in the following sentence: "Nevertheless, with the shyness which simple competence often shows in the presence of conventional shams, these wits have not taken their native wisdom very seriously"; and wrote beside it: "note alliteration," which indeed is cunningly employed here.

A little further along, on page 8, Santayana put me on guard as to his choice of words. He wrote: "A philosophy may have a high value, other than its truth to things, in its truth to method and to the genius of its author; it may be a feat of synthesis and imagination, like a great poem, expressing one of the eternal possibilities of being, although one which the creator happened to reject when he made this world." I am wary of that word "value"; my marginal objection, in fact, says, "Value is not the word for a drug"; but of course here we are dealing more with content than with style.

My next note pertains to a paragraph too long to quote, but the reader may see pages 13 and 14 of the text, if he wishes. It is an example of Santayana's irony. The writing is very quietly done here, and the comment has often been made that irony appears to best advantage in quietude.

Then I began to notice Santayana's partiality for allusive writing—an evidence of a mind rich in literary associations. "Enough for the day was the good thereof" and "it leads to the heroic egotism of Fichte or Nietzsche rather than to any green pastures beside any still waters" were the two obvious examples I checked off.

Just before the end of this first chapter I came upon the most important stylistic mannerism of all. It is Santayana's trick of veiling ideas in poetic sentiment. Here are charming instances: "But this strain of subjectivity is not in all respects an evil; it is a warm purple dye"; "Nature is like a beautiful woman that may be as delightfully and as truly known at a certain distance as upon a closer view; as to knowing her through and through, that is nonsense in both cases, and might not reward our pains." It is well to let this trait of embellishing and perhaps obscuring logic with art strike one forcibly, for it eventually must lead to the inquiry by the reader of the philosophic writer, "Do I wish to be charmed or to be convinced by you?" But before settling down to the attempt to define the relation between the philosopher and his reader, let us take a backward glance at the half-dozen or so scattered notations about Santayana's style: they will show that already we have learned a great deal about the general constitution of that style.

CREDITS AND DEBITS

We have to do with an urbane, velvety, courtly style, gracious and elevated. There is subtlety in its necromancy, specified in the minute points of skilled alliteration and quiet ironic phrasing—and, as we shall find out by reading further, in the mellow tonality of the humor. The style reflects the store of literary and philosophic associations of the writer's mind, and the allusive sentence or phrase for enriching the reader's impressions is often resorted to. On the crests of the style metaphors and poetic sentiments alight, plume themselves, and dazzle the student whose eyes have been fixed on some line of hard reasoning. "It was a fresh morning in the life of reason, cloudy but brightening" is the final sentence of Santayana's chapter on "The Academic Environment" in *Character and Opinion in the United States* and distills into a metaphor all the thought of the chapter, causing the reader to hold his breath just slightly at the perfectly timed change from thinking to feeling.

But on the debit side Santayana's perspicuity of diction is occasionally lost in sinuous transitions from phase to phase of his subject: his choice of words does not always satisfy, but on the contrary arouses doubt: and his reasoning at critical places is likely to hide beneath draperies of charming sentiment. He has another fault not yet disclosed. Unfortunately the specimen pages that reveal it are too long for reproduction here, since it is the very nature of this defect to be tedious and drawn out. I mean an inability to let go of an idea after it has once been lucidly presented to the reader.

FORMAL BALANCE

All in all, Santayana is a seductive stylist and he often wins the reader to overlook his shortness of weight of idea. He seems so sane, so fluent in his intellectual postures, so serene about it all, that it is only when we analyze the form of his essays that we notice there is little thrust of his own mind. For his is a balancing mind, and his form operates like a complicated set of scales, now weighted here, now counterbalanced there, until at the close there is a discreet preponderance on one of the trays. Is it possible, then, that Santayana's air of serenity derives not from strength of reason but from finesse in balance?

RECOURSE TO PLATO

By now we should be ready to make the effort for an understanding *au fond* of what intellectual style, whether adapted for literary criticism, science, or philosophy, should be. However, a rapid historical survey of our literature does not quite yield up the desired intellectual style *par excellence*. In American criticism I do not believe that any definite advance since Poe can be shown. Poe was high and Eliot stylistically ranks with him; there has naturally been some change but it is on the given level. I am obviously speaking only of leaders, for certainly the rank and file of contemporary American critics write better than the journalists of Poe's day. Turning to science, we have seen that it has been sufficiently though not gloriously served in America by James's instrument, and we have studied the elevation of philosophic style. Emerson offered an incongruous oratory; James gave philosophy a meritorious journalism; Santayana prepared for it a rich, unguented, ceremonious body of words. Each incarnation has enabled American philosophy to exist in rarer air.[1] But we are still

---

[1] I am not considering in this book the complex noetic style of John Dewey. This style is associated with some original and important ideas, but it actually requires treatment by a specialist before it can become lucid behavior for the ordinary experienced reader, let alone the general public.

led to ask if the intellectual style in its perfection is bare, chaste, and essentially utilitarian, if the language of ideas by its very nature is incompatible with and therefore to be strictly divorced from sensuous and emotional appeals to the reader? I may appear to have given warrant for belief in an affirmative answer to these questions, and certainly when I add that there is in Santayana's style an element of disloyalty to true philosophic writing, I must seem altogether committed to an ascetic viewpoint. But fortunately there is the style of Plato to reveal how liberally a thinker may help himself with the beauties of art.

What is the particular relation uniting philosopher and reader? If this is seen, then a good philosophic style can be defined, and our quandaries about Beauty and Use in intellectual writing may vanish. It happens, moreover, that the hearer-speaker (or reader-writer) relation was constantly specified in Plato's dialogues.

In them we have a master intelligence, that of Socrates, discoursing with disciples, inquirers, and opponents. If you look for it you will certainly be impressed by the attitude which Socrates consistently takes toward them: his advice to Crito when he sets forth his reasons for abiding by the death sentence of Athens will do excellently. "Ask yourself then and answer," Socrates says to Crito. ". . . Let us think about it together, my friend, and if you have anything to say in answer to me, say it. . . . So will you examine the first steps in the inquiry, to see if you consider it established. . . . And, Crito, you must be careful in agreeing to this, not to say that you agree unless you really do. . . . Therefore look, and look carefully, to see if you stand on the same ground as I, and hold the same opinion, and then we may begin our inquiry with this belief."

By these recurrent exhortations you perceive that Socrates always remained aware that philosophy embodies itself in the language of thought and makes its appeal as directly as it can to the mind of the reader. That is the primal necessity, and nothing must be allowed to interfere with or confuse this appeal to the reader's judgment. Since the philosopher invites the reader to try constantly if he has thought aright, all emotional and sensory appeals must not only be subsidiary to the intellectual content, but, if made, must actually assist the entrance of the ideas into the reader's mind.

Study the amazingly fine construction of the "Crito" and you must be admiration-struck by the consummate art with which Plato has rendered the reader susceptible to what Socrates has to say about the true nature of laws. Plato wished to make the reader deeply serious about the ideas to be uttered, and to putting him into a mood of tense seriousness all his rhetorical skill has been directed. Yet there is not the slightest obscuration of his content by his art.

THE FUNDAMENTAL HERESY OF SANTAYANA'S PROSE

Perhaps it will be seen now why I regard Santayana's style as inclined to heresy. In themselves one does not object to its æsthetic appeals; by no means! But one objects because Santayana seems subtly to violate the terms on which writers of philosophy and their readers come together. His velvety urbanity, for instance, has this effect on me: I feel, not that the author is really detached and serene, but that he is comfortable and unconcerned about his problems. This, considering the dilemmas of philosophers, is like a clubman enjoying a game of billiards in a building quivering with premonitions of an earthquake. In Santayana's style there is no sense of any real dangers for the human race.

The most flagrant breakdowns in relationship occur when, as happens several times at crucial points, Santayana substitutes a caress of the reader's sensibility, a bid for the reader's vague emotion of the "Beautiful," for the clear exposition of an idea. *Exempli gratia:*

> "But good and evil, like light and shade, are ethereal; all things, events, persons and conventional virtues are in themselves utterly valueless, save as an immaterial harmony (of which mind is an expression) plays about them on occasion, when their natures meet propitiously, and bathes them in some tint of happiness or beauty."

Socrates was fond of asking, "Shall we say this, or what shall we say?" Usually the alert minds about him agreed with his statement, but had they heard the sentence above, they would surely have said that it was more charming than convincing and would the master consent to be more definite in his meaning?

Finally, in pursuance of my thesis that style is a perfect register of content, I cannot forbear noting that Santayana's philosophy subsides into a kind of intellectual Epicurean enjoyment at just the point in his thinking analogous to the point where in the style his philosophic appeal shifts from the mind to the sensibility of the reader. Thus, "all that is requisite is that we should pause in living to enjoy life, and should lift up our hearts to things that are pure goods in themselves, so that once to have found and loved them, whatever else may betide, may remain a happiness that nothing can sully."

ON WEIGHING THOUGHT

I recall now an obligation to fulfill a promise made earlier, and in doing so we shall touch (but not see, for it is invisible) the passage of behavior into substance. Somewhere in the weighing of thoughts and emotions one becomes aware that style and form have vanished before one's gaze and matter has succeeded to full view; one knows that here is the fusion, but one cannot detect any boundary between them. At the conclusion of our consideration of prose for fiction some principles for weighing emotions will be advanced; our present concern is with the weight of thought.

It is not by chance that we speak of a light thought, or weighty thinking, or solid reasoning. Our language gives ample proof of the fact that our forefathers recognized a certain materiality of ideas, but what are the criteria for determining the mass, density, and so on of the matter called thought? The following will infallibly enable us to be much more exact in our measurements of this class of material.[2]

A thought is to be estimated for its degree of definition or clarity. This has to do with the individuality of the thought expressed. Is it exactly stated, is it really defined, limned, separated from other thoughts?

In the second place, attempt to discover the range or scope of the thought. It is important to remember that our planet is not all of the world and that human life is not all of existence. In other words, ask of a thought what area it

---

[2] I am indebted to Mr. A. R. Orage for them. He presented them in New York during a series of novel psychological exercises conducted in June, 1927.

covers of existence in general and of the universe at large.

Next test the thought for fullness. That is, how completely does it say the last word on whatever it has set out to formulate?

Fourth, illumination. Some thoughts shed little light, others much. To what degree does the thought being tested light up surrounding truths?

The fifth is the test for applicability. Does the thought tend to retreat to a vacuum or does it emerge, as one studies it more and more, into life? To what extent is it a practical thought, to what extent can it be applied?

After that, question the thought to see if it is or is not inexhaustible. It may cover only its own field: on the other hand, it may continually reach out in many other fields, yielding up for years significance after significance to the persistent ponderer. (This is, in truth, the principle of the parable.)

Lastly, weigh the thought for its truth. It should be the repetition in thought of objective fact. Is there an exact parallel between the object and the thought? Here is the hardest of all the criteria, naturally, for the tester must first learn to distinguish between the subjective and the objective in his own experience, and in our day that distinction has been almost lost.

This sounds very set and formal, and in fact, at the beginning it is necessary to be strictly formal in procedure. But after a little experience in deliberately measuring thoughts, one will be able to do almost simultaneously what one has had to practice step by step. As a start, here are four thoughts to estimate. They are chosen for their obvious inequality so as not to tax the student's powers of discrimination too severely at the first trial, and they are not intended

to reveal anything about the general standing of each philosopher when his whole system is weighed in the balance.

(a) "But good and evil, like light and shade, are ethe-
real; all things, events, persons, and conventional
virtues are in themselves utterly valueless, save as
an immaterial harmony (of which mind is an expression) plays about them on occasion, when their
natures meet propitiously, and bathes them in some
tint of happiness or beauty."—Santayana.

(b) "Above all we find *consistency* satisfactory, consistency between the present idea and the entire rest
of our mental equipment, including the whole order
of our sensations, and that of our intuitions of
likeness and difference, and our whole stock of previously acquired truths."—William James.

(c) "There are two parts in every being: the Actual,
which is the expressed, and the Inactual, which is
the unexpressed, and they grow together, infinitely,
the one out of the other."—Denis Saurat.[3]

(d) "A foolish consistency is the hobgoblin of little
minds, adored by little statesmen and philosophers
and divines."—Emerson.

[3]Quoted from *The Three Conventions,* by Denis Saurat (The
Dial Press).

WILLIAM JAMES[4]

By George Santayana

William James enjoyed in his youth what are called advantages: he lived among cultivated people, travelled, had teachers of various nationalities. His father was one of those somewhat obscure sages whom early America produced: mystics of independent mind, hermits in the desert of business, and heretics in the churches. They were intense individualists, full of veneration for the free souls of their children, and convinced that every one should paddle his own canoe, especially on the high seas. William James accordingly enjoyed a stimulating if slightly irregular education: he never acquired that reposeful mastery of particular authors and those safe ways of feeling and judging which are fostered in great schools and universities. In consequence he showed an almost physical horror of club sentiment and of the stifling atmosphere of all officialdom. He had a knack for drawing, and rather the temperament of the artist; but the unlovely secrets of nature and the troubles of man preoccupied him, and he chose medicine for his profession. Instead of practising, however, he turned to teaching physiology, and from that passed to psychology and philosophy.

In his earlier years he retained some traces of polyglot

[4]From *Character and Opinion in the United States,* by George Santayana and reprinted by permission of Charles Scribner's Sons, Publishers.

student days at Paris, Bonn, Vienna, or Geneva; he slipped sometimes into foreign phrases, uttered in their full vernacular; and there was an occasional afterglow of Bohemia about him, in the bright stripe of a shirt or the exuberance of a tie. On points of art or medicine he retained a professional touch and an unconscious ease which he hardly acquired in metaphysics. I suspect he had heartily admired some of his masters in those other subjects, but had never seen a philosopher whom he would have cared to resemble. Of course there was nothing of the artist in William James, as the artist is sometimes conceived in England, nothing of the æsthete, nothing affected or limp. In person he was short rather than tall, erect, brisk, bearded, intensely masculine. While he shone in expression and would have wished his style to be noble if it could also be strong, he preferred in the end to be spontaneous, and to leave it at that; he tolerated slang in himself rather than primness. The rough, homely, picturesque phrase, whatever was graphic and racy, recommended itself to him; and his conversation outdid his writing in this respect. He believed in improvisation, even in thought; his lectures were not minutely prepared. Know your subject thoroughly, he used to say, and trust to luck for the rest. There was a deep sense of insecurity in him, a mixture of humility with romanticism: we were likely to be more or less wrong anyhow, but we might be wholly sincere. One moment should respect the insight of another, without trying to establish too regimental a uniformity. If you corrected yourself tartly, how could you know that the correction was not the worse mistake? All our opinions were born free and equal, all children of the Lord, and if they were not consistent that was the Lord's business, not theirs. In reality, James was consistent enough, as even Emerson (more extreme in this sort of irresponsibility) was too. Inspiration has its limits, sometimes very narrow ones. But James was not consecutive, not insistent; he turned to a subject afresh, without egotism or pedantry; he dropped his old points, sometimes very good ones; and he modestly looked for light from others, who had less light than himself.

His excursions into philosophy were accordingly in the nature of raids, and it is easy for those who are attracted by one part of his work to ignore other parts, in themselves perhaps more valuable. I think that in fact his popularity does not rest on his best achievements. His popularity rests on three somewhat incidental books, *The Will to Believe,* *Pragmatism,* and *The Varieties of Religious Experience,* whereas, as it seems to me, his best achievement is his *Principles of Psychology.* In this book he surveys, in a way which for him is very systematic, a subject made to his hand. In its ostensible outlook it is a treatise like any other, but what distinguishes it is the author's gift for evoking vividly the very life of the mind. This is a work of imagination; and the subject as he conceived it, which is the flux of immediate experience in men in general, requires imagination to read it at all. It is a literary subject, like autobiography or psychological fiction, and can be treated only poetically; and in this sense Shakespeare is a better psychologist than Locke or Kant. Yet this gift of imagination is not merely literary; it is not useless in divining the truths of science, and it is invaluable in throwing off prejudice and scientific shams. The fresh imagination and vitality of William James led him to break through many a false convention. He saw that experience, as we endure it, is not a mosaic of distinct sensations, nor the expression of separate hostile faculties, such as reason and the passions, or sense and the categories; it is rather a flow of mental dis-

course, like a dream, in which all divisions and units are
vague and shifting, and the whole is continually merging
together and drifting apart. It fades gradually in the rear,
like the wake of a ship, and bites into the future, like the
bow cutting the water. For the candid psychologist, carried
bodily on this voyage of discovery, the past is but a questionable report, and the future wholly indeterminate; everything is simply what it is experienced as being.

At the same time, psychology is supposed to be a science,
a claim which would tend to confine it to the natural history of man, or the study of behavior, as is actually proposed by Auguste Comte and by some of James's own
disciples, more jejune if more clear-headed than he. As
matters now stand, however, psychology as a whole is not
a science, but a branch of philosophy; it brings together the
literary description of mental discourse and the scientific
description of material life, in order to consider the relation between them, which is the nexus of human nature.

What was James's position on this crucial question? It is
impossible to reply unequivocally. He approached philosophy as mankind originally approached it, without having
a philosophy, and he lent himself to various hypotheses in
various directions. He professed to begin his study on the
assumption of common sense, that there is a material
world which the animals that live in it are able to perceive
and to think about. He gave a congruous extension to this
view in his theory that emotion is purely bodily sensation,
and also in his habit of conceiving the mind as a total shifting sensibility. To pursue this path, however, would have
led him to admit that nature was automatic and mind simply
cognitive, conclusions from which every instinct in him recoiled. He preferred to believe that mind and matter had
independent energies and could lend one another a hand,

matter operating by motion and mind by intention. This dramatic, amphibious way of picturing causation is natural to common sense, and might be defended if it were clearly defined; but James was insensibly carried away from it by a subtle implication of his method. This implication was that experience or mental discourse not only constituted a set of substantive facts, but the *only* substantive facts; all else, even that material world which his psychology had postulated, could be nothing but a verbal or fantastic symbol for sensations in their experienced order. So that while the door was kept open to any hypothesis regarding the conditions of the psychological flux, in truth the question was prejudged. The hypotheses, which were parts of this psychological flux, could have no object save other parts of it. That flux itself, therefore, which he could picture so vividly, was the fundamental existence. The *sense* of bounding over the waves, the *sense* of being on an adventurous voyage, was the living fact; the rest was dead reckoning. Where one's gift is, there will one's faith be also; and to this poet appearance was the only reality.

This sentiment, which always lay at the back of his mind, reached something like formal expression in his latest writings, where he sketched what he called radical empiricism. The word experience is like a shrapnel shell, and bursts into a thousand meanings. Here we must no longer think of its setting, its discoveries, or its march; to treat it radically we must abstract its immediate objects and reduce it to pure data. It is obvious (and the sequel has already proved) that experience so understood would lose its romantic signification, as a personal adventure or a response to the shocks of fortune. "Experience" would turn into a cosmic dance of absolute entities created and destroyed *in vacuo* according to universal laws, or perhaps by chance.

No minds would gather this experience, and no material agencies would impose it; but the immediate objects present to any one would simply be parts of the universal fireworks, continuous with the rest, and all the parts, even if not present to anybody, would have the same status. Experience would then not at all resemble what Shakespeare reports or what James himself had described in his psychology. If it could be experienced as it flows in its entirety (which is fortunately impracticable), it would be a perpetual mathematical nightmare. Every whirling atom, every changing relation, and every incidental perspective would be a part of it. I am far from wishing to deny for a moment the scientific value of such a cosmic system, if it can be worked out; physics and mathematics seem to me to plunge far deeper than literary psychology into the groundwork of this world; but human experience is the stuff of literary psychology; we cannot reach the stuff of physics and mathematics except by arresting or even hypostatizing some elements of appearance, and expanding them on an abstracted and hypothetical plane of their own. Experience, as memory and literature rehearse it, remains nearer to us than that: it is something dreamful, passionate, dramatic, and significative.

Certainly this personal human experience, expressible in literature and in talk, and no cosmic system however profound, was what James knew best and trusted most. Had he seen the developments of his radical empiricism, I cannot help thinking he would have marvelled that such logical mechanisms should have been hatched out of that egg. The principal problems and aspirations that haunted him all his life long would lose their meaning in that cosmic atmosphere. The pragmatic nature of truth, for instance, would never suggest itself in the presence of pure data; but a romantic mind soaked in agnosticism, conscious of its own habits and assuming an environment the exact structure of which can never be observed, may well convince itself that, for experience, truth is nothing but a happy use of signs— which is indeed the truth of literature. But if we once accept *any* system of the universe as literally true, the value of convenient signs to prepare us for such experience as is yet absent cannot be called truth: it is plainly nothing but a necessary inaccuracy. So, too, with the question of the survival of the human individual after death. For radical empiricism a human individual is simply a certain cycle or complex of terms, like any other natural fact; that some echoes of his mind should recur after the regular chimes have ceased, would have nothing paradoxical about it. A mathematical world is a good deal like music, with its repetitions and transpositions, and a little trill, which you might call a person, might well peep up here and there all over a vast composition. Something of that sort may be the truth of spiritualism; but it is not what the spiritualists imagine. Their whole interest lies not in the experiences they have, but in the interpretation they give to them, assigning them to troubled spirits in another world; but both another world and a spirit are notions repugnant to a radical empiricism.

I think it is important to remember, if we are not to misunderstand William James, that his radical empiricism and pragmatism were in his own mind only methods; his doctrine, if he may be said to have had one, was agnosticism. And just because he was an agnostic (feeling instinctively that beliefs and opinions, if they had any objective beyond themselves, could never be sure they had attained it), he seemed in one sense so favorable to credulity. He was not credulous himself, far from it; he

was well aware that the trust he put in people or ideas
might betray him. For that very reason he was respectful
and pitiful to the trustfulness of others. Doubtless they
were wrong, but who were we to say so? In his own person
he was ready enough to face the mystery of things, and
whatever the womb of time might bring forth; but until
the curtain was rung down on the last act of the drama
(and it might have no last act!) he wished the intellectual
cripples and the moral hunchbacks not to be jeered at; perhaps they might turn out to be the heroes of the play. Who
could tell what heavenly influences might not pierce to these
sensitive half-flayed creatures, which are lost on the thick-
skinned, the sane, and the duly goggled? We must not suppose, however, that James meant these contrite and romantic suggestions dogmatically. The agnostic, as well
as the physician and neurologist in him, was never quite
eclipsed. The hope that some new revelation might come
from the lowly and weak could never mean to him what it
meant to the early Christians. For him it was only a right
conceded to them to experiment with their special faiths; he
did not expect such faiths to be discoveries of absolute fact,
which everybody else might be constrained to recognize.
If any one had made such a claim, and had seemed to have
some chance of imposing it universally, James would have
been the first to turn against him; not, of course, on the
gound that it was *impossible* that such an orthodoxy should
be true, but with a profound conviction that it was to be
feared and distrusted. No: the degree of authority and
honor to be accorded to various human faiths was a moral
question, not a theoretical one. All faiths were what they
were experienced as being, in their capacity of faiths;
these faiths, not their objects, were the hard facts we must
respect. We cannot pass, except under the illusion of the

moment, to anything firmer or on a deeper level. There was accordingly no sense of security, no joy, in James's apology for personal religion. He did not really believe; he merely believed in the right of believing that you might be right if you believed.

It is this underlying agnosticism that explains an incoherence which we might find in his popular works, where the story and the moral do not seem to hang together. Professedly they are works of psychological observation; but the tendency and suasion in them seems to run to disintegrating the idea of truth, recommending belief without reason, and encouraging superstition. A psychologist who was not an agnostic would have indicated, as far as possible, whether the beliefs and experiences he was describing were instances of delusion or of rare and fine perception, or in what measure they were a mixture of both. But James—and this is what gives such romantic warmth to these writings of his—disclaims all antecedent or superior knowledge, listens to the testimony of each witness in turn, and only by accident allows us to feel that he is swayed by the eloquence and vehemence of some of them rather than of others. This method is modest, generous, and impartial; but if James intended, as I think he did, to picture the *drama* of human belief, with its risks and triumphs, the method was inadequate. Dramatists never hesitate to assume, and to let the audience perceive, who is good and who bad, who wise and who foolish, in their pieces; otherwise their work would be as impotent dramatically as scientifically. The tragedy and comedy of life lie precisely in the contrast between the illusions or passions of the characters and their true condition and fate, hidden from them at first, but evident to the author and the public. If in our diffidence and scrupulous fairness we refuse to take this judicial attitude, we shall be led to strange conclusions. The navigator, for instance, trusting his "experience" (which here, as in the case of religious people, means his imagination and his art), insists on believing that the earth is spherical; he has sailed round it. That is to say, he has seemed to himself to steer westward and westward, and has seemed to get home again. But how should he know that home is now where it was before, or that his past and present impressions of it come from the same, or from any, material object? How should he know that space is as trim and tri-dimensional as the discredited Euclidians used to say it was? If, on the contrary, my worthy aunt, trusting to her longer and less ambiguous experience of her garden, insists that the earth is flat, and observes that the theory that it is round, which is only a theory, is much less often tested and found useful than her own perception of its flatness, and that moreover that theory is pedantic, intellectualistic, and a product of academies, and a rash dogma to impose on mankind for ever and ever, it might seem that on James's principle we ought to agree with her. But no; on James's real principles we need not agree with her, nor with the navigator either. Radical empiricism, which is radical agnosticism, delivers us from so benighted a choice. For the quarrel becomes unmeaning when we remember that the earth is *both* flat and round, if it is experienced as being both. The substantive fact is not a single object on which both the perception and the theory are expected to converge; the substantive facts are the theory and the perception themselves. And we may note in passing that empiricism, when it ceases to value experience as a means of discovering external things, can give up its ancient prejudice in favor of sense as against imagination, for imagination and thought are immediate experiences as much as sensation is : they are therefore, for absolute empiricism, no less actual ingredients of reality.

In *The Varieties of Religious Experience* we find the same apologetic intention running through a vivid account of what seems for the most part (as James acknowledged) religious disease. Normal religious experience is hardly described in it. Religious experience, for the great mass of mankind, consists in simple faith in the truth and benefit of their religious traditions. But to James something so conventional and rationalistic seemed hardly experience and hardly religious ; he was thinking only of irruptive visions and feelings as interpreted by the mystics who had them. These interpretations he ostensibly presents, with more or less wistful sympathy for what they were worth ; but emotionally he wished to champion them. The religions that had sprung up in America spontaneously—communistic, hysterical, spiritistic, or medicinal—were despised by select and superior people. You might inquire into them, as you might go slumming, but they remained suspect and distasteful. The picking up of genteel skirts on the part of his acquaintance prompted William James to roll up his sleeves—not for a knock-out blow, but for a thorough clinical demonstration. He would tenderly vivisect the experiences in question, to show how living they were, though of course he could not guarantee, more than other surgeons do, that the patient would survive the operation. An operation that eventually kills may be technically successful, and the man may die cured ; and so a description of religion that showed it to be madness might first show how real and how warm it was, so that if it perished, at least it would perish understood.

I never observed in William James any personal anxiety or enthusiasm for any of these dubious tenets. His concep-

tion even of such a thing as free-will, which he always
ardently defended, remained vague; he avoided defining
even what he conceived to be desirable in such matters. But
he wished to protect the weak against the strong, and what
he hated beyond everything was the *non possumus* of any
constituted authority. Philosophy for him had a Polish
constitution; so long as a single vote was cast against the
majority, nothing could pass. The suspense of judgment
which he had imposed on himself as a duty, became almost
a necessity, I think it would have depressed him if he had
to confess that any important question was finally settled.
He would still have hoped that something might turn
up on the other side, and that just as the scientific hangman
was about to despatch the poor convicted prisoner, an unexpected witness would ride up in hot haste, and prove him
innocent. Experience seems to most of us to lead to conclusions, but empiricism has sworn never to draw them.

In the discourse on "The Energies of Men," certain
physiological marvels are recorded, as if to suggest that
the resources of our minds and bodies are infinite, or can be
infinitely enlarged by divine grace. Yet James would not,
I am sure, have accepted that inference. He would, under
pressure, have drawn in his mystical horns under his scientific shell; but he was not naturalist enough to feel instinctively that the wonderful and the natural are all of a piece,
and that only our degree of habituation distinguishes them.
A nucleus, which we may poetically call the soul, certainly
lies within us, by which our bodies and minds are generated
and controlled, like an army by a government. In this
nucleus, since nature in a small compass has room for anything, vast quantities of energy may well be stored up,
which may be tapped on occasion, or which may serve like
an electric spark to let loose energy previously existing in

the grosser parts. But the absolute autocracy of this central power, or its success in imposing extraordinary trials on its subjects, is not an obvious good. Perhaps, like a democratic government, the soul is at its best when it merely collects and coördinates the impulses coming from the senses. The inner man is at times a tyrant, parasitical, wasteful, and voluptuous. At other times he is fanatical and mad. When he asks for and obtains violent exertions from the body, the question often is, as with the exploits of conquerors and conjurers, whether the impulse to do such prodigious things was not gratuitous, and the things nugatory. Who would wish to be a mystic? James himself, who by nature was a spirited rather than a spiritual man, had no liking for sanctimonious transcendentalists, visionaries, or ascetics; he hated minds that run thin. But he hastened to correct this manly impulse, lest it should be unjust, and forced himself to overcome his repugnance. This was made easier when the unearthly phenomenon had a healing or saving function in the everyday material world; miracle then re-established its ancient identity with medicine, and both of them were humanized. Even when this union was not attained, James was reconciled to the miracle-workers partly by his great charity, and partly by his hunter's instinct to follow a scent, for he believed discoveries to be imminent. Besides, a philosopher who is a teacher of youth is more concerned to give people a right start than a right conclusion. James fell in with the hortatory tradition of college sages; he turned his psychology, whenever he could do so honestly, to purposes of edification; and his little sermons on habit, on will, on faith, and this on the latent capacities of men, were fine and stirring, and just the sermons to preach to the young Christian soldier. He was much less sceptical in morals than in science. He

seemed to have felt sure that certain thoughts and hopes—
those familiar to a liberal Protestantism—were every man's
true friends in life. This assumption would have been hard
to defend if he or those he habitually addressed had ever
questioned it; yet his whole argument for voluntarily cultivating these beliefs rests on this assumption, that they are
beneficent. Since, whether we will or no, we cannot escape
the risk of error, and must succumb to some human or
pathological bias, at least we might do so gracefully and
in the form that would profit us most, by clinging to those
prejudices which help us to lead what we all feel is a good
life. But what is a good life? Had William James, had the
people about him, had modern philosophers anywhere, any
notion of that? I cannot think so. They had much experience of personal goodness, and love of it; they had standards of character and right conduct; but as to what might
render human existence good, excellent, beautiful, happy,
and worth having as a whole, their notions were utterly
thin and barbarous. They had forgotten the Greeks, or
never known them.

This argument accordingly suffers from the same weakness as the similar argument of Pascal in favor of Catholic
orthodoxy. You should force yourself to believe in it, he
said, because if you do so and are right you win heaven,
while if you are wrong you lose nothing. What would
Protestants, Mohammedans, and Hindus say to that?
Those alternatives of Pascal's are not the sole nor the true
alternatives; such a wager—betting on the improbable because you are offered big odds—is an unworthy parody of
the real choice between wisdom and folly. There is no
heaven to be won in such a spirit, and if there was, a
philosopher would despise it. So William James would have
us bet on immortality, or bet on our power to succeed, be-

cause if we win the wager we can live to congratulate ourselves on our true instinct, while we lose nothing if we have made a mistake; for unless you have the satisfaction of finding that you have been right, the dignity of having been right is apparently nothing. Or if the argument is rather that these beliefs, whether true or false, make life better in this world, the thing is simply false. To be boosted by an illusion is not to live better than to live in harmony with the truth; it is not nearly so safe, not nearly so sweet, and not nearly so fruitful. These refusals to part with a decayed illusion are really an infection to the mind. Believe, certainly; we cannot help believing; but believe rationally, holding what seems certain for certain, what seems probable for probable, what seems desirable for desirable, and what seems false for false.

In this matter, as usual, James had a true psychological fact and a generous instinct behind his confused moral suggestions. It is a psychological fact that men are influenced in their beliefs by their will and desires; indeed, I think we can go further and say that in its essence belief is an expression of impulse, of readiness to act. It is only peripherally, as our action is gradually adjusted to things, and our impulses to our possible or necessary action, that our ideas begin to hug the facts, and to acquire a true, if still a symbolic, significance. We do not need a will to believe; we only need a will to study the object in which we are inevitably believing. But James was thinking less of belief in what we find than of belief in what we hope for: a belief which is not at all clear and not at all necessary in the life of mortals. Like most Americans, however, only more lyrically, James felt the call of the future and the assurance that it could be made far better, totally other, than the past. The pictures that religion had painted of heaven or the

millenium were not what he prized, although his Sweden-
borgian connection might have made him tender to them,
as perhaps it did to familiar spirits. It was the moral suc-
cour offered by religion, its open spaces, the possibility of
miracles *in extremis,* that must be retained. If we recoiled at
the thought of being dupes (which is perhaps what nature
intended us to be), were we less likely to be dupes in disbe-
lieving these sustaining truths than in believing them? Faith
was needed to bring about the reform of faith itself, as
well as all other reforms.

In some cases faith in success could nerve us to bring
success about, and so justify itself by its own operation.
This is a thought typical of James at his worst—a worst
in which there is always a good side. Here again psychological observation is used with the best intentions to hearten
oneself and other people; but the fact observed is not at all
understood, and a moral twist is given to it which (besides
being morally questionable) almost amounts to falsifying
the fact itself. Why does belief that you can jump a ditch
help you to jump it? Because it is a symptom of the fact
that you *could* jump it, that your legs were fit and that the
ditch was two yards wide and not twenty. A rapid and just
appreciation of these facts had given you your confidence,
or at least had made it reasonable, manly, and prophetic;
otherwise you would have been a fool and got a ducking for
it. Assurance is contemptible and fatal unless it is self-
knowledge. If you had been rattled you might have failed,
because that would have been a symptom of the fact that
you were out of gear; you would have been afraid because
you trembled, as James at his best proclaimed. You would
never have quailed if your system had been reacting
smoothly to its opportunities, any more than you would
totter and see double if you were not intoxicated. Fear is

a sensation of actual nervousness and disarray, and confidence a sensation of actual readiness; they are not disembodied feelings, existing for no reason, the devil Funk and the angel Courage, one or the other of whom may come down arbitrarily into your body, and revolutionize it. That is childish mythology, which survives innocently enough as a figure of speech, until a philosopher is found to take that figure of speech seriously. Nor is the moral suggestion here less unsound. What is good is not the presumption of power, but the possession of it: a clear head, aware of its resources, not a fuddled optimism, calling up spirits from the vasty deep. Courage is not a virtue, said Socrates, unless it is also wisdom. Could anything be truer both of courage in doing and of courage in believing? But it takes tenacity, it takes *reasonable* courage, to stick to scientific insights such as this of Socrates or that of James about the emotions; it is easier to lapse into the traditional manner, to search natural philosophy for miracles and moral lessons, and in morals proper, in the reasoned expression of preference, to splash about without a philosophy.

William James shared the passions of liberalism. He belonged to the left, which, as they say in Spain, is the side of the heart, as the right is that of the liver; at any rate there was much blood and no gall in his philosophy. He was one of those elder Americans still disquieted by the ghost of tyranny, social and ecclesiastical. Even the beauties of the past troubled him; he had a puritan feeling that they were tainted. They had been cruel and frivolous, and must have suppressed far better things. But what, we may ask, might these better things be? It may do for a revolutionary politician to say: "I may not know what I want—except office—but I know what I don't want"; it will never do for a philosopher. Aversions and fears imply principles of preference, goods acknowledged; and it is the philosopher's business to make these goods explicit. Liberty is not an art, liberty must be used to bring some natural art to fruition. Shall it be simply eating and drinking and wondering what will happen next? If there is some deep and settled need in the heart of man, to give direction to his efforts, what else should a philosopher do but discover and announce what that need is?

There is a sense in which James was not a philosopher at all. He once said to me: "What a curse philosophy would be if we couldn't forget all about it!" In other words, philosophy was not to him what it has been to so many, a consolation and sanctuary in a life which would have been unsatisfying without it. It would be incongruous, therefore, to expect of him that he should build a philosophy like an edifice to go and live in for good. Philosophy to him was rather like a maze in which he happened to find himself wandering, and what he was looking for was the way out. In the presence of theories of any sort he was attentive, puzzled, suspicious, with a certain inner prompting to disregard them. He lived all his life among them, as a child lives among grown-up people; what a relief to turn from those stolid giants, with their prohibitions and exactions and tiresome talk, to another real child or a nice animal! Of course grown-up people are useful, and so James considered that theories might be; but in themselves, to live with, they were rather in the way, and at bottom our natural enemies. It was well to challenge one or another of them when you got a chance; perhaps that challenge might break some spell, transform the strange landscape, and simplify life. A theory while you were creating or using it was like a story you were telling yourself or a game you were playing; it was a warm, self-justifying thing then; but when the glow of creation or expectation was over, a theory was a phantom, like a ghost, or like the minds of other people. To all other people, even to ghosts, William James was the soul of courtesy; and he was civil to most theories as well, as to more or less interesting strangers that invaded him. Nobody ever recognized more heartily the chance that others had of being right, and the right they had to be different. Yet when it came to understanding what they meant, whether they were theories or persons, his intuition outran his patience; he made some brilliant impressionistic sketch in his fancy and called it by their name. This sketch was as often flattered as distorted, and he was at times the dupe of his desire to be appreciative and give the devil his due; he was too impulsive for exact sympathy; too subjective, too romantic, to be just. Love is very penetrating, but it penetrates to possibilities rather than to facts. The logic of opinions, as well as the exact opinions themselves, were not things James saw easily, or traced with pleasure. He liked to take things one by one, rather than to put two and two together. He was a mystic, a mystic in love with life. He was comparable to Rousseau and to Walt Whitman; he expressed a generous and tender sensibility, rebelling against sophistication, and preferring daily sights and sounds, and a vague but indomitable faith in fortune, to any settled intellectual tradition calling itself science or philosophy.

A prophet is not without honor save in his own country; and until the return wave of James's reputation reached America from Europe, his pupils and friends were hardly aware that he was such a distinguished man. Everybody liked him, and delighted in him for his generous, gullible nature and brilliant sallies. He was a sort of Irishman among the Brahmins, and seemed hardly imposing enough for a great man. They laughed at his erratic views and his undisguised limitations. Of course a conscientious professor ought to know everything he professes to know, but then, they thought, a dignified professor ought to seem to know everything. The precise theologians and panoplied idealists, who exist even in America, shook their heads. What sound philosophy, said they to themselves, could be expected from an irresponsible doctor, who was not even a college graduate, a crude empiricist, and vivisector of frogs? On the other hand, the solid men of business were not entirely reassured concerning a teacher of youth who seemed to have no system in particular—the ignorant rather demand that the learned should have a system in store, to be applied at a pinch; and they could not quite swallow a private gentleman who dabbled in hypnotism, frequented mediums, didn't talk like a book, and didn't write like a book, except like one of his own. Even his pupils, attached as they invariably were to his person, felt some doubts about the profundity of one who was so very natural and who after some interruption during a lecture—and he said life was a series of interruptions—would slap his forehead and ask the man in the front row, "What *was* I talking about?" Perhaps in the first years of his teaching he felt a little in the professor's chair as a military man might feel when obliged to read the prayers at a funeral. He probably conceived what he said more deeply than a more scholastic mind might have conceived it; yet he would have been more comfortable if some one else had said it for him. He liked to open the window, and look out for a moment. I think he was glad when the bell rang, and he could be himself again until the next day. But in the midst of this routine of the class-room the spirit would sometimes come upon him, and, leaning his head on his hand, he would let fall golden words, picturesque, fresh from the heart, full of the knowledge of good and evil. Incidentally there would crop up some humorous characterization, some candid confession of doubt or of instinctive preference, some pungent scrap of learning; radicalisms plunging sometimes into the sub-soil of all human philosophies; and, on occasion, thoughts of simple wisdom and wistful piety, the most unfeigned and manly that anybody ever had.

Part Three

IMAGINATIVE PROSE

CHAPTER VIII

PROSE FOR FICTION: HERMAN MELVILLE

THE NECESSITY FOR SIMULTANEOUS ATTENTION

STEVENSON, in his essay on Style, compared the literary artist to an adroit juggler with oranges, and he remarked that the greater the number of oranges the juggler keeps in play, the more his audience is delighted. Thus the juggling figure I am about to appropriate has a history in stylistic commentary but he has hitherto stood for the artist, not for the reader as now. This book would become very unwieldy if I should attempt in each chapter to perform all the rites of an inquiry into style instead of concentrating on a few. But it should be understood that when we are looking at only certain aspects of an author's style, we should be keeping aloft in our minds throughout our study five or six general ideas. It is imperative to remember that our mental dexterity is requisitioned not to let drop these major considerations, just as a juggler remains conscious of all his oranges while catching one of them.

On recapitulation of these guiding ideas, it turns out that we have paid some heed to prose as exemplifying the principle of Variety and considerable attention to prose as the chosen vehicle for thought, and we have initiated some work on prose as intellectual behavior (one of the aspects of the meaning of Buffon's statement, "Style is the man himself"). But with two other leading ideas we have not proceeded very far. They are the meaning of form and Stendhal's definition of style, and these I propose to emphasize in the present chapter.

THAT DIFFICULT PHRASE, "AS IF"

We are passing now from the literature of thought to imaginative prose, and the difference is as striking as moving from a polar zone to a temperate zone. The aim of literary criticism, science, and philosophy is truth before God and in the presence of one's enemies. The aim of imaginative literature is to create an *as if*.

The artist in fiction, for example, labors to write as if he were present at the events he describes, as if his imagined situations were actual. It has happened from time to time that a master of art has had to employ all his skill in an emergency arising in his own life. A stock instance is Demosthenes. He received the best oratorical training of his time from the Pythagorean teacher, Isocrates: he became celebrated by his Philippics: and he was through most of his political life involved in a very bitter rivalry with an orator second only to himself, Æschines. After Macedon conquered Greece, Demosthenes was placed on trial for treason, and the formidable Æschines was his opponent. The former's speech in defense is a masterpiece of response to this most dangerous situation for his person, and he saved his life by it. He was obliged to use all the resources of his art, all his mastery of technic, for the sake of his life.

Now if we imagine this occasion treated as the great scene in a historical novel we shall see that the writer must write as if he were Demosthenes, must write as if he had really to extricate himself from danger.[1] In other words, the writer of fiction with nothing personally at stake must by the sheer power of his imagination write as if everything were in question. Only thus can he fully compel the reader to share in his imaginary experiences, to feel, throughout his being, as if he also were actually present.

There is an illuminating point to make here. Only very young readers truly identify themselves with imagined characters and live inside their skins and in their very hearts, so to speak. That rarely happens with the mature except in the following way. If we see somebody in distress or danger we sympathetically identify ourselves with that person, not by saying, as a young reader might, "Hamlet seems to be my very self," but by fancying *ourselves* in their boots. Very often, however, we are not sympathetically identified in this suppose-it-were-happening-to-me fashion, but usually find ourselves cast by the author in the rôle of absorbed spectators invisibly privy to his narrative. We are there, but we do not participate. Now in life we are present as watchers in innumerable happenings, and we know that we are present because our five senses, our emotions, our minds receive impacts from them. We are present, therefore, in a complex variety of ways, and if in reading fiction we are to be made to feel that we are actually *there,* we must be affected by the author in numerous ways. Hence, the appeal of imaginative prose is necessarily broader than that of the language of ideas: it must play upon our senses, it must excite our emotions, it must engage our minds if we are to feel fully caught up in an imitation of life.

---

[1] The speech of Mark Antony ("He was my friend, faithful and just to me," etc.) in *Julius Cæsar* is of course a supreme example of *as if* creation.

RETURNING TO STENDHAL

One of the common ways by which this state of trance in the reader is procured is by the application of the Stendhalian formula, "Style is this: to add to a given thought all the circumstances fitted to produce the whole effect that the thought ought to produce." I intimated in the second chapter that in essence this statement means the evocation of the general by the specific, and I gave a very ordinary impromptu example. Here, now, are some superior examples from *Mardi,* that extraordinary rehearsal of his genius which Herman Melville performed before sitting down to write the greatest work of American literature, *Moby Dick.*

In the first chapter of *Mardi,* Melville makes us feel the birth in the narrator of a mood of longing to desert the whaling ship. He might have written simply this: "One evening, watching a glorious sunset, I was seized with a wild desire to quit the *Arcturion.*" But our author does not do things in that flat, ineffective manner. I have italicized in the first sentence of his passage the words that render vivid the narrator's loathing of his ship. After that the reader should supply his own italics for the little, all-important, particularizing words. The reader should further observe that when Melville opens his second paragraph he does it as though he were deliberately setting a trumpet to his lips to blow. Then comes verbal magnificence and the mood of longing finds its symbol in the lone bird flying through a distant arch of the sunset's cloudy architecture.

"I cast my eyes downward to the *brown* planks of the *dull plodding* ship, *silent* from stem to stern: then abroad.

"In the distance what visions were spread! The entire western horizon, high piled with gold and crimson clouds; airy arches, domes and minarets, as if the yellow, Moorish sun were setting behind some vast Alhambra. Vistas seemed leading to worlds beyond. To and fro and all over the towers of this Nineveh in the sky, flew troops of birds. Watching them long, one crossed my sight, flew through a low arch, and was lost to view. My spirit must have sailed in with it; for directly, as in a trance, came upon me the cadence of mild billows, laving a beach of shells, the waving of boughs, and the voices of maidens, and the lulled beatings of my own dissolved heart, all blended together."

In another short passage I have singled out, the "thought" for which the evocative circumstances are to be found is the picture of the old Viking, Jarl, and the narrator adrift in a longboat. Subtract the detail of the bobbing Guayaquil hat and the picture will be killed.

"When playing the sempstress, Jarl's favorite perch was the triangular little platform in the bow, which, being the driest and most elevated part of the boat, was best adapted to his purpose. Here for hours and hours together the honest old tailor would sit darning and sewing away, heedless of the wide ocean around, while for ever his slouched Guayaquil hat kept bobbing up and down against the horizon."

This is precise writing of another kind than precise intellectual writing. There has been a shift in vocabulary, and the composer of fiction exercises his powers of precision among sensational and emotional words. Another important change is that the fiction writer's opportunities for constructing forms are much more expanded and diverse.

MAJOR AND MINOR FORMS IN "MARDI"

May I for a moment introduce Kenneth Burke on this subject of form? In an essay previously recommended to the reader Burke makes a minute analysis of scene four, act one of *Hamlet* and then says: "I have gone into this scene at some length, since it illustrates so perfectly the relationship between psychology and form, and so aptly indicates how the one is to be defined in terms of the other. That is, the psychology here is not the psychology of the *hero,* but the psychology of the *audience.* And by that distinction, form would be the psychology of the audience. Or, seen from another angle, form is the creation of an appetite in the mind of the auditor, and the adequate satisfying of that appetite. This satisfaction—so complicated is the human mechanism—at times involves a temporary set of frustrations, but in the end these frustrations prove to be simply a more involved kind of satisfaction, and furthermore serve to make the satisfaction of fulfilment more intense. If, in a work of art, the poet says something, let us say, about a meeting, writes in such a way that we desire to observe that meeting before us—that is form. While obviously, that is also the psychology of the audience, since it involves desires and their appeasements."

With this explanation in hand, let us now try to resolve into their elements and functions some of the minor forms of *Mardi,* for to analyze in detail the form of the book as a whole would be a disproportionate task. It is sufficient to note that *Mardi* is an allegorical novel. The first hundred pages are the preparation for the allegory and tell us of the sailor who narrates the story, of his escape with a companion, Jarl, while the ship is plodding bootlessly along in the Pacific Ocean, and of their voyage to the west in a longboat. Strange things, such as the encounter with the wandering brigantine, begin to multiply, and they culminate when Jarl and the sailor capture the maiden Yillah from the sea-voyaging savages. All this, to those who feel æsthetic form geometrically, is linear, a straightforward flight. Now the form bellies out, becomes round and expansive. Melville has been preparing us to enter a New World, a fantastic model of our own. The archipelago of Mardi is discovered and the sailor-narrator, now named Taji, voyages through it in pursuit of Yillah, who has been abducted.

The book now becomes Rabelaisian in quality, a horseplay of extravagant humor on the surface but a continual thrust of satire beneath. The form is loosely handled and permits the numerous episodes, digressions, panegyrics, apostrophes, and songs almost to run riot in Melville's mind. But there are certain connecting threads—the pursuit of Yillah, the messengers of Queen Hautia, the three vengeance-sworn pursuers of Taji—which hold the tale together until finally the story dissolves in a mysterious ending that is a foretaste of the perfect closing of *Moby Dick*.

This is an inadequate account of the form of *Mardi* which taken as a whole is a failure—but a failure on a lofty level of fiction. Because it is an extraordinary exercise in virtuosity,[2] and because it is in the final analysis a too

---

[2]Since virtuosity is a term now very often used to cast a slur, it is not amiss to remind ourselves that a virtuoso is one who is skilled in the mechanical side of a fine art, and to that measure praiseworthy. One of the chief reasons why Herman Melville is a

utterly wayward excursus of Melville's powers, the explanation of *Mardi's* full workings and excesses would be too involved.

But how many of our contemporary novelists, I wonder, could manage such a chapter as the one entitled: "Taji Sits Down to Dinner with Five-and-Twenty Kings, and a Royal Time They Have"? It opens quietly.

> "It was afternoon when we emerged from the defile. And informed that our host was receiving his guests in the House of the Afternoon, thither we directed our steps."

This is the tone and the rhythm in which the celebrated descriptions of battles usually begin, and throughout this *tour de force* its Rabelaisian humor will depend upon the narrative of the banquet being set to the form of a battle piece. Melville was aware of this for, midway in his account of Donjalolo's banquet, he remarks:

> "And like unto some well-fought fight, beginning calmly, but pressing forward to a fiery rush, this well-fought feast did now wax warm."

I wish to indicate the way in which the form "steps up" and "steps down" from plane to plane of writing, and I think it can be done by quoting the passages in which the "stepping" takes place. There is, first the Approach of

---

master of American prose is his virtuosity. Another reason for his greatness has to do with the quality of his purpose, for the fulfillment of which he made levy on all his resources of skill. In both respects American prose to-day falls short of Melville: it has not exhibited the variety of style and form he did, nor does it work for so high an aim.

Taji and Media, the calmness of which has already been noted. Next, there is the Reception by the Kings of the Newcomers.

> "Still advancing unperceived, in social hilarity we descried their Highnesses, chatting together like the most plebeian of mortals; full as merry as the monks of old. But marking our approach, all changed. A pair of potentates, who had been playfully trifling, hurriedly adjusted their diadems, threw themselves into attitudes, looking stately as statues. Phidias turned not out his Jupiter so soon."

Third—and this starts the progression proper of the piece—there is the Drinking of the Morando.

> "A nutty, pungent flavor it had; like some kinds of arrack distilled in the Philippine Islands. And a marvellous effect did it have, in dissolving the crystallization of the brain; leaving nothing but precious drops of good humor, beading round the bowl of the cranium."

This wild wine, the Morando, performs the same office for the reader as it does for the feasters: after the *apéritif* both are eager to proceed. Melville turns to his task with gusto: he gives us a crescendo of courses of food and drink until the Marzilla, the Royal Particular, is served as a liqueur, and he gives us a rising series of panegyrics for the banquet until he breaks forth in a rousing drinking song as the Marzilla is quaffed—for these kings quaff their liqueurs. The following quotations will show the bold rise in his treatment.

Fourth—the Porphyry-hued Basin.

". . . the basin being filled to within a few inches of the lizards, the attendants fell to launching therein divers goodly-sized trenchers, all laden with choice viands— wild boar meat; humps of grampuses; embrowned bread-fruit, roasted in odoriferous fires of sandal wood, but suffered to cool; gold fish, dressed with the fragrant juices of berries; citron sauce; rolls of the baked paste of yams; juicy bananas, steeped in a saccharine oil; mar-malade of plaintains; jellies of guava; confections of the treacle of palm sap; and many other dainties; besides numerous stained calabashes of Morando, and other beverages, fixed in carved floats to make them buoyant.

"The guests assigned seats, by the woven handles at-tached to his purple mat, the prince, our host, was now gently moved by his servitors to the head of the porphyry-hued basin. Where, flanked by lofty crowned-heads, white-tiaraed, and radiant with royalty, he sat; like snow-turbaned Mont Blanc, at sunrise presiding over the head waters of the Rhône; to right and left, looming the gilded summits of the Simplon, the Gothard, the Jung-frau, the Great St. Bernard, and the Grand Glockner.

"Yet turbid from the launching of its freight, Lake Como tossed to and fro its navies of good cheer, the shadows of the king-peaks wildly flitting thereupon."

Fifth—the Browsing and Tusking of the Kings at their Viands.

". . . from hand to hand the trenchers sailed: no sooner gaining one port, than dispatched over sea to another. . . . At last, the whole flotilla of trenchers—

wrecks and all—were sent swimming to the further end
of Lake Como; and thence removed, gave place to ruddy
hillocks of fruit, and floating islands of flowers."

Sixth, the Praise of the Wine.

"Nor did the wine cease flowing. That day the Juam
grape did bleed; that day the tendril ringlets of the vines,
did all uncurl; and grape by grape, in sheer dismay, the
sun-ripe clusters dropped. Grape-glad were five-and-
twenty kings: five-and-twenty kings were merry."

Seventh, the Calabash of Marzilla.

"All Hail, Marzilla! King's Own Royal Particular!
A vinous Percy! Dating back to the Conquest! Distilled
of yore from purple berries growing in the purple valley
of Ardair. Thrice hail!"

Eighth, the Drinking Chorus.

'Ha, ha! gods and kings! fill high, one and all;
Drink, drink! shout and drink! mad respond to the call;
Fill fast, and fill full; 'gainst the goblet ne'er sin;
Quaff there, at high tide, to the uttermost rim:—
     Flood-tide, and soul tide to the brim!" Etc., etc.

This is the highest pitch in the form. "Mad and crazy
revellers," Melville apostrophizes them, "how ye drank
and roared! but kings no more: vestures loosed; and
sceptres rolling on the ground. . . . The mirth now blew a
gale . . . the goblets danced fandangos; and Donjalolo,
clapping his hands" announces the subsidence of the action.

Ninth, the Dancing Women.

"Swimming in the air, emerged the nymphs, lustrous arms interlocked like Indian jugglers' glittering snakes. Round the cascade they thronged; then paused in its spray. Of a sudden, seemed to spring from its midst, a young form of foam, that danced into the soul like a thought. At last, sideways floating off, it subsided into the grotto, a wave."

Tenth, the Two Mute Damsels of Service.

". . . one with a gourd of scented waters; the other with napkins. Bending over Donjalolo's steaming head, the first let fall a shower of aromatic drops, slowly absorbed by her companion. Thus, in turn, all were served; nothing heard but deep breathing."

Lastly, and giving perfectly the *coup de grâce* to the form, the Sedative Fumes of the Aina.

"Steeped in languor, I strove against it long; essayed to struggle out of the enchanted mists. But a syren hand seemed ever upon me, pressing me back.

"Half-revealed, as in a dream, and the last sight that I saw, was Donjalolo; eyes closed, face pale, locks moist, borne slowly to his sedan, to cross the hollow, and wake in the seclusion of his harem."

The other expert manipulations that go on in this chapter are too numerous to mention, but space enough for naming two of them is requisitioned. Melville here as elsewhere excites the reader's sense of the marvelous by the use of grandiose metaphors (see the passage in which the kings about the porphyry-hued basin become Alpine peaks looking down upon Lake Como), and he secures counterpoint by describing the melting away of regal formality as the banquet progresses until at the end the monarchs are simply "royal good fellows."

The chapter is an "exercise" in writing. Another such "exercise," "The Supper of King Abrazza," is reprinted from *Mardi* at the close of my remarks, and the reader may find it amusing to plot out its form and discover for himself Melville's astounding powers of variation. If more of our living novelists could manage to accomplish such "exercises" as a gratuitous test of their skill their novels when they came to write them would show a great gain in variety, for which, Heaven knows, there is an unsatisfied hunger.

AN ANALYSIS OF LETTER VALUES

Our business, however, is not to make pious wishes, but to keep down to tacks. Style and form are not mysterious, but they are elusive. You almost grasp their complexities but never quite, and for the reason that you have to see all the strokes at once, and continually you are losing sight of one or the other of the fascinating movements that contribute to the triumph of all. Therein, however, is the principal excitement of this form of study.

We have not as yet gazed into and wondered at the harmony of vowel and consonantal relationships—without reference to rhythm. Melville was very sensitive in this respect, and having begun this chapter with nothing less than an attempt to put into simple language the meaning of the phrase "imitation of life," I shall close it by descending to the utmost particularity, namely, the effects of individual letters.

I doubt very much if anyone interested in style can read

the following sentences from *Mardi* without experiencing a thrill of delight. The effect is one of coolness and readiness to dance.

"How glorious a morning! The new-born (k)clouds all dappled with gold and streaked with violet; the sun in high spirits, and the pleasant air (k)cooled overnight by the blending cir(k)cumambient fountains for ever playing all round the reef; the lagoon within the (k)coral-rimmed basin, into which they poured, subsiding hereabouts into green tran(kw)quillity."[3]

Without going deeply into this fortunate conjunction of vowels and consonants we can very quickly outline its general plan. First, the labialized consonants such as b, p, m, v, f, etc., are very subdued, and we note the absence of the PVF combination that Stevenson extolled. Second, the sensations of coolness and dancing are conveyed by the open vowels and the short vowels. The long o's and i's and e's, but especially the o's, exhale coolness, while the phrase, the "blending circumambient fountains" and particularly the world "circumambient," which in itself is a dance of short vowels, imparts a quick graceful air to the whole passage. Thirdly, the "k" sounds are determinative, and in fact the prose is here skilfully gutturalized.

----

[3]For simplicity's sake I have noted only the more important letter values and have avoided phonetic spelling except for the injection of a few k's. The system of notation is one underscoring for guttural consonants, a double underscoring for long vowels, and the usual half-circle for short vowels. R. L. Stevenson gives full details for this sort of analysis.

But what of it, many readers undoubtedly will murmur. Well, if you will stop to analyze in this fashion runs of prose that have affected you with gayety or pathos or melancholy or some other mood, you will find the answer sooner than you expect. This is not to imply that the writer consciously plots out his letters, though some like De Quincey have been meticulous to that degree, but it is saying that there is no chance about the effects on the reader. For those effects there are causes, and the writer by design or instinct or chance has supplied the causes.

THE SUPPER OF KING ABRAZZA[4]

By Herman Melville

That night, in his regal hall, King Abrazza received us. And in merry good time a fine supper was spread.

Now, in thus nocturnally regaling us, our host was warranted by many ancient and illustrious examples.

For old Jove gave suppers; the god Woden gave suppers; the Hindu deity Brahma gave suppers: chiefly venison and game.

Ahasuerus gave suppers, Xerxes gave suppers; Montezuma gave suppers; Powhattan gave suppers; the Jews' Passovers were suppers; the Pharaohs gave suppers; Julius Cæsar gave suppers:—and rare ones they were; Great Pompey gave suppers; Nabob Crassus and Heliogabalus, surnamed the Gobbler, gave suppers.

It was a common saying of old, that King Pluto gave suppers; some say he is giving them still. If so, he is keeping tip-top company, old Pluto; Emperors and Czars; Great Moguls and Great Khans; Great Lamas and Grand Dukes; Prince Regents and Queen Dowagers; Tamerlane hob-a-nobbing with Bonaparte; Antiochus with Solyman the Magnificent; Pisistratus pledging Pilate; Semiramis eating bon-bons with Bloody Mary, and her namesake of Medicis; the Thirty Tyrants quaffing three to one with the Council of Ten; and Sultans, Satraps, Viziers, Hetmans, Soldans,

---

[4]Reprinted from *Mardi*.

Landgraves, Bashaws, Doges, Dauphins, Infantas, Incas,
and Caciques looking on.

Again: at Arbela, the conqueror of conquerors, conquer-
ing son of Olympia by Jupiter himself, sent out cards to his
captains—Hephestion, Antigonus, Antipater, and the rest
—to join him at ten P. M., in the Temple of Belus; there,
to sit down to a victorious supper, off the gold plate of
the Assyrian High Priests.

Spread, heaped up, stacked with good things; and re-
dolent of citrons and grapes, hilling round tall vases of wine;
and here and there, waving with fresh orange-boughs,
among whose leaves, myriads of small tapers gleamed like
fire-flies, in groves—Abrazza's glorious board showed like
some banquet in Paradise; Ceres and Pomona presiding;
and jolly Bacchus, like a recruit with a mettlesome rifle,
staggering back as he fires off the bottles of vivacious
champagne.

"This way, my dear Media! this seat at my left. Noble
Taji! my right. Babbalanja—Mohi—where you are. But
where's pretty Yoomy?—Gone to meditate in the moon-
light! Ah! very good. Let the banquet begin. A blast there!"
And charge all did.

But as yet, Babbalanja joined not in the revels. His mood
was on him; and apart he sat; silently eyeing the banquet;
and ever and anon muttering "Fogle-foggle, fugle-fi . . ."

The first fury of the feast over, said King Media, pour-
ing out from a heavy flagon into his goblet, "Abrazza, these
suppers are wondrous fine things."

"Ay, my dear lord, much better than dinners."

"So they are, so they are. The dinner-hour is the summer of the day; full of sunshine, I grant; but not like the
mellow autumn of supper. A dinner, you know, may go on
rather stiffly; but invariably suppers are jovial. At din-

ners, 'tis not till you take in sail, furl the cloth, bow the lady-passengers out, and make all snug; 'tis not till then that one begins to ride out the gale with complacency. But at these suppers—Good Oro! your cup is empty, my dear demi-god! But at these suppers, I say, all is snug and shipshape before you begin; and when you begin, you waive the beginning, and begin in the middle. And as for the cloth,—but tell us, Braid-Beard, what that old king of Franko, Ludwig the Fat, said of that matter. The cloth for suppers, you know. It's down in your chronicles."

"My lord," wiping his beard, "old Ludwig was of opinion, that at suppers the cloth was superfluous, unless on the back of some jolly good friar. Said he, 'For one, I prefer sitting right down to the unrobed table.' "

"High and royal authority, that of Ludwig the Fat," said Babbalanja; "far higher than the authority of Ludwig the Great: the one, only great by courtesy; the other, fat beyond a peradventure. But they are equally famous; and in their graves, both on a par. For after devouring many a fair province, and grinding the poor of his realm, Ludwig the Great has long since, himself, been devoured by very small worms, and ground into very fine dust. And after stripping many a venison rib, Ludwig the Fat has had his own polished and bleached in the Valley of Death; yea, and his cranium chased with corrodings, like the carved flagon once held to its jaws."

"My lord! my lord!" cried Abrazza to Media, "this ghastly devil of yours grins worse than a skull. I feel the worms crawling over me. By Oro, we must eject him!"

"No, no, my lord. Let him sit here, as of old the Death's-head graced the feasts of the Pharaohs—let him sit—let him sit—for Death but imparts a flavor to life. Go on; wag your tongue without fear, Azzageddi! But come, Braid-Beard, let's hear more of the Ludwigs."

"Well, then, your highness, of all the eighteen royal Ludwigs of Franko——"

"Who, like so many ten-pins, all in a row," interposed Babbalanja, "have been bowled off the course by grim Death!"

"Heed him not," said Media; "go on."

"The Debonnaire, the Pious, the Stammerer, the Do-Nothing, the Juvenile, the Quarreller; of all these, I say, Ludwig the Fat was the best table-man of them all. Such a full-orbed paunch was his, that no way could he devise of getting to his suppers but by getting right into them. Like the Zodiac his table was circular, and full in the middle he sat, like a sun; all his jolly stews and ragouts revolving round him."

"Yea," said Babbalanja, "a very round sun was Ludwig the Fat. No wonder he's down in the chronicles; several ells about the waist, and King of cups and Tokay. Truly, a famous king; three hundred weight of lard, with a diadem on top; lean brains and a fat doublet—a demijohn of a demigod!"

"Is this to be longer borne?" cried Abrazza, starting up. "Quaff that sneer down, devil! on the instant! down with it to the dregs! This comes, my lord Media, of having a slow drinker at one's board. Like an iceberg, such a fellow frosts the whole atmosphere of a banquet, and is felt a league off. We must thrust him out. Guards!"

"Back! touch him not, hounds!" cried Media. "Your pardon, my lord, but we'll keep him to it; and melt him down in this good wine. Drink! I command it; drink, Babbalanja!"

"And am I not drinking, my lord? Surely you would not

that I should imbibe more than I can hold. The measure being full, all poured in after that is but wasted. I am for being temperate in these things, my good lord. And my one cup outlasts three of yours. Better to sip a pint, than pour down a quart. All things in moderation are good; whence, wine in moderation is good. But all things in excess are bad; whence wine in excess is bad."

"Away with your logic and conic sections! Drink!—But no, no, I am too severe. For of all meals a supper should be the most social and free. And going thereto we kings, my lord, should lay aside our sceptres. Do as you please, Babbalanja."

"You are right, you are right, after all, my dear demigod," said Abrazza. "And to say truth, I seldom worry myself with the ways of these mortals; for no thanks do we demi-gods get. We kings should be ever indifferent. Nothing like a cold heart; warm ones are ever chafing, and getting into trouble. I let my mortals here in this isle take heed to themselves; only barring them out when they would thrust in their petitions. This very instant, my lord, my yeoman-guard is on duty without to drive off intruders. Hark! what noise is that? Ho, who comes?"

At that instant there burst into the hall, a crowd of spearmen, driven before a pale, ragged rout, that loudly invoked King Abrazza.

"Pardon, my lord king, for thus forcing an entrance! But long in vain have we knocked at thy gates! Our grievances are more than we can bear! Give ear to our spokesman, we beseech!"

And from their tumultuous midst, they pushed forward, a tall, grim, pine-tree of a fellow, who loomed up out of the throng, like the Peak of Teneriffe among the Canaries.

"Drive the knaves out! Ho, cowards, guards, turn about!

charge upon them! Away with your grievances! Drive
them out, I say; drive them out! High time, truly, my lord
Media, when demi-gods are thus annoyed at their wine.
Oh! who would reign over mortals!"

So at last, with much difficulty, the ragged rout were
ejected; the Peak of Teneriffe going last, muttering about
some black time that was coming.

While the hoarse murmurs without still echoed through
the hall, King Abrazza refilling his cup, thus spoke, "You
were saying, my dear lord, that of all meals a supper is
the most social and free. Very true. And of all suppers those
given by us bachelor demi-gods are the best. Are they not?"

"They are. For Benedict mortals must be home betimes;
bachelor demi-gods are never away."

"Ay, your highness, bachelors are all the year round at
home," said Mohi; "sitting out life in the chimney corner,
cozy and warm as the dog, whilome turning the old-
fashioned roasting-jack."

"And to us bachelor demi-gods," cried Media, "our to-
morrows are as long rows of fine punches ranged on a
board, and waiting the hand."

"But, my good lords," said Babbalanja, now brightening with wine, "if, of all suppers those given by bachelors
be the best: of all bachelors, are not your priests and monks
the jolliest? I mean, behind the scenes? Their prayers all
said, and their futurities securely invested, who so care-free
and cozy as they? Yea, a supper for two in a friar's cell in
Maramma, is merrier far, than a dinner for five-and-
twenty, in the broad right wing of Donjalolo's great Palace
of the Morn."

"Bravo, Babbalanja!" cried Media; "your iceberg is
thawing. More of that, more of that. Did I not say we
would melt him down at last, my lord?"

"Ay," continued Babbalanja, "bachelors are a noble fraternity: I'm a bachelor myself. One of ye, in that matter, my lord demi-gods. And if unlike the patriarchs of the world, we father not our brigades and battalions; and send not out into the battles of our country whole regiments of our own individual raising; yet do we oftentimes leave behind us goodly houses and lands; rare old brandies and mountain Malagas; and more especially warm doubtlets and togas, and spatterdashes, wherewithal to keep comfortable those who survive us; casing the legs and arms, which others beget. Then compare not invidiously Benedicts with Bachelors, since thus we make equal division of the duties which both owe to posterity."

"Suppers for ever," cried Media. "See, my lord, what yours has done for Babbalanja. He came to it a skeleton; but will go away every bone padded!"

"Ay, my lord demi-gods," said Babbalanja, drop by drop re-filling his goblet. "These suppers are all very fine, very pleasant, and merry. But we pay for them roundly. Every thing, my good lords, has its price, from a marble to a world. And easier of digestion and better for both body and soul, are a half-haunch of venison and a gallon of mead, taken under the sun at meridian than the soft bridal breast of a partridge, with some gentle negus, at the noon of night!"

"No lie that!" said Mohi. "Beshrew me, in no well-appointed mansion doth the pantry lie adjoining the sleeping chamber. A good thought; I'll fill up, and ponder on it."

"Let not Azzageddi get uppermost again, Babbalanja," cried Media. "Your goblet is only half-full."

"Permit it to remain so, my lord. For whoso takes much wine to bed with him, has a bed-fellow, more restless than a somnambulist. And though Wine be a jolly blade at the

board, a sulky knave is he under a blanket. I know him of
old. Yet, your highness, for all this, to many a Mardian,
suppers are still better than dinners, at whatever cost pur-
chased; forasmuch, as many have more leisure to sup, than
dine. And though you demi-gods may dine at your ease,
and dine it out into the night; and sit and chirp over your
Burgundy, till the morning larks join your crickets, and
wed matins to vespers; far otherwise, with us plebeian mortals. From our dinners, we must hie to our anvils; and
the last jolly jorum evaporates in a cark and a care."

"Methinks he relapses," said Abrazza.

"It waxes late," said Mohi; "your highnesses, is it not
time to break up?"

"No, no!" cried Abrazza; "let the day break when it
will; but no breakings for us. It's only midnight. This way
with the wine; pass it along, my dear Media. We are young
yet, my sweet lord; light hearts and heavy purses; short
prayers and long rent-rolls. Pass round the Tokay! We
demi-gods have all our old age for a dormitory. Come!
Round and round with the flagons! Let them disappear like
mile-stones on a race-course!"

"Ah!" murmured Babbalanja, holding his full goblet
at arm's length on the board, "not thus with the hapless
wight, born with a hamper on his back, and blisters in his
palms. Toil and sleep—sleep and toil, are his days and
his nights. He goes to bed with a lumbago, and wakes
with the rheumatics; I know what it is; he snatches lunches,
not dinners, and makes of all life a cold snack! Yet praise
be to Oro, though to such men dinners are scarce worth
eating; nevertheless, praise Oro again, a good supper is
something. Off jackboots; nay, off shirt, if you will, and go
at it. Hurrah! the fagged day is done: the last blow is an
echo. Twelve long hours to sunrise! And would it were

an Antarctic night, and six months to a to-morrow. But, hurrah! the very bees have their hives, and after a day's weary wandering, hie home to their honey. So they stretch out their stiff legs, rub their lame elbows, and putting their tired right arms in a sling, set the others to fetching and carrying from dishes to dentals, from foaming flagons to the demijohn, which never pours out at the end you pour in. Ah! after all, the poorest devil in Mardi lives not in vain. There's a soft side to the hardest oak plank in the world!"

"Methinks! I have heard some such sentimental gabble as this before from my slaves, my lord," said Abrazza to Media. "It has the old gibberish flavor."

"Gibberish, your highness? Gibberish? I'm full of it— I'm a gibbering ghost, my right worshipful lord! Here, pass your hand through me—here, here, and scorch it where I most burn. By Oro! King! but I will gibe and gibber at thee, till thy crown feels like another skull clapped on thy own. Gibberish! Ay, in hell we'll gibber, king! we'll howl, and roast, and hiss together!"

"Devil, that thou art, begone! Ho, guards! seize him!"

"Back, curs!" cried Media. "Harm not a hair of his head. I crave pardon, King Abrazza, but no violence must be done Babbalanja."

"Trumpets there!" said Abrazza; "so: the banquet is done, lights for King Media! Good-night, my lord!"

Now, thus, for the nonce, with good cheer, we close. And after many fine dinners and banquets—drawing nigh to the evening end of these wanderings wild—meet is it that all should be regaled with a supper.

CHAPTER IX

PROSE FOR FICTION: STEPHEN CRANE

THE IMPORTANCE OF TONE

So MUCH has been said about *le mot juste* and so little about *le ton juste!* Yet failure or success in writing depends more upon the latter than upon the first. By an edifying accident, in the collection of Stephen Crane's short stories known in the Modern Library series as *Men, Women and Boats,* his greatest short story, "The Open Boat," was immediately followed by his worst failure, "The Reluctant Voyagers."

The plot of "The Reluctant Voyagers" was good. Two men bicker with each other at the seaside; they swim out to a raft and bask there; in their semiconscious loafing they fail to notice that the raft has drifted too far from shore; during the ensuing night they are picked up by a schooner and taken to New York Bay; as they, still in their bathing costumes, are being transported by rowboat to the wharf, they quarrel anew and capsize the boat; they are rescued by another boat and landed but for a time it appears as though their oarsman had been drowned.

Such a plot is at once seen to be amenable to a variety of treatments; Crane himself wished to present it humorously, to write a comic story. But he spoiled his intention as soon as he started the tale.

"Two men sat by the sea waves.

" 'Well, I know I'm not handsome,' said one gloomily.

He was poking holes in the sand with a discontented cane.

"The companion was watching the waves play. He seemed overcome with perspiring discomfort as a man who is resolved to set another man right.

"Suddenly his mouth turned into a straight line.

" 'To be sure you are not,' he cried vehemently."[1]

No light touch here! The sparseness of the diction, the brief rhythm, the heavy tone, cause one to expect something tense, as in "The Open Boat": yet what follows is obviously meant to be diverting. In fact, throughout the entire tale Crane never found the right tone for it, and consequently the reader is continually misled. Therefore, "The Reluctant Voyagers" seems unreal, forced, bad in every respect, whereas it is bad in only one: wrong tonality.

Indeed, an erratic sense of tone was one of Crane's besetting sins as a craftsman. He strikes his tone right in "The Open Boat," but even in that powerful story there are little stumbles into negligent journalese.

A DIGRESSION ON REALITY

But so strong is the taste of reality in "The Open Boat" that it could survive much graver faults than these little slips. I should like to digress on this theme, the taste of reality, and for another reason than just once again to illustrate the difference between a subject-matter approach and a stylistic approach to the same piece of work. The digression is aimed point-blank at you, the readers of this book. Most of you are Americans and undoubtedly subscribe, if not in words, then in the still more meaningful

[1]Reprinted from *Men, Women and Boats,* by Stephen Crane, coyright 1921, by and with the permission of and special arrangement with Alfred A. Knopf, Inc., authorized publishers.

language of your wishes and actions, to our supreme national cult of comfort. Of you who read this book—for
your means, leisure, and habits can be inferred from your
interest in our subject—it can be said as an absolute fact:
you seldom or perhaps never get a full taste of reality. Generally speaking, though our lives are precariously led, we
don't have to pay much attention to the perils—as we would
in a time of revolution. It happens to be our lot to experience
comfortable lives and to be mercifully treated by circumstances. This is simply a matter of luck, and it may well
be that most of us will never feel what it is to stand alone
in the universe and to be called upon to make a maximum
effort to preserve ourselves.

Stephen Crane may be defined as a writer who wished
passionately to taste reality, and he devoted many hours
with the pen to the task of at least imagining individual
men thoroughly up against it, as we say. (That Crane was
eager to take greater risks than literary composition affords
is shown by his career as a war correspondent.) He had a
stern conception of reality, and it may be, I should like to
add, that the situations in which his characters found themselves are quite comparable to the real situation of utmost
danger in which the human race may actually be. Blinded
by comfort, we do not perhaps see that we human beings,
collectively considered, are castaways, up against it, and
must fight against virtually impossible odds to win any
foothold in the universe. This is going far from our selected field, but I have advised you that this is a digression
—with a point.

Here is a situation for a story which Stephen Crane
would have loved to write. A friend once said to me:
"Imagine that you and I are two travelers approaching a
village in Tibet. We are weary from our struggle through

a high mountain pass. We do not know the language of the country. We have no money. There is the village a few miles away and night only a few hours off. Furthermore, we cannot stay outdoors in the cold night air of this lofty plateau. We should simply and certainly freeze to death. So we must do something, we must devise a plan, we must tax all our resources, we must make the effort of our lives. Imagine then our emotional state in this situation. Well," he concluded, "on this occasion we should get a taste of what reality is."

"The Open Boat"[2] is the story of a struggle by four shipwrecked human beings against odds as great as those depicted above. A filibustering steamer has gone down off Florida, and the captain, with his arm broken, the cook, the oiler, and a war correspondent find themselves in a small boat. For two nights and a day, without food, they battle to reach shore against a very heavy sea. The agony of this backbreaking and heartbreaking effort is the theme of the tale.

Such a theme in itself cannot fail to grip the reader, but if the reader reads it as he should, *with his experience,* its effect will be no transient one, but forever memorable among one's encounters with printed pages. But do not think that one reads with one's experience simply by wishing to do so. There are a technic and discipline necessary, and as these as much as any analysis of style and form are a portion of the art of reading, I shall present them rather thoroughly.

---

[2]This story happens to be based on an actual experience of shipwreck suffered by Crane. That he could have conceived it without the experience is shown by *The Red Badge of Courage,* which, written before Crane saw warfare, is a remarkable triumph of "as if-ness" for him.

THE RESENSUALIZATION OF WORDS

We all know that each one of us has associations with words, and that we cannot help having these associations aroused whenever we read. But apparently it seldom occurs to anyone to make a critical scrutiny of his associations with words. This is rather strange, since we do in fact discriminate between two kinds of associations. Of So-and-so we shall say, "His understanding of the matter is purely verbal," or "He's just saying words, words, words: he has no experience to back them with." Or, conversely, we say of somebody: "His words testified that he has actually been through what he has described. He knows whereof he speaks. There was weight behind his speech." Better yet: make an individual experiment. Contrast the associations with words that one has in speaking of some interval of ennui with the associations called upon in speaking of immortality. The second are sure to be verbal, mere associations with other words, all clustered about a given topic; whereas the former are associations with one's own experience, in this case not a word but a certain state of the emotions. Another experiment can be tried. Make a list of emotional terms: surprise, horror, irritation, anger, fury, panic, reverence, awe, ecstasy, etc. Then in all candor inquire of oneself for each term: have I experienced something for which this word was invented? Quite likely we have not in a number of cases. There are many people, for instance, who have never experienced or seen that extreme emotional state called panic, and for whom therefore panic is merely a word. And as for awe or sublimity, how many can truthfully say, "Yes, in my own life I have found out what these words stand for"?

So we can say that we have two types of associations:

verbal and experiential. Now let us put the proposition. The active reader reads with his experience, whereas the passive reader reads with his word associations. To see how this would work out, take the opening lines of Keats's "Ode to a Nightingale."

"My heart aches, and a drowsy numbness pains
    My sense, as though of hemlock I had drunk,
Or emptied some dull opiate to the drains
    One minute past, and Lethe-wards had sunk:
'T is not through envy of thy happy lot,
    But being too happy in thine happiness,—
        That thou, light-wingèd Dryad of the trees,
In some melodious plot
    Of beechen green, and shadows numberless,
        Singest of summer in full-throated ease."

I can read this in the ordinary way. That is, I first of all understand the words, and my mind grasps the contrasted statements that the poet is emotionally and even physically depressed and heavy, whereas the nightingale is light, happy, and buoyant with song. I am also somewhat affected emotionally. The music of the lines has drenched me. I do not know exactly what I feel, but the poet is beginning to manipulate me, and certainly I am induced to read on.

But I resist and instead read over the lines again: this time I attempt to read with my experience. "My heart aches": I try to summon what actual experience I have had of the meaning of "my," of the feeling of ownership. For some readers such a feeling may be connected with some article of property, but it just happens that of late I have been too much impressed with the transiency of such articles to feel that I in any sense own them. My feelings of ownership have, in fact, to do with my own body, and I recall one particular morning lying in bed and vividly realizing that the outstretched form was *mine*. For the next word, "heart," I assemble certain sensations I have received from the feeling of my own heartbeat. "Aches" happens to recall a specific sharp experience of a toothache last summer, but for this I substitute the delayed recollection of an experience of "heartache" which I underwent six years ago. And so I proceed through the stanza.

When I come to "hemlock" I am, of course, stopped by a gap in my experience. I have no taste sensations to recall, but at least there are visual memories of hemlocks. Nor have I any concrete experience of Dryads a few lines further: the best I can do there is to recollect a few bits of mythological lore and a picture or two.

Obviously, this is a slow way to read—for a time, anyway. But it should be noted that the specimen lines from Keats are very difficult. Let the reader now try a simple descriptive passage from Thoreau, visualizing for each word of a pictorial character, recalling the song of the wood thrush if happily one's ears have ever been delighted by it, and reëxperiencing the sensations of looking into distance and of standing on tiptoe. Each one of our senses has its history, as has also each of our emotions and frames of mind: our repertory of previous responses to life should be at our disposal when reading.

"This small lake was of most value as a neighbor in the intervals of a gentle rain storm in August, when, both air and water being perfectly still, but the sky overcast, mid-afternoon had all the serenity of evening, and the wood-thrush sang around, and was heard from shore to shore. A lake like this is never smoother than at such a time; and the clear portion of the air above it being shallow and darkened by clouds, the water, full of light and reflections, becomes a lower heaven itself so much the more important. From a hill top near by, where the wood had been recently cut off, there was a pleasing vista southward across the pond, through a wide indentation in the hills which form the shore there, where their opposite sides sloping toward each other suggested a stream flowing out in that direction through a wooded valley, but stream there was none. That way I looked between and over the near green hills to some distant and higher ones in the horizon, tinged with blue. Indeed, by standing on tiptoe I could catch a glimpse of some of the peaks of the still bluer and more distant mountain ranges in the northwest, those true-blue coins from heaven's own mint, and also of some portion of the village."

With practice one comes to be much swifter in relating an item of one's own sensory or emotional or mental history with a given word, but always it requires the expenditure of effort. Effort making, however, can be said to be the distinction between the active devouring reader and the passive devoured reader. And one of the results of this effort directed to the resensualizing of words, the matching of them with the composition of the stream of one's life, is that what is read in this way sticks in one's memory. But, more important than that, one comes to know oneself in a fuller measure, for this method of reading necessitates a growing familiarity with one's past life and makes that past experience accessible.

The gain then is double. The active reader takes a stronger and clearer impression from each word of a writer, and at the same time he revivifies his previous experience.[3]

This experiencing of words is really the foundation of the art of reading. Above it, as the second stage, comes the observation of literary behavior, that penetration into style and form which is the object of this volume. Above that comes a stage, the most important of all, which, however, I have repeatedly pointed out, does not concern us in our present restricted studies. It is pondering on the meanings, the values, the ends of literature; and on the discipline of pondering, a lengthy treatise could be written. The reader who resensualizes words, who divines the technic, who ponders the substance, can be said really to read: but less than that is either titillation or like playing chess or the attempt to value without accumulating the data for weighing.

THE ANATOMY OF "THE OPEN BOAT"

One can, to be sure, study the form of "The Open Boat" as one pores over the moves in a chess game, but in what ensues remember that the difference between an art and a game is this: art is a means, whereas the game itself is the end. Anatomically considered, here is the outline of the plot of "The Open Boat." But the reader is asked to take this skeleton and clothe it with the functions that each member

---

[3]Warning: This book contains a fair number of practical suggestions. That is, things to do. They can and should be tried out at once. But many readers have a habit of postponing action on ideas that seem plausible and perhaps beneficial to the furtherance of their aims. Usually postponement is fatal. The new idea is held for a while and then the life goes out of it: it is taken for granted and never really used. In this way, while one's stock of merely verbal information grows, one's experience remains the same, and in the end one becomes incapable of putting ideas into practice.

performs in the story, for, to repeat, form is a plot functioning.

(1) There is a description of the situation that makes the story: a frail boat, four men in it, and the heavy waves continually charging at the little cockleshell.

(2) The conversation of the cook, the oiler, and the correspondent ending on a note of grim doubt: "We're not there yet."

(3) The conversation of the cook, the oiler, and the captain revolving about the terrible question: "Do you think we've got much of a show now, boys?"

(4) The omen of the sea gull.

(5) The sighting of the lighthouse.

(6) The subtle brotherhood that springs up in the boat.

(7) Raising of the sail and the sighting of land.

(8) The smoking of the four dry cigars.

(9) The ominous exchange of home addresses by the four men as they near the surf.

(10) The reflections of the men as they approach the danger of the surf.

(11) The turning back from the shore and the rowing out to sea.

(12) The running man on the beach and the disappointment that follows.

(13) Out to sea again and the gripping of hunger.

(14) The feeling between the oiler and the correspondent voiced in the meek question, "Will you spell me for a while?"

(15) While the men take turns sleeping in the bilge water of the boat, a roving shark appears.

(16) The growth of a feeling of indifference toward human fate on the part of nature.

(17) Dawn comes and the suspicion of nature's aloofness is enhanced.

(18) The men take their boat into the surf and it is swamped.

(19) Swimming in the surf and the additional dangers of an unfavorable current and the wild swamped boat.

(20) Rescue.

(21) The death of the oiler.

(22) The terse conclusion.

REMARKS ON THE OUTLINE

The problem, which I am for the most part handing over to the reader, is to assign functions to each one of these items. It is easy to see from the outline that the story moves on two planes. On the physical plane it is developed by re-iterated descriptions of the hugeness and might of the waves and the smallness of the boat. On the emotional plane the development proceeds by alternation, the alternation of hopefulness and despair.

In the end I believe all who study the story will concede that it is itself wavelike in form. The reader's sympathy is firmly attached to the four men because of their utmost exertions in fighting the sea, and because of this sympathy the reader shares their suspense and is carried by hope up to the crest of an emotional wave only to tumble into the trough of despair as some new hostile element enters. Finally, in a surf of excited feelings, the story grounds on the shore of its conclusion.

Here then is an exercise which, if completed, should reveal better than any full account by a critic how organic literary form is. But while engaged in that, do not overlook our many other technical concerns with this story.

Notice how limited the vocabulary is to words that denote sensible objects and to words that denote emotions. Notice the particularization of the circumstances of the struggle, Crane's much applauded sense of the telling detail. And notice the tone of the story—a tone of seriousness and anxiety. *Le ton juste!*

CHAPTER X

PROSE FOR FICTION: WALDO FRANK

HISTORICAL NOTE ON THE NOVEL

So STRICTLY contemporary is the fiction of Waldo Frank that before we look directly at it a historical setting is essential. Melville and Crane, although, needless to state, they do not exhaust the previous evolution (or perhaps involution) of the novel, are sufficiently representative of two of its principal phases, and Frank is worthy of careful scrutiny as an exemplar of the most recent phase this form has entered.

Originally, the novel was a blend of tale, drama, and essay. It was a large and varied form when Melville took it up, and perhaps its profuse variety of opportunities (for narrative, for dialogue, for auctorial comment) was germane to the true nature of the novel. Failure to achieve variety would then mean failure to be a novelist. Later times, however, have regarded the early novel as an impure form. It is true that it is a blend, but our contemporaries prefer to say, a mixture of *genres,* and they debate whether the novel can become "pure" by minimizing or eliminating such elements as scenic and character descriptions, expository paragraphs, the direct presentation of the author's point of view, and so on. The outcome has been what we now call the modern subjective novel with James Joyce as its most conspicuous practitioner in the Western world and Waldo Frank as the most advanced American transformer of the novel's character. Between these stages, the early and the late novel, came the naturalistic and so-called realistic examples of fiction . . . such as the stories of Stephen Crane.

To recur to Melville: as John Freeman[1] has said, "Melville began by being a writer of simple direct prose, reminding one partly of Defoe and partly of Borrow, and he became a writer of eloquent elaborated prose wantoning in its strength and movement as his whales wanton in water." Melville in *Mardi* and in *Moby Dick* furnishes a marvelous example of highly rhythmed pure prose, the best example, and the only one taken in this book, of the Grand Ornate Style in American literature. At the top of his powers Melville employed a very large design for his novels, one that had amplitude for all manner of variation in styles and minor forms such as dramatic interludes, apostrophes, poems, fantasies, and prose hymns, one that allowed him exuberance and vehemence and even lavish unrestraints. There is something Elizabethan, even Shakespearean, about the largesse Melville proffers the reader. What is more, in *Moby Dick* he elevates the novel to the realm of the myth.

If we waive for a moment the question of purity we shall be unimpeded in seeing the fiction of Stephen Crane as a contraction in scale and freedom from Melville's titanic constructions. Realistic and naturalistic tendencies in fiction give us approximations, still, however, more or less removed, to camera studies. The novelist deliberately resigns as participant: it has been said that Thackeray, to take a good example, stalked through his own pages with his hands in his pockets, saying his say as the situation moved him[2]: but the naturalist will be none of that but simply a reporter,

---

[1] *Herman Melville.* By John Freeman. Macmillan.
[2] Sherlock Bronson Gass.

an observer. So he narrows his lens, collects information, makes his style more sensational in its diction.

After him looms up the subjective novelist of the present day. But we must be clear on this matter of subjectivity. All novels are ultimately subjective, and it is only by tacit consent that people say that Crane's writing, for instance, is objective. Each and every novelist, in fact, is the recipient of certain gifts unequally apportioned in him: each has been molded by his environment and sociological influences: each, so far as he has been concerned, has been played upon by circumstance at hazard: and each has reacted to circumstance with chance associations. So it is that beneath the most rigidly naturalistic prose we can still detect the author's prejudices and attitudes doing their work of selecting, sifting, rearranging his materials.

But there is this striking difference between the older naturalist and the contemporary subjectivist. The naturalist tried to limit himself to external facts of human life, which, however, he could not avoid perceiving subjectively. But the modern advanced novelist tries to deal more and more exclusively with the internal facts of human existence: he transfers his gaze from the external to the internal environment, the "inner life" of man. Of course, he looks within man by means of introspection: that is, he sees, or thinks he sees, a "stream of consciousness" which external behavior does not imply. This is subjectivity viewed subjectively, and because both its field of attention and its method are subjective, the modern novel has itself come to be named such.

AGAINST SELF-EXPRESSION

But we need more background than this to explain the recent novel. The doctrine of self-expression has been rampant in the last thirty years in American literature: it came to a head several decades earlier in European letters: and only now is it beginning to wane. It should really be studied in connection with the philosophy and art of romanticism, but for our purposes in this discussion the doctrine can be simplified. Self-expression as an artistic theory holds that it is the function of the artist to express himself (in blunter words, simply to manifest himself) *as he is now*. It is assumed that what he is now is worthy of expression, and it is further argued that his duty of communication with the reader, his office of conveying himself, is entirely secondary or to be disregarded. The entire onus of comprehension is shifted to the reader, and the writer is thus free to proceed without reference to the reader's psychology. This has been taken advantage of by many writers who have indulged themselves in odd styles, perversities of thought and feeling, peculiar subject-matter, in private discourses, in short. Much "modern" writing is disguised soliloquizing but with the fervent and incongruous hope that there will be many who will pay for the invitation to eavesdrop.

This is a departure from the tradition and discipline of the art of literature and from an older point of view it means the shirking of the difficulties of communication.[3] To-day, for many readers self-expression, the babbling in private tongues, has meant the dehumanization of literature. How has this come to pass? Humanly considered, literature is a development of common speech, and writers and

---

[3]To those readers who wish to delve into the metaphysics of communication, I recommend Chapter V, "Nature, Communication and Meaning," in *Experience and Nature,* by John Dewey. Dewey concludes by saying: "Language is primarily a mode of action used for the sake of influencing the conduct of others in connection with the speaker."

readers are substitutes for speakers and hearers. But the trend of self-expression is to sever the ties between our mother tongue and what literature should be, our father tongue,[4] and to exalt instead a bastard species of self-indulgence in words—which sheds more light on the author than on the reader. Having written for himself as audience instead of for an intended reader, the self-expressionist then regards his product either sentimentally or superstitiously as inspired, and abuses the public for not sharing his private feelings about it.

Arnold Bennett has written a sound little handbook, *Literary Taste: How to Form It,* from which some of the less experienced readers of this text could derive a certain amount of profit. The following quotation is apt at this moment. "It is extremely important that the beginner in literary study should always form an idea of the man behind the book. The book is nothing but the expression of the man. The book is nothing but the man trying to talk to you, trying to impart to you some of his feelings. An experienced student will divine the man from the book, will understand the man by the book, as is, of course, logically proper. But the beginner will do well to aid himself in understanding the book by means of independent information about the man. He will thus at once relate the book to something human, and strengthen in his mind the essential notion of the connection between literature and life. The earliest literature was delivered orally direct by the artist to the recipient. In some respects this arrangement was ideal. Changes in the constitution of society have rendered it impossible. Nevertheless, we can still, by the exercise of the imagination, hear mentally the accents of the artist

---

[4] On this point consult the chapter on Reading in Thoreau's *Walden.*

speaking to us. We must so exercise our imagination as to feel the man behind the book."

The congeniality between self-expression and the program of the subjective novelist is obvious, but in fairness one justification for the eccentric modern artist should be advanced. The spread of democratic education and the tireless clattering of the printing press have produced an appalling confusion of audiences. To-day any kind of book may fall into the hands of any kind of reader. Yet great books have not been written for *any* audience, but only for a certain audience. For whom were the classics composed? We can easily find to-day the assumption that they were written for anybody: hence, the effort to vulgarize their meanings and to cajole the unfit reader into regarding them as domestic diversions. Another result of the spread of literacy has been the promotion of an utterly debased journalism. From this state of affairs the self-expressing highly subjective writer recoils, quite rightly, but he recoils too far. Instead of selecting his public within the great overgrown literate public and directing his skill at manipulating the psychology of that definite inner group, he withdraws disdainfully and altogether and boasts: "I write to please myself alone."

INVASION BY THE LITERARY CHEMIST

Mingled with the glorification of subjectivism and self-manifestation is another important trend, that of literary experimentation. It is assumed that many forms are by now exhausted and research must be undertaken for the invention of new forms. To set up a literary laboratory is legitimate and even valuable, but it should be understood that workshop experiments are primarily for the literary profes-

sion. They are trials at new effects which it is not reasonable
to suppose will, in nine cases out of ten, interest other than
specialists. The *Ulysses* of James Joyce is a great feat for
writers to study, but from the standpoint of the general
intelligent reader the book can be only an enormous curiosity.

FRANK'S ORGANIZING POWER AS SHOWN IN "HOLIDAY"

Now, to take up the work of Waldo Frank wholly in the
unfavorable light of the foregoing paragraphs would be
unjust to the author of *Rahab, City Block* and *Holiday*. If
one wished to point out an American artist who has been
ruined by these currents of our time, there is Sherwood
Anderson. Frank rises well above the faults induced by the
acceptance of such theories, but he has not lived unscathed
by our present literary environment. His writing does raise
the very questions we have just outlined, but in one whole
side of his work Frank tends to transcend literary experiment, personal expression and subjective entanglements.
The forms of Frank's novels are admirable.

Read his novel of the South, *Holiday,* from which a
chapter is later extracted as a specimen of his prose for
our study. In its lowest terms *Holiday* is the story of one
day's events in the town of Nazareth. We are first given
pictures of the parallel communities of blacks and whites
on an Indian summer's eve. In Niggertown the workers
return home and eat supper. Later they go to church. In
Whitetown the mass of its population flows down to the
wharf to meet the Gulf steamer, a Negro falls overboard
and is let drown because no white man will plunge to the
rescue, the whites flow back to Main Street and to their
harsh church. During these scenes two characters, John

Cloud, Negro, and Virginia Hade, white girl, emerge as protagonists. The next morning, since Negroes must go into town to work for their white masters, witnesses the convergence of the lives of the two races. Because of the intense heat, a holiday is declared at noon, and separately John Cloud and Virginia Hade roam to the bay's shore in quest of coolness. A crucial meeting occurs there between them and its aftermath is the winding into Niggertown of a gang of white lynchers. John Cloud is borne to the village square, hanged, and burned at dusk.

But even this naked summary suggests the possibilities for formal organization which Frank has so boldly worked out; intricately and subtly as well. Modern though the texture of the book is, in its antiphonal form it is akin, distantly, perhaps, but clearly so, to Greek tragedy. For the novel is a momentous play of two masses which at first are balanced by contrast, then by opposition. The design is sketched in the first sentences.

"Sunset at Nazareth.[5]

"Niggers go home through the copperglow of pines. Niggers sing home.

"White men stand lean in the doors of paintless houses. White men stand still."

The fair highly colored setting in which the drama is to be played out and which Frank is to emphasize as the events turn horrible is brushed in by the ensuing sentence. "The waters of the bay go red to the blue Gulf where swims the bloody sun . . . sunset on Nazareth."

Frank then proceeds to endow his contrasted masses with

---

[5]From *Holiday,* by Waldo Frank, and reprinted by permission of Horace Liveright, Publisher.

a life appropriate to each, until they are able to respond as communities to each other, almost as opposed choruses. Here is a specimen of the antiphonal impassioned voicing of the "unconscious"[6] of each community at the moment Frank changes their relationship from contrast to opposition.

> "BLACKTOWN : *Whar are you? Why should I stay down?*
> *O our village is singin' strong,*
> *An' de crops is in,*
> *An' de cotton's made,*
> *An' de watermelon's ripe.*
> *We goes rollin' into one*
> *Down de red street to de moon*
> *—She stands dere like a melon in de sky—*
> *We goes rollin', we goes strong,*
> *We is a great big thunderin' song!*
> *Whar are you?*
> *Whar are yo'-all?*
> *White town? Da's funny. I's heard tell o' dat.*
> *Dim, dim, dim, white town.*
> *Why, sho! I's done heard tell o' dat.*
> "WHITETOWN : I'll crush you! If you're color and love, watch my white hate. I'll hold you! If you are seed and fruit, watch my white drouth exalt the dry well and the blind eyes of my women!"

[6]It is on the æsthetic side alone that Frank suggests Greek tragedy, for certainly the unconscious articulation of Frank's choral masses and the somnambulistic thoughts and actions of his chief characters are remote from the temper of Greek drama.

Now the book halts in a restless suspense that shall give birth to its tragic cumulation.

"Noon. The sun halts vibrant. Rays pour through the tremor of equilibrant heat. Animals, leaves, caked clay stand in the same suspension with the sun. Under the sun reaches the western sky that sun must fall through, die through into dusk. Now momently sun stands—and the world stands with it."

Then the energies coiled into the plot commence to unwind fatally. Black mass and white mass swell out in conflict.

> *"The fire in the sky slides down*
> *Nazareth fire mounts"*

The sun descends fatefully while human hatred ascends to its consummation at nightfall, when in turn the night wells up and "Nazareth plunges down" into it. This is dynamic form in which Frank excels.

The agents of the conflict are John Cloud and Virginia Hade, moving out from the responding masses until they touch each other, converse, and exchange knives in an oddly exalted, partially incomprehensible, and altogether extraordinary scene. This foreground scene is the highest pitch of the book, and its implications are such that the white men, smoldering from an ineffectual revival meeting, are inflamed into a destructive unit : the lynching party. All potentialities of action innate in the form are burned away in this bursting forth of pent-up energies, and the design dies into an absolute rest, ashen and lifeless.

"The fire tongues fall back from the charred body of John Cloud.

"Nazareth beneath him peers with grimed eyes through the murk of its spent lust.

"Virginia, soothed by the silence, sleeps in her bed.

"The *Psyche* stands at the empty pier that points from Nazareth out into the world."

FRANK'S WORLD-CONCEPTION

Inadequate as this account of formal machinery is, it will have to do full duty here, since disproportionate space would be required for all the complications. Recall that it is not Frank alone, but the contemporary radical novel which he ably represents, that we are endeavoring to come to quarters with, and that justifies me in probing into this particular example as much as I have. But I have another reason—it is connected with the close of my third chapter—for persisting in this examination. Is there a relation between form and the world view of the author? Let Waldo Frank speak on the significance of the form of *Holiday*.[7]

"*Holiday* is a story as simple and direct as I could make it, of one of the greatest of American dramas: the struggle in the South between the white race and the black. . . . The truths of the white race are pitted in merciless conflict against the truths of the negro. From this meeting of fundamental forces there arises a tragedy which has haunted me long. . . .

"There are no villains in *Holiday*, no heroes. The two protagonists are White Town and Black Town; the white girl, Virginia, and the black man, John, are significant in so far as forces, hungers, passions, and ideals vastly greater than themselves run through them and grow articulate in their deeds. For here is a dual world, each part of which

[7] Quoted from *Brentano's Book Chat*, Thanksgiving, 1923.

yearns in its racial way for self-expression, for joy, for life, for God; each part of which *profoundly loves and needs what the other part possesses,* and through the fateful circumstances of American life, all this energy of desire is locked into opposition and distrust so that it becomes chanelled not in some fair communion but in an orgy of blood and horror. This ironic state is tragedy, surely, but tragedy quite as profound for the white oppressors and lynchers (victims of their own hate and love) as for their negro victims."

But Frank has more than an ironic vision of life: he sees beyond an interlocking and conflict of relative truths and desires destined to achieve the opposite of what they initiate. He is pronouncedly mystical in his inclinations, and this governs his ambitious æsthetic. He maintains that the ordinary world is not the true world. The senses give but a succession of fragments: the mind limits and compartmentalizes. But intuition leaps beyond sensationalism and rationalism. Man has in fact a sense of a Whole, immobile and ordered, of which our ordinary world is but the moving surfaces. The Whole is irrational judged by our customary consciousness. So it comes about that Frank's object as an artist is to make the reader leap the gap from the confined and the rational to the "irrational" and free sense of the Whole. Hence the dynamism of his forms. As in *Holiday,* he builds solidly and rationally his earlier forms, gives them momentum, and hopes that their cumulative force will carry the reader upward and through such puzzling scenes as the exchange of knives between John Cloud and Virginia. Some readers have testified that they have been able to accept this scene because of the power generated in advance and so have experienced a moment in an uncreate Dionysian world.

FRANK'S INTENSELY PERSONAL STYLE

But a greater number of readers have admitted their total failure to make any such flight, or rather they have indulged in reproaches directed at Waldo Frank's methods. We can understand their outcries if we glance at the style of *Holiday*. The mobility of its language is of considerable interest to professional writers, but this does not signify that it has the same degree of interest to the general reader whose part I am about to espouse. For the means taken to gain mobility are experimental: the dropping of particles, the cutting away of connective tissue, the sudden injections of unspoken thoughts or feelings, the lyrical crystallizations, the incessant activity of the verbs, the continuous short stroking of the sentences, make the professional speculate on the extent to which Frank's method can be driven, but according to evidence they irritate the reader. Probably less, however, than the liberties taken with word associations. The reader's mind trips when Frank converts an adjective into a noun or vice versa ("He feels the warm of her body") ; he gets little but perplexity when Frank introduces the vocabulary of physics into a word painting ("The clay in striant measure responds to the heat rays, casts a tyric tension back into the air where the flexed waves are swirling between the vertices of sun and earth"). These are, to the reader, objectionable details, but what makes Frank's prose hardest for him to enjoy is the fluidity that Frank constantly bestows on the clearest cut objects of sense. He emotionalizes the sensory world: objects lose their fixities, their architectural qualities, and begin to churn, to liquefy, to veer and race and gyre and strew themselves about his pages. Sometimes this loosing the visible world from its anchorage is extremely effective, but as a continuous device the reader protests that it is a nervous distortion of fact.

"White Nazareth thrusts down longing to the bay. Main Street narrows in resolution. The frame stores, tin fronted, lose their pride, lose half their being. The red street dips and all its will is bayward. The stores, crowded, are shoddier. The street is strident with cacophony of gutter, of twisting rut and groove. On the loose-beam bridge street leaps a gulley, red through water oak and holly: street flares into a tongue of wide moist land which is the way to the pier. The longing of white Nazareth is the pier: Nazareth longing for a towered world, a world of trolleys and department stores and liners from Honduras plethoric with fruit."

This is in Frank's characteristic manner, and that manner makes no concessions to the psychology of the reader who is not in the habit of ascribing volition and dynamic qualities to natural objects like a street. It is, in fact, a subtle instance of self-expression and subjective interpretation. But why not? Because Frank wishes passionately to communicate his world view, his sense of the Whole, his religious vision, to an audience. Yet his paradox is that he writes in such a way that most of his readers cannot see his form for the style, cannot, this is to say, grasp his message, that of a human being valiantly striving to solve the meaning and aim of existence, because of the intrusion of his personality. He does not wish to be simply a writer's writer nor a self-communer who happens to please a coterie: yet he does not pay the price of consciously manipulating the reader's psychology and so conducting him *through* his

ordinary impressions, associations, and prejudices to a
new insight.

There is another way, a very simple one, of estimating
Waldo Frank's style. After Bagehot, it has often been said
of Gibbon's undulant style: "It is impossible to tell the
truth in such a style." We can ask of Waldo Frank's style
or of any other personal style, "What things can it do and
what things are impossible in such a style?" The student
should be able to make a list of those things Frank can perform well, such as descriptive passages of moving objects
(the docking of the *Psyche* in *Holiday*), the melting of a
crowd into a single state of emotionalism (the Negro
church scene), and dramatic crises (the taking of John
Cloud by the lynchers). But it seems to me that in his
present style Frank can never achieve impressiveness,
weight, majesty, and sublime grandeur. The style is too
swift and light for that, yet these are the very qualities that
a religious writer must be able to create.

A PARADOX FOR STUDY

Here, then, are indicated exceptional materials for further study. Frank has a less naïve view of man in relation to
the cosmos than the majority of his contemporaries, and
he strives to formulate this view, to become aware of it. As
an artist, he is distinguished in his conceptions of form: all
his books have an astutely planned unity of larger organization. The two are related. Equally related are one's personality (a product mainly of education, taking that word in
its widest sense) and style. And Frank's style shows so
markedly the effects of artistic theories current to-day that
it defeats his more profound intentions. For it is easy
enough to say that a modern artist must create the taste by

which he is to be judged, but on second thought one should see that it would take a god to change the genius of the language since that would mean transforming the psychology of those who speak and read it.

ON WEIGHING EMOTIONS

I shall conclude this chapter with what has apparently become a habit in this book: I find myself resorting again to the inevitable subjoining. How would you estimate the following passages, picked more or less at random from the works of our three novelists, for weight of emotion?

(a) "From earth to heaven! High above me was Night's shadowy bower, traversed, vine-like, by the Milky Way, and heavy with golden clusterings. Oh, stars! oh, eyes that see me wheresoe'er I roam: serene, intact, inscrutable for aye, tell me, Sybils, what am I? Wondrous worlds on worlds! Lo, round and round me, shining, awful spells: all glorious, vivid constellations, God's diadem ye are! To you, ye stars, man owes his subtlest raptures, thoughts unspeakable, yet full of faith."—From *Mardi,* by Herman Melville.[8]

(b) "If I am going to be drowned—if I am going to be drowned—if I am going to be drowned, why, in the name of the seven mad gods who rule the sea, was I allowed to come thus far and contemplate sand and trees? Was I brought here merely to have my nose dragged away as I was about to

[8]Notice Melville's lapses into meter.

nibble the sacred cheese of life?"[9]—From "The Open Boat," by Stephen Crane.

(c) "I stand still: a shudder swarms my skin, draws my throat taut, uprises in my hair. . . .

". . . the white room larded with books: the face noble and reticent, and the swift births of amaze, of pity, of horror . . . indecorous death. Pale hands fluttering up like rebellious dreams—and fallen.

"My own hands bar my eyes. . . . How do I know this is not morbid nonsense?"—From *Chalk Face*, by Waldo Frank.

An interesting difficulty at once appears. For full measurement of the emotions informing these passages, we need the context that precedes each one. Extracts from poems would do better, and this ought to illuminate again the difference between prose and poetry. Prose is more dependent upon the idea that supports the work, and even a very emotional passage detached from the general idea does not cry out to us so clearly as a similar detached fragment of poetry would. But the application of the ensuing tests[10] will still be of value even when we are ignorant of the intellectual framework within which the prose emotion has been built.

(1) What kind of emotion—anger, hatred, benevolence, bathos, pathos, sublimity, et cetera—has been expressed? Classifying is our first concern. Then ask your-

---

[9]Reprinted from *The Open Boat and Other Tales* by Stephen Crane, by and with permission of and special arrangement with Alfred A. Knopf, Inc., authorized publishers.

[10]Permit me again to offer thanks to Mr. A. R. Orage.

self what emotions do we put in the highest place, what scale of emotions does the common sense of man agree upon? To be specific, which do we rank higher: courage or cowardice, reverence or irritation?

(2) Is the emotion appropriate? Is the occasion or cause for the emotion a justifiable one? This is a way to track down sentimentalities which are emotions in excess of the facts that excite them.

(3) How intense is the emotion? Intensity is always of value, regardless of the kind of emotion that is raised in its vibratory rate. For intensity is dependent upon the purity of the emotion being felt and upon the strength of the person's springs, or natural constitution, of feeling.

(4) What is the elevation of the emotion? This can be determined by considering the objects with which the emotion is connected. A simple illustration is envy, which may be exercised toward a great thing or a small.

(5) To what degree is the emotion expressed? Oftentimes intensity of feeling and incoherence of utterance accompany each other: scores of inferior writers actually believe that it is "strong" writing to put their characters into a state of incoherence. But in contrast to them consider the sonnets of Shakespeare and their perfect expression of the intensest jealousy.

(6) How universal is the emotion? Universal here means appearing in all men at some time or other. The ranking emotions must be of universal validity and proper to mankind.

(7) Is the emotion individual or unique? This does not, as it seems before one has thought about it, contradict the sixth question. Is the emotion absolutely *characteristic* of the person experiencing it? It may be a universal emotion but it should be felt in an individual way.

Just as in the case of the four thoughts we weighed at the close of the chapter on Santayana, we found that there was only one possible order for them which, by the way, was c (the weightiest), then b, then a, then d (the lightest), so you will find that there is only one possible gradation for the three emotional passages culled from Melville, Crane, and Frank.

AFTER THE REVIVAL MEETING[11]

By Waldo Frank

They are coming out of the Revival Tent. The preacher's rasp has scaled its height and fallen. They flutter to their feet, lean drab-clothed men and women: from their throats the buzzing voices swarm toward the common note. Opulent words of love and faith are pushed by their thin voices up into the air. The Deacon has made his announcements:—Church goes on. Time falls with all its glittering prohibitions into the drab eternity of Church. His voice is high. Gloating and rebuke waft his stale messages of meetings, sewing circles and collection with a voice as verdant as the words of the preacher who has a voice that rasps. "You should have heard me more," goes with the Deacon's voice. And they are coming out from the Revival Tent. The preacher has rasped his climax, he is tumbling down. Brave words of faith and love have been high wafted out of leaden throats. Eager eyes, voices almost fierce, have asserted the victory of meekness, helped the preacher hoist them . . . *rasp rasp frenzy, rasp up, rasp eye, blood, passion up* . . to the release of vision: love there, love allowed, rasp up to love allowed. And they are coming out from the Revival Tent. The rasp of the preacher has not hoisted them quite: high words lead-winged have not hoisted them quite. There for a spell they dangled, off the

[11]From *Holiday*, by Waldo Frank and reprinted by permission of Horace Liveright, Publisher.

Nazareth ground, the choked tent and their vision off the ground; yet under the free sweet spaces of the Lord his rasping and their own song-words jerked them toward. Not quite. There they suspended . . *rasp rasp up up . . there they strained . . lift me a bit a bit more heft to that pull . .* there they stayed . . *rasp rasp rasp rasp* DOWN . . . They are coming out of the Revival Tent. Sluggish blood not whipped to foam. Clottish blood shutting out sun and making their faces sallow, hard . . *blood should foam, blood should flood* . . . They are coming clottish thick from the Revival Tent: and the preacher has failed.

—God ain't so easy to reach like He used to be. Y' don't ketch on to His bootstraps easy, no mo'. Got to h'ist yo'self up, nowadays, by yo' own bootstraps.

Men and women, boys and girls come out. A remnant lingers. The preacher subdued is speaking to them yet. *They* ain't so hard to h'ist up. His voice rasps less. His little yellow eyes glow thankfully. His smile dwells on the Remnant who stay, who have been h'isted up. —Nothing else counts. The Remnant. I am the Remnant. His little paunch is rounder as his round hands clasp it, and the yellow eyes warm out upon his Remnant. His voice is different: thin like a paper strip, but waxen smooth, now he no longer strives to make of it a banner of the Lord across the Southern skies. He chats colloquially to the clustered Remnant: familiar with them (he does not know he has failed): familiar with God (—I am God's and God can't fail. If God chooses only a Remnant, I cannot fail). He chats. But under the warming beam of his eyes a glance, furtive and fearful, vaults the little group who press about his pulpit, takes in the long rows of wooden emptiness whence Nazareth has drifted from the Tent: and in even measures, harsh and cold, the benches speak their word to the wistful glance covert within his eyes. His lips purse and his voice a little rasps once more, glowing a benison upon the Remnant.

Men, the solid men of Nazareth, mark and support the crowd that forms at the Tent's mouth. It is a clot of tangential pressures held together. It shuttles in and out upon itself. It is hard with words and intercourse of gesture. It is the Town of Nazareth pressing upon itself for an eye, for a direction. There are tall lean men silk-haired, cadaverous, whose words come hard like steel pins. There are heavy men with flaring brows and the mustachios of musketeers whose words are a roar. There are men with shallow eyes not looking; there are men with ripe red lips, too ripe . . . Men make the structure of the outlet crowd. The women stand and shred among them, pale light beams, emanant escapes of the hard male hungers. Men dry as bone, vacillant stiff like autumn grass, men lush and hard like the salt marshes baked by the sun: and their women among them, disembodied, making in their separate wistfulness the duality of Nazareth that is its Law.

The edge of the crowd shifts, flutters. It is the place of the women. A solid clot the center where the men talk affairs. But the affairs they talk, the opalescent gossip of the women are feelers of atoms nostalgic to be close. The substance that bulged the Tent mourns for its dwindling unity. Under the sky, solidity runs out and clots afresh: words rustle, hands clasp, eyes hold, that the substance of the Tent live longer.

—Fo' yo' ain't h'isted us up. *Rasp Rasp*. Yo' ain't h'isted us away!

It is tumescence cheated. In the mass threatened with dispersal lives still the glow that should have come to flame.

—What is God for? Jesus, what are you for?

—Ain't it a shame God's got so hard to git holt on?

Nazareth lingers, dangerously half-roused: in its soul's dark smolders a sore spot that is fire.

—It is time to die.

It is time to be getting home.

Let the spark that mustn't catch glim out.

—It is time to die.

Always, it is time to die.

Birth is a sin, and sun is a mocking sin.

—Sun . . sun . . eternal Orgasm,

What more do you want?

Myriad men sparks make you:

Glowing women make you.

Where is the Lord that'll h'ist us up to Him?

—The sun don't care.

O no!

He sucks my men, he sucks my women white.

Sun laughs!

I'm cheated by white sky . . .

. . . But they smile at each other: holding together still: loth to let go and die.

"A good sermon."

"Well, that's over."

"O yes, pretty good."

"Now the Reverend Mack, *he* was good."

"What's become of him?"

"Why he's dead, Mrs. Brewster. Done died last year . . ."

"You don' say! My! So young. He was fine, that parson."

"Overdid himself, Ah reckon. Broke a bloodvessel in his brain, a-preachin'."

"Too much thinkin'."

"Pretty good sermon, after all."

"Well, that's over."

"Will you be comin' round, George, after supper?"

"Reckon I might."

"Then says I to her: Why, my dear, you're a married woman!"

"Doesn't she think folks has eyes?"

"Nor ears. Why, what I heard by the South Gully!"

"They're sending an Orficer down, Bast tells me."

"No: you won't find *that* in the Gazette."

"Come roun' and I'll give you mine. O a fiver should do."

"No, Stoughton. The assessment's ten, this year."

"Everything goes up . . goes up . . even Revenoo Orficers."

"Now if we could elect a President."

"Dey's nothin' but niggers up No'th."

"Sure. Pretty good. Now, the Reverend Mack."

"They oughtn't to allow 'em to have Revival."

"Het 'em up too durn much."

"Willoughby came round shoutin'."

"We'll tar him, ef."

"Nothin' but Voodoo drunk, that's all it is."

"Well, why shouldn't Peters stay on? He's fair. He's played fair . . ."

"The assessing of that turpentine grove by Lounsville."

"O they is alright."

"Yes indeed, Ma'am. Good evenin' to *you*, Ma'am."

"Splendid sermon."

"Now, the Reverend Mack."

"O couldn't ha' been better."

"Dignified."

"What he needs."

"Mind talks nowadays."

"And yet . . ."

. . Voices thickly dryly twine a straw tangle through the slow mass moving up to Main Street; angular bodies bowing faint gesticulant sharp pent kets of easelessness at play up out from the horizontal pace to Main street; maze of eye-seek, lip-curl, finger-twist-and-jerk within the sluggish forward of the way to Main Street; choked breast, clamped heart-leap, gnaw of the spark a cancer in their brains throb shuttle thresh deliberate slow to Main Street: HALT

Virginia Hade

She stands at ease in the center of the street. Her white height thrusts its red heart at them. Athwart her head, the town fades: they feel the stroke of her eyes. Staccato roofs, porches on piles drag to the right, lurch to the left . . are gone. She, hard and sure, stands and is real. On her brow they see a smudge of blood. And in her hand upheld, they see a knife.

The crowd compresses upon itself. She watches her work as terror and amaze wipe blandness from eyes, inject an angular rush upon these somnolent muscles. Terror and amaze cover eyes an instant and are gone. Mist of stirring: a release faint and hopeful curls like a first flame in the mass of Nazareth. She sees now freedom and gladness. She is at ease with her hard eyes blacksmiling, while her magic works.

The crowd breaks into integrate parts. It is a crowd maturing. From its hearty will eyes muscles limbs are fleshed: with a young joy muscles and limbs move to the creating of its will. Judge Hade and Bob Hade step from the crowd. They come up to Virginia.

The father places his hands upon her arms. But she is firm, resting in the magic of her work.

Bob Hade takes the knife from her hand.

He looks at it: and from that instant he looks at his sister no more. He clasps the knife as if it were some absolute deep Thing, making his sister dim.

He is alive with a nervous luminous glow. He turns to the crowd, he is the crowd's sharp spirit: he is the culminant word of the crowd grown to voice. His lips move freely, tasting their masterful words. And from his eyes comes a splendor as of revelation.

"Men," his voice is mellow. "Men . . this knife . . I know this knife. John Cloud."

He does not lift his voice. He does not urge. His words are free. They have wings. They have faith. They bear with them a glamorous life all dawning. They career, sure of themselves, low-paning to the ears of the men who hear them.

The crowd is a birth of colors interwhirled. Murmur and suspense and hunger flush the dim crowd to life. It moves upon itself: fertile, condign. It breaks out fluently from its drab smolder. It opens, passionate, giving out its men: giving the wealth of its substance.

Men part from the crowd's vague, moving in vibrancy across the space (the sun lifts the clay into red oscillant tremors) to where the two men and the girl stand sheer. Like blood, men rise from the crowd's belly to the crowd's high head. Boys pale and tense with lips that curl; mature young men stoop-shouldered, necks craned stiff; heavy men hunched on themselves; hard men whose wills impressed come out in the flint of their eyes. They are the substance of Bob Hade's words. They join the words of the Head. The crowd stands living in its Head. They move, they go forth spreading sure and at work, the words of the Head.

The men have scattered: no true scattering. The men have gone forth from the crowd like its will, like hands of a body to reach for certain tangible things.

Virginia stands alone beside her father, Bob is gone. He looks at her. The men and the crowd, after the look that kindled them, see her no more. She leans a little on her father's arm. A little thought lies crooked in her mind, that if she had a mother he could now be with the men.

A buckboard clatters up: the mules prance: they too are of the dawning ecstasy. The wood of the wagon gleams in the sun.

"Better step in, daughter."

Only her father is a soft discord in the steel lilt of the world.

"Come." It is a mother's firmness. "Come. I'll help you home."

She steps forward free of her father's arms. She sees him.

"Must I go home?"

"Yes, daughter. Come."

From the distance, the scattered men draw in again. Boys tense-lipped carry rope. Heavy men carry slender guns. All are sure, all are laved in a glum rhythm as of a dawn scarce broken and yet certain to rise and to spread.

Virginia sees them. A smile touches her face: It is a smile of gentle reminiscence. And its touch upon her eyes and lips is like a whip on them. Her face contorts. She sees her father there.

"Father," she says. "I'm all right." Her hand is at her breast. "A bit of a wound."—*Stay here!*

"Daughter, step in."

"Father, stay here!"—Why do I want him here?

They do not mind her. She has brought to them what now these boys and men and women carry like a love, sinister gay, above their heads as they cluster, as they plan. Rope, guns and knives of the men are one with the draw of the women's eyes, with the glint of the women's words.

Virginia steps into the buckboard. She steps in slow and heavy: the mules prance away.

The men form a knot apart. They confer with their white brows clustered.

The Tent flaps debile. It is empty. Nazareth is empty. The crowd has drawn unto itself all of the Tent, all of Nazareth.

But the men are apart. They are an organ thrust forth from the crowd. They are bleak and dark. They do not glow and exclaim like the crowd itself. They are silent, muttering low. They are a promise: a larval joy. The crowd .. women, children, old men, sick men .. look on the knot of men with their ropes and guns, and love its darkling ugliness. It is an instrument for them of joy and of flame.

From the Tent's flapping mouth a little man appears. He is black-frocked. He stands a moment in the droop of canvas which he has tried to swell with the word of Christ: his eyes wince as he catches the crowd's dark note. His hands flutter before him. He rushes with pattering feet to the knot of men.

"Men! Brothers!" he butts against them shrilling. "What are you going to do? What are those guns for, brothers? You have just come from Christ. What are those guns?"

Backs fend him off. His hands whimmer.

This larval knot must burst in its own time.

He turns. He is a little sleek plump man. His eyes blink, he suffers. With whimmering hands, he is drawn away from the knot of men . . into the men-drained crowd. Flutter and press of women take him in, make him theirs. In saccade fragments, women's phrases agglutinate his will. His hands droop silent.

"I have done my duty."

Talk binds them close: the women who are one, waiting the stroke of the men.

—Dark engine: ugly: full of sweetness
    We wait for you
Burst us open with your bursting flame-might
    We wait.
We murmur and talk, we cheat and lie,
Our hands upraised in protest cheat and lie,
    We are waiting. Burst us.
Our words cheat time, for we must wait:
    We are waiting.

—Time and suspense we cover.
(That's what the protest's for,
That's what the words and gestures and the screams
Serve) : Serve us!
    We are waiting.

—We'll rouse you!
With resistance.
With the resisting word and the resisting hand to touch
    and fire your passion,
Ugly men!
Larval pushing men!
    Burst us. e are waiting.

For the men have made a rope of themselves. Bob Hade is the head. He strides and the men are a rope, taut, writhing after. Thick men and lean men and callow youths, strange to their first ecstasy, rope out and are away toward Niggertown.

The crowd remains:—*Burst us. We wait.*

Part Four

OTHER FORMS OF PROSE

CHAPTER XI

PROSE FOR HUMOR AND SATIRE: MARK TWAIN, FINLEY PETER DUNNE, AND DONALD OGDEN STEWART

ANOTHER LITTLE ADDRESS TO THE READER

As WE start a fresh division of this book I find myself regretting the absence of certain opportunities that a course of lectures gives. I imagine that I am writing to intelligent but untrained readers who feel, a little uneasily, perhaps, that they would like to develop a more critical attitude toward the books that come into their hands. But since I cannot question you face to face, you must question yourselves. Ask yourselves how you are getting along. Are you really beginning to alter your reading habits? Do you find illustrations of the various principles of prose in the books you have taken up since opening this volume? Is a critical attitude forming in you?

Only if—and there can be no dodging this necessity— one makes effort can one solidify a new attitude. Criticism means work, and he who would become a critic must, in the language of a leading American psychologist, be a "go-doer." I am making my text as practical as I am able, but exercises which are suggested to, but not performed by, the reader are—it is worth repeating—deleterious to his morale in this field.

The rule is, to act on your own as much as possible. I have done a certain amount of preparation for writing this chapter. The active reader will also prepare himself to read it. He will pause and collect his own thoughts on the subject before he submits himself to another man's reasoning. A handy way to prepare for the present chapter is to look over the vocabulary of the subject, writing down such words as wit, satire, comedy, humor, farce, burlesque, nonsense, amusement, the comic, and then search for your own definitions and understanding of these terms and for your distinctions between one and another of them.

WIT, SATIRE, HUMOR, ETC.

Having done that, then look for a basic principle tying together all these types of writing. It is apparent that there is an element of the unexpected in all of them, and that each deals with incongruities. The appeal is to our risibilities (for the most part) by the swift revelation of an unexpected incongruity.

But the appeal is made in widely different fashion. We associate intellect with wit. Satire, too, is generally regarded as intellectual in character but propelled by a strong emotion which is usually indignation. Humor is more mixed; less intellectual than wit or satire and broader, as we say, by which we mean more emotional: the feeling is very often benevolent. We descend the scale further when we consider farce. A minimum of intellect is utilized here, the emotions are simple, and the instinctive enters as a principal ingredient. Hence it is that farce flourishes best on the stage where physical actions may become more important than the text.

From a psychological standpoint the lack of purity in

these forms is most interesting, for it means that these forms stem from a compound produced by thought and feeling or by feeling and action, very much as intuitions are compound judgments. Properly speaking, there is no emotion of amusement or humor, but only a compound state of thinking and feeling.

These remarks pretend to be no more than surface indications of where to begin to dig deeper. Now let us change the venue and come closer to our subject of prose. Are satire and humor in their nature better adapted for prose expression than for verse? They can of course be employed in verse. Yet in front of even the satire of Juvenal and Horace it can still be maintained that they are essentially prosaic in their inherent tendencies. For in reality humor and satire are based on calculation, which is a cool mental exercise. The humorist calculates the distance from the average sense of man of some incongruity in the scheme of society and genially displays it: the greater satirists measure and calculate, too, but the distance they are concerned with is distance from a norm, not an average. "Satire," as J. Middleton Murry has said, "is not a matter of personal resentment, but of impersonal condemnation," and he adds, "The satirist is engaged in measuring the monstrous abberration from the ideal." I am not claiming that satire and even humor are inappropriate to verse: the compound character of them lately referred to does in fact explain why, if the emotional temperature reaches a high enough point (*"Facit indignatio versus"*), they do make excellent verse: but the calculating element inclines them more to prose than otherwise.

I have made use for the purposes of this chapter of the prose of Mark Twain, Finley Peter Dunne, and Donald Ogden Stewart because I think they show very well a certain curve in American humor and satire. Unfortunately, no thorough and excellent study has yet been written of the American wits, satirists, and humorists, yet here is an exceptionally rich field in our native letters for criticism to explore and map. Artemas Ward, James Russell Lowell, Eugene Field, George Ade, Gelett Burgess—these names and many more, including some of the present-day columnists, invite one to an enjoyable task.

MARK TWAIN

It will be enjoyable because a humorist can be almost anything he chooses provided he is not a bad craftsman, and honest craft always gives a pleasure of its own. There is no opportunity for the indulgences of self-expression, for if you aim to make the reader chuckle and smile you must eliminate all the risks of boring him with the gratuitous intrusions of your own personality. Nor can you be eccentric in your choice of words: the simple style is best. After all that has been written in praise of Mark Twain's masterpieces, *Adventures of Tom Sawyer* and *Huckleberry Finn,* we can, from our angle, return to two plain statements: Mark Twain wrote a simple fresh vernacular style (it is difficult to write vernacularly) and he was an adept in craftsmanship.

Your true craftsman does not care whether you are interested in his subject or his characters or his theme. He will compel your interest. He will take a superstition that you laugh at and force you under its spell until you shiver with horror as Bram Stoker does in *Dracula,* or he will take the antics of a small boy like Tom Sawyer (in whom I for one have not an atom of interest) and carry you eagerly from one episode to the next. He knows that all he has to do is to pique your curiosity, excite the associations that he wants, tell a good story, and he has you captive. But the humorist is lost if he forgets about you, the reader, and begins to amuse only himself.

THE RAPPORT BETWEEN MR. DOOLEY AND MR. HENNESSY

Finley Peter Dunne, the creator of Mr. Dooley, vies with Mark Twain in point of craftsmanship. His finesse in keeping in touch with his audience's psychology is remarkable. In fact, he put his audience into his pieces in the form of Mr. Hennessy, and remarks in his preface to *Mr. Dooley in Peace and War* that Mr. Dooley's "impressions are transferred to the desensitized plate of Mr. Hennessy's mind, where they can do no harm." In actuality, Mr. Dooley never soliloquizes, though he does practically all the talking, but throughout he is addressing Mr. Hennessy and very attentive he is to that gentleman's limitations, prejudices, and mental habits. Criticism of Finley Peter Dunne must not forget that he wrote for the newspaper press: that is, his audience was the barbarians of America, so well described by him as "moderately but firmly governed, encouraged to passionate votings for the ruling race, but restrained from the immoral pursuit of office." When this is kept in mind it will be seen that Dunne was not less masterly in his conception of Mr. Hennessy than in his creation of the bartender-philosopher.

Finley Peter Dunne is, I judge, the type of humorist America patently needs in this age. His genial benevolence is winning to the larger public. At the same time he is very much above his public in intelligence. He does not prostitute his mind in his intercourse with his readers but uses it to persuade the average citizen to part with some of his sentimentality and bigotry. His humor does not cater to Mr. Hennessy's prejudices, but gently dissolves them in laughter. A very good example of Dunne's Machiavellian treatment of the mob in wartime is "Prayers for Victory," which makes ridiculous the sentimental props to the war spirit and thereby reduces war to the stark brutal outrage that it is.

In reading "Prayers for Victory" take note of the subtle and restrained distortion of the language (Mr. Dooley's brogue, pronunciation, and idioms), for it is an important factor in Dunne's style. His restraint is such that he never sacrifices clarity and ease in reading to distorted spelling: at the same time he gets precisely the flavor of a speech that one enjoys listening to simply for the sake of its variance from the ordinary. Again, he shows himself the expert craftsman in the remarkable economy of structure of his brief essays. One more point before we consider the twist in American humorous writing that Donald Ogden Stewart illustrates: the trick of Mr. Dooley is to transpose the facts that Mr. Hennessy regards with an unquestioning solemnity into ridiculous facts, as this on our occupation of the Philippine Islands: "We import juke, hemp, cigar wrappers, sugar an' fairy tales fr'm th' Ph'lippeens, an' export six-inch shells an' th' like. Iv late th' Ph'lippeens has awaked to th' fact that they're behind th' times, an' has received much American ammunition in their midst."

THE LATEST TENDENCY IN AMERICAN HUMOR

In such a novel as *The Crazy Fool* Stewart revels in a kingdom of sophisticated nonsense. Once again we have the simple style to which the madcap or jesting or mirthful writer must adhere, but the framework of the book just mentioned is fantastic. It gives plenty of scope for parodying the Little Rollo books, for burlesquing the methods of modern business, modern publicity, and the motion pictures, and for extended gambols among free associations. This is sophistication indulging in fancy, and in places reminds one of that cult of absurdity in France a few years ago which went by the name of Dadaism. Here is a page of sheer "dada" appropriately occurring in Charlie Hatch's insane asylum (the milieu of *The Crazy Fool*) and beginning a mock business "conference."

"There was a moment of silence—then a knock on the door.

" 'Come in,' said Charlie.

"Mr. King entered.

" 'Why did *you* knock?' asked Charlie.

" 'It's a relic of my old married days,' replied Mr. King and his eyes became moist. 'Dear Florence. What a girl *she* was. I can see her now.'

" 'Did you shoot the snake?' asked Charlie. 'I would have.'

" 'There were so many snakes,' replied Mr. King. 'I felt like St. Patrick.'

"Mrs. Barbee laughed.

" 'I don't see what there is to laugh at,' said Charlie, and he went over to Mr. King and put his hand on his shoulder. 'I'm sorry, old pal,' he said.

" 'Thanks, old fellow,' said Mr. King. 'That's awfully white of you. It's this beastly tropical sun—it gets in your blood.' "[1]

---

[1] Reprinted from *The Crazy Fool,* by Donald Ogden Stewart, Horace Liveright, Publisher.

Stewart began as a parodist (one of his most successful parodies is appended to this chapter) and he chose to ridicule a variety of provincial authors. Then he turned to ridicule of American society from the standpoint of one well versed in the politer modes and manners of the Twentieth Century, but embedded in this sophisticated criticism of the social shortcomings of Americans there is a humane attitude which Stewart holds with considerable fierceness. Existence, he seems to say, is a sorry affair and the best we can do is to take what mad enjoyment we can get on this lunatic planet called Earth. In *The Crazy Fool* when the masquerade ball starts, Mrs. Barbee calls out to an idiot who fancies that he is Dante: "Don't you see they're right and you're wrong? They don't want to be told they're tragic. They want to dance. And they're right. My God— life's terrible enough, isn't it, without you trying to make us feel sorry for ourselves—or scaring us to death—come on, dance. That's all you *can* do—dance and laugh." This appears to be Stewart's own conclusion about life and explains why it is logical that his forms should be so illogical and absurd.

In petto, this is the history of American humor and satire. Mark Twain is the monarch of a period of ebullient sympathy with young scamps who played hob with the conventions of respectability: Finley Peter Dunne is the best of those who later by means of genial good sense tried to persuade the newspaper-reading hordes to look on life with tolerant eyes: Donald Ogden Stewart represents our contemporary wits and columnists and Merry Andrews who feel that life is terrible enough and nothing can be done about it but act, *deo volente,* the savage playboy.

LACK OF PROFUNDITY IN AMERICAN HUMOR

America has not yet had a great humorist or a great satirist because there has been no greatness of attitude toward life among her humorists and satirists. For without profound seriousness on the major issues of life there can be no profound humor or satire. Frank Moore Colby used to maintain that the American genius was for fun, not for humor, and that seems to be accurate. Our writers are too modest in their conceptions of the possible or ideal life of man, too trivial often in the objects they pick for ridicule, too constricted in their framework of general ideas—and very skilled in their craftsmanship. They have not been men of large minds, as you will see if you ask of them the questions which we employed in trying to understand the mental structure of Poe and Eliot. Here (another subjoining!) is as good a place as any to indicate the corresponding questions for emotional build. They have to do with the motor characteristics of emotional life: the health of the emotions: and their strength. Are the emotions vivacious, quick in movement, or are they slow and persistent in their states? Some people sulk for hours, while others have a flare of anger and then respond brightly to the next pleasant stimulus. This means a difference in the mobility of their feelings. Emotional health we can sum up in the word, humanity or humane-ity, while emotional strength is exhibited in the force of feeling. To my way of thinking, it is much more useful to chart Mark Twain's emotions in such a manner as this than it is to go maundering on about alleged "inferiority complexes," "frustrations," and "repressions."

THE GLORIOUS WHITEWASHER[2]

By Mark Twain

Saturday morning was come, and all the summer world was bright and fresh, and brimming with life. There was a song in every heart; and if the heart was young the music issued at the lips. There was cheer in every face and a spring in every step. The locust trees were in bloom and the fragrance of the blossoms filled the air. Cardiff Hill, beyond the village and above it, was green with vegetation, and it lay just far enough away to seem a Delectable Land, dreamy, reposeful, and inviting.

Tom appeared on the sidewalk with a bucket of whitewash and a long-handled brush. He surveyed the fence, and all gladness left him and a deep melancholy settled down upon his spirit. Thirty yards of board fence nine feet high. Life to him seemed hollow, and existence but a burden. Sighing he dipped his brush and passed it along the topmost plank; repeated the operation; did it again; compared the insignificant whitewashed streak with the far-reaching continent of unwhitewashed fence, and sat down on a tree-box discouraged. Jim came skipping out at the gate with a tin pail, and singing "Buffalo Gals." Bringing water from the town pump had always been hateful work in Tom's eyes, before, but now it did not strike him so. He remembered that there was company at the pump. White,

[2]From *The Adventures of Tom Sawyer,* by Mark Twain, and reprinted by permission of Harper and Brothers, Publishers.

mulatto, and negro boys and girls were always there waiting their turns, resting, trading playthings, quarreling,
fighting, skylarking. And he remembered that although
the pump was only a hundred and fifty yards off, Jim never
got back with a bucket of water under an hour—and even
then somebody generally had to go after him. Tom said:

"Say, Jim, I'll fetch the water if you'll whitewash some."

Jim shook his head and said:

"Can't, Mars Tom. Ole missis, she tole me I got to go an
git dis water an' not stop foolin' roun' wid anybody. She
say she spec' Mars Tom gwine to ax me to whitewash, an'
so she tole me go 'long an' 'tend to my own business—she
'lowed *she'd* 'tend to de whitewashin'."

"Oh, never you mind what she said, Jim. That's the way
she always talks. Gimme the bucket—I won't be gone only
a minute. She won't ever know."

"Oh, I dasn't, Mars Tom. Ole missis she'd take an' tar
de head off'n me. 'Deed she would."

"*She!* She never licks anybody—whacks 'em over the
head with her thimble—and who cares for that, I'd like to
know. She talks awful, but talk don't hurt—anyways it
don't if she don't cry. Jim, I'll give you a marvel. I'll give
you a white alley!"

Jim began to waver.

"White alley, Jim! And it's a bully taw."

"My! Dat's a mighty gay marvel, I tell you! But, Mars
Tom, I's powerful 'fraid ole missis——"

"And besides, if you will I'll show you my sore toe."

Jim was only human—this attraction was too much for
him. He put down his pail, took the white alley, and bent
over the toe with absorbing interest while the bandage was
being unwound. In another moment he was flying down the

street with his pail and a tingling rear, Tom was white-washing with vigor, and Aunt Polly was retiring from the field with a slipper in her hand and triumph in her eye.

But Tom's energy did not last. He began to think of the fun he had planned for this day, and his sorrows multiplied. Soon the free boys would come tripping along on all sorts of delicious expeditions, and they would make a world of fun of him for having to work—the very thought of it burnt him like fire. He got out his worldly wealth and examined it—bits of toys, marbles, and trash; enough to buy an exchange of *work,* maybe, but not half enough to buy so much as half an hour of pure freedom. So he returned his straitened means to his pocket, and gave up the idea of trying to buy the boys. At this dark and hopeless moment an inspiration burst upon him! Nothing less than a great, magnificent inspiration.

He took up his brush and went tranquilly to work. Ben Rogers hove in sight presently—the very boy, of all boys, whose ridicule he had been dreading. Ben's gait was the hop-skip-and-jump—proof enough that his heart was light and his anticipations high. He was eating an apple, and giving a long, melodious whoop, at intervals, followed by a deep-toned ding-dong-dong, ding-dong-dong, for he was personating a steamboat. As he drew near, he slackened speed, took the middle of the street, leaned far over to starboard and rounded to ponderously and with laborious pomp and circumstance—for he was personating the *Big Missouri,* and considered himself to be drawing nine feet of water. He was boat and captain and engine bells combined, so he had to imagine himself standing on his own hurricane-deck giving the orders and executing them:

"Stop her, sir! Ting-a-ling-ling!" The headway ran almost out and he drew up slowly toward the sidewalk.

"Ship up to back! Ting-a-ling-ling!" His arms straightened and stiffened down his sides.

"Set her back on the stabboard! Ting-a-ling-ling! Chow! ch-chow-wow! Chow!" His right hand, meantime, describing stately circles—for it was representing a forty-foot wheel.

"Let her go back on the labboard! Ting-a-ling-ling! Chow-ch-chow-chow!" The left hand began to describe circles.

"Stop the stabboard! Ting-a-ling-ling! Stop the labboard. Come ahead on the stabboard! Stop her! Let your outside turn over slow! Ting-a-ling-ling! Chow-ow-ow! Get out that head-line! *Lively* now! Come—out with your spring-line—what're you about there! Take a turn round that stump with the bight of it! Stand by that stage, now—let her go! Done with the engines, sir! Ting-a-ling-ling! *Sh't! sh't! sh't*" (trying the gauge cocks).

Tom went on whitewashing—paid no attention to the steamboat. Ben stared a moment and then said:

"Hi-*yi! You're* up a stump, ain't you!"

No answer. Tom surveyed his last touch with the eye of an artist, then he gave his brush another gentle sweep and surveyed the result, as before. Ben ranged up alongside of him. Tom's mouth watered for the apple, but he stuck to his work. Ben said:

"Hello, old chap, you got to work, hey?"

Tom wheeled suddenly and said:

"Why, it's you, Ben! I warn't noticing."

"Say—I'm going in a-swimming, I am. Don't you wish you could? But of course you'd druther *work*—wouldn't you? Course you would!"

Tom contemplated the boy a bit, and said:

"What do you call work?"

"Why, ain't *that* work?"

Tom resumed his whitewashing, and answered carelessly:

"Well, maybe it is, and maybe it ain't. All I know is, it suits Tom Sawyer."

"Oh come, now, you don't mean to let on that you *like* it?"

The brush continued to move.

"Like it? Well, I don't see why I oughtn't to like it. Does a boy get a chance to whitewash a fence every day?"

That put the thing in a new light. Ben stopped nibbling his apple. Tom swept his brush daintily back and forth— stepped back to note the effect—added a touch here and there—criticized the effect again—Ben watching every move and getting more and more interested, more and more absorbed. Presently he said:

"Say, Tom, let *me* whitewash a little."

Tom considered, was about to consent; but he altered his mind:

"No—no—I reckon it wouldn't hardly do, Ben. You see, Aunt Polly's awful particular about this fence—right here on the street you know—but if it was the back fence I wouldn't mind and *she* wouldn't. Yes, she's awful particular about this fence; it's got to be done very careful; I reckon there ain't one boy in a thousand, maybe two thousand, that can do it the way it's got to be done."

"No—is that so? Oh come, now—lemme just try. Only just a little—I'd let you, if you was me, Tom."

"Ben, I'd like to, honest injun; but Aunt Polly—well, Jim wanted to do it, but she wouldn't let him; Sid wanted to do it, and she wouldn't let Sid. Now don't you see how I'm fixed? If you was to tackle this fence and anything was to happen to it——"

"Oh, shucks, I'll be just as careful. Now lemme try. Say
—I'll give you the core of my apple."

"Well, here—No, Ben, now don't. I'm afeard——"

"I'll give you *all* of it!"

Tom gave up the brush with reluctance in his face, but
alacrity in his heart. And while the late steamer *Big Missouri* worked and sweated in the sun, the retired artist sat
on a barrel in the shade close by, dangled his legs, munched
his apple, and planned the slaughter of more innocents.
There was no lack of material; boys happened along every
little while; they came to jeer, but remained to whitewash.
By the time Ben was fagged out, Tom had traded the next
chance to Billy Fisher for a kite, in good repair; and when
he played out, Johnny Miller bought in for a dead rat and
a string to swing it with, and so on, and so on, hour after
hour. And when the middle of the afternoon came, from
being a poor poverty-stricken boy in the morning, Tom was
literally rolling in wealth. He had beside the things before
mentioned, twelve marbles, part of a jews'-harp, a piece of
blue bottle-glass to look through, a spool cannon, a key that
wouldn't unlock anything, a fragment of chalk, a glass
stopper of a decanter, a tin soldier, a couple of tadpoles, a
door-knob, a dog-collar—but no dog—the handle of a knife,
four pieces of orange-peel, and a dilapidated old window-
sash.

He had a nice, good, idle time all the while—plenty of
company—and the fence had three coats of whitewash on
it! If he hadn't run out of whitewash, he would have bank-
rupted every boy in the village.

Tom said to himself that it was not such a hollow world,
after all. He had discovered a great law of human action,
without knowing it—namely, that in order to make a man
or a boy covet a thing, it is only necessary to make the thing

difficult to attain. If he had been a great and wise philosopher, like the writer of this book, he would now have comprehended that Work consists of whatever a body is obliged to do, and that Play consists of whatever a body is not obliged to do. And this would help him to understand why constructing artificial flowers or performing on a treadmill is work, while rolling tenpins or climbing Mont Blanc is only amusement. There are wealthy gentlemen in England who drive four-horse passenger-coaches twenty or thirty miles on a daily line, in the summer, because the privilege costs them considerable money; but if they were offered wages for the service, that would turn it into work and then they would resign.

The boy mused awhile over the substantial change which ·had taken place in his worldly circumstances, and then wended toward headquarters to report.

MR. DOOLEY ON PRAYERS FOR VICTORY[3]

By Finley Peter Dunne

"It looks to me," said Mr. Dooley, "as though me frind Mack'd got tired iv th' Sthrateejy Board, an' was goin' to lave th' war to th' men in black."

"How's that?" asked Mr. Hennessy, who has at best but a clouded view of public affairs.

"Well," said Mr. Dooley, "while th' sthrateejans have been wearin' out their jeans on cracker-boxes in Wash'n'-ton, they'se been goin' on th' mos' deadly conflict iver heerd tell iv between th' pow'rful preachin' navies iv th' two counthries. Manila is nawthin' at all to th' scenes iv carnage an' slaughter, as Hogan says, that's been brought about be these desthroyers. Th' Spanyards fired th' openin' gun whin th' bishop iv Cades, a pow'rful turreted monitor (ol' style), attackted us with both for'ard guns, an' sint a storm iv brimstone an' hell into us. But th' victhry was not f'r long with th' hated Spanyard. He was answered be our whole fleet iv preachers. Thin he was jined be th' bishop iv Barsaloona an' th' bishop iv Mahdrid an' th' bishop iv Havana, all battle-ships iv th' first class, followed be a fleet iv cruisers r-runnin' all th' way fr'm a full-ar-rmored vicar gin'ral to a protected parish priest. To meet thim, we sint th' biship iv New York, th' bishop iv Philadelphia, th' bishop iv Baltimore, an' th' bishop iv Chicago, accompanied

[3]From *Mr. Dooley in Peace and War,* by Finley Peter Dunne, and reprinted by permission of the author.

be a flyin' squadhron iv Methodists, three Presbyteryan monitors, a fleet iv Baptist submarine desthroyers, an' a formidable array iv Universalist an' Unitaryan torpedo boats, with a Jew r-ram. Manetime th' bishop iv Manila had fired a solid prayer, weighin' a ton, at San Francisco; an' a masked batthry iv Congregationalists replied, inflictin' severe damage. Our Atlantic fleet is now sarchin' f'r th' inimy, an' the biship iv New York is blockadin' th' bishop iv Sandago de Cuba; an' they'se been an exchange iv prayers between th' bishop iv Baltimore an' th' biship iv Havana without much damage.

"Th' Lord knows how it'll come out. First wan side prays that th' wrath iv Hiven'll descind on th' other, an' thin th' other side returns th' compliment with inthrest. Th' Spanish bishop says we're a lot iv murdherin', irreligious thieves, an' ought to be swept fr'm th' face iv th' earth. We say his people ar-re th' same, an' manny iv thim. He wishes Hivin to sink our ships an' desthroy our men an' we hope he'll injye th' same gr-reat blessin'. We have a shade th' best iv him, f'r his fleets ar-re all iv th' same class an ol' style, an' we have some iv th' most modhern prayin' machines in the warruld; but he prays har-rd, an' 'tis no aisy wurruk to silence him."

"What d'ye think about it?" asked Mr. Hennessy.

"Well," said Mr. Dooley, "I dinnaw jus' what to think iv it. Me own idee is that war is not a matther iv prayers so much as a matther iv punchin'; an' th' on'y place a prayer book stops a bullet is in th' story books. 'Tis like what Father Kelly said. Three weeks ago las' Sundah he met Hogan; an' Hogan, wantin' to be smart, ast him if he'd offered up prayers f'r th' success iv th' cause. 'Faith, I did not,' says th' good man. 'I was in too much iv a hurry to get away.' 'What was th' matther?' ast Hogan. 'I had me uniform to brush up and me soord to polish,' says Father Kelly. 'I am goin' with th' rig'mint to-morrah,' he says; an' he says, 'If ye hear iv me waitin' to pray,' he says, 'anny time they'se a call f'r me,' he says, 'to be in a fight,' he says, 'ye may conclude,' he says, 'that I've lost me mind, an' won't be back to me parish,' he says. 'Hogan', he says, 'I'll go into th' battle with a prayer book in wan hand an' a soord in th' other', he says; 'an' if th' wurruk calls f'r two hands, 'tis not th' soord I'll dhrop,' he says. 'Don't ye believe in prayer?' says Hogan. 'I do', says th' good man; 'but,' he says, 'a healthy person ought,' he says, 'to be ashamed,' he says, 'to ask f'r help in a fight,' he says."

"That's th' way I look at it," said Mr. Hennessy. "When 'tis an aven thing in th' prayin', may th' best man win."

"Ye're r-right, Hinnissy," said Mr. Dooley, warmly. "Ye're r-right. An' th' best man will win."

HOW LOVE CAME TO GENERAL GRANT[1]

IN THE MANNER OF HAROLD BELL WRIGHT

By Donald Ogden Stewart

On a brisk winter evening in the winter of 1864 the palatial Fifth Avenue "palace" of Cornelius van der Griff was brilliantly lighted with many brilliant lights. Outside the imposing front entrance a small group of pedestrians had gathered to gape enviously at the invited guests of the "four hundred" who were beginning to arrive in elegant equipages, expensive ball-dresses and fashionable "swallow-tails."

"Hully gee!" exclaimed little Frank, a crippled news-boy who was the only support of an aged mother, as a par-ticularly sumptuous carriage drove up and a stylishly dressed lady of fifty-five or sixty stepped out accompanied by a haughty society girl and an elderly gentleman in cleri-cal dress. It was Mrs. Rhinelander, a social leader, and her daughter Geraldine, together with the Rev. Dr. Gedney, pastor of an exclusive Fifth Avenue church.

"What common looking people," said Mrs. Rhinelander, surveying the crowd aristocratically with her lorgnette.

"Yes, aren't they?" replied the clergyman with a condes-cending glance which ill befit his clerical garb.

"I'm glad you don't have people like that *dans votre*

---

[1]From *A Parody Outline of History,* by Donald Ogden Stewart, copyright 1921, George H. Doran Company.

église, Dr. Gedney," said young Geraldine, who thought it was "smart" to display her proficiency in the stylish French tongue. At this moment the door of the van der Griff residence was opened for them by an imposing footman in scarlet livery and they passed into the abode of the "elect."

"Hully gee!" repeated little Frank.

"What's going on to-night?" asked a newcomer.

"Gee—don't youse know?" answered the newsboy. "Dis is de van der Griffs' and to-night dey are giving a swell dinner for General Grant. Dat lady wot just went in was old Mrs. Rhinelander. I seen her pitcher in de last Harper's Weekly and dere was a story in de paper dis morning dat her daughter Geraldine was going to marry de General."

"That isn't so," broke in another. "It was just a rumor."

"Well, anyway," said Frank, "I wisht de General would hurry up and come—it's getting cold enough to freeze the tail off a brass monkey." The onlookers laughed merrily at his humorous reference to the frigid temperature, although many cast sympathetic looks at his thin threadbare garments and registered a kindly thought for this brave boy who so philosophically accepted the buffets of fate.

"I bet this is him now," cried Frank, and all waited expectantly as a vehicle drove up. The cabman jumped off his box and held the carriage door open.

"Here you are, Miss Flowers," he said, touching his hat respectfully.

A silver peal of rippling laughter sounded from the interior of the carriage.

"Why Jerry," came in velvet tones addressed to the coachman, "You mustn't be so formal just because I have come to New York to live. Call me 'Miss Ella,' of course, just like you did when we lived out in Kansas," and with these words Miss Ella Flowers, for it was she, stepped out of the carriage.

A hush fell on the crowd as they caught sight of her face —a hush of silent tribute to the clear sweet womanhood of that pure countenance. A young man on the edge of the crowd who was on the verge of becoming a drunkard burst into tears and walked rapidly away to join the nearest church. A pr-st---te who had been plying her nefarious trade on the avenue, sank to her knees to pray for strength to go back to her aged parents on the farm. Another young man, catching sight of Ella's pure face, vowed to write home to his old mother and send her the money he had been expending in the city on drinks and dissipation.

And well might these city people be affected by the glimpse of the sweet noble virtue which shone forth so radiantly in this Kansas girl's countenance. Although born in Jersey City, Ella had moved with her parents to the west at an early age and she had grown up in the open country where a man's a man and women lead clean sweet womanly lives. Out in the pure air of God's green places and amid kindly, simple, big hearted folks, little Ella had blossomed and thrived, the pride of the whole country, and as she had grown to womanhood there was many a masculine heart beat a little faster for her presence and many a manly blush of admiration came into the features of her admirers as she whirled gracefully with them in the innocent pleasure of a simple country dance. But on her eighteenth birthday, her parents had passed on to the Great Beyond and the heart-broken Ella had come East to live with Mrs. Montgomery, her aunt in Jersey City. This lady, being socially promi-nent in New York's "four hundred," was of course quite ambitious that her pretty little niece from the West should also enter society. For the last three months, therefore,

Ella had been fêted at all the better class homes in New
York and Jersey City, and as Mrs. van de Griff, the Fifth
Avenue social leader, was in the same set as Ella's aunt, it
was only natural that when making out her list of guests
for the dinner in honor of General Grant she should in-
clude the beautiful niece of her friend.

As Ella stepped from the carriage, her gaze fell upon little Frank, the crippled newsboy, and her eyes quickly filled
with tears, for social success had not yet caused her to forget that "blessed are the weak." Taking out her purse, she
gave Frank a silver dollar and a warm look of sympathy
as she passed into the house.

"Gee, there went an angel," whispered the little cripple,
and many who heard him silently echoed that thought in
their hearts. Nor were they far from wrong.

But even an angel is not free from temptation, and by
letting Ella go into society her aunt was exposing the girl
to the whisperings of Satan—whisperings of things material rather than things spiritual. Many a girl just as pure
as Ella has found her standards gradually lowered and her
moral character slowly weakened by the contact with the so-
called "refined" and "cultured" infidels one meets in fashionable society. Many a father and mother whose ambition
has caused them to have their daughter go out in society
have bitterly repented of that step as they watched the poor
girl gradually succumbing to the temptation of the world.
Let her who thinks it is "smart" to be in society consider
that our brothels with their red plush curtains, their hard-
wood floors and their luxurious appointments, are filled
largely with the worn out belles and débutantes of fashionable society.

The next minute a bugle call sounded down the street and
up drove a team of prancing grays. Two soldiers sprang

down from the coachman's box and stood at rigid attention while the door of the carriage opened and out stepped General Ulysses S. Grant.

A murmur of admiration swept over the crowd at the sight of his manly inspiring features, in which the clean cut virility of a life free from dissipation was accentuated by the neatly trimmed black beard. His erect military bearing—his neat well fitting uniform—but above all his frank open face proclaimed him a man's man—a man among men. A cheer burst from the lips of the onlookers and the brave but modest general lowered his eyes and blushed as he acknowledged their greeting.

"Men and women," he said, in a voice which although low, one could see was accustomed to being obeyed, "I thank you for your cheers. It makes my heart rejoice to hear them, for I know you are not cheering me personally but only as one of the many men who are fighting for the cause of liberty and freedom, and for—" the general's voice broke a little, but he mastered his emotion and went on—"for the flag we all love."

At this he pulled from his pocket an American flag and held it up so that all could see. Cheer after cheer rent the air, and tears came to the general's eyes at this mark of devotion to the common cause.

"Wipe the d--d rebels off the face of the earth, G--d d-- 'em," shouted a too enthusiastic member of the crowd who, I fear, was a little the worse for drink. In an instant General Grant had stepped up to him and fixed upon him those fearless blue eyes.

"My man," said the general, "It hurts me to hear you give vent to those oaths, especially in the presence of ladies. Soldiers do not curse, and I think you would do well to follow their example."

The other lowered his head shamefacedly. "General," he said, "You're right and I apologize."

A smile lit up the general's handsome features and he extended his hand to the other.

"Shake on it," he said simply, and as the crowd roared its approval of this speech the two men "shook."

Meanwhile within the van der Griff house all were agog with excitement in expectation of the arrival of the distinguished guest. Expensively dressed ladies fluttered here and there amid the elegant appointments; servants in stylish livery passed to and fro with trays of wine and other spirituous liquors.

At the sound of the cheering outside, the haughty Mrs. Rhinelander patted her daughter Geraldine nervously, and between mother and daughter passed a glance of understanding, for both felt that to-night, if ever, was Geraldine's opportunity to win the handsome and popular general.

The doorbell rang, and a hush fell over the chattering assemblage; then came the proud announcement from the doorman—"General Ulysses S. Grant"—and all the society belles crowded forward around the guest of honor.

It had been rumored that the general, being a soldier, was ignorant of social etiquette, but such proved to be far from the case. Indeed, he handled himself with such ease of manner that he captivated all, and for each and every young miss he had an apt phrase or a pretty compliment, greatly to their delight.

"Pleased to know you"—"Glad to shake the hand of such a pretty girl"—"What a nice little hand—I wish I might hold it all evening"—with these and kindred pleasantries the general won the way into the graces of Mrs. van de Griff's fair guests, and many a female heart fluttered in her bosom as she gazed into the clear blue eyes of the soldier, and listened to his well chosen tactful words.

"And how is the dear General this evening?"—this in the affected tone of old Mrs. Rhinelander, as she forced her way through the crowd.

"Finer than silk," replied he, and he added, solicitously, "I hope you have recovered from your lumbago, Mrs. Rhinelander."

"Oh quite," answered she, "and here is Geraldine, General," and the ambitious mother pushed her daughter forward.

"Comment vous portez-vous, mon Général," said Geraldine in French, "I hope we can have a nice *tête-à-tête* tonight," and she fawned upon her prey in a manner that would have sickened a less artificial gathering.

Were there not some amid all that fashionable throng in whom ideals of purity and true womanhood lived—some who cared enough for the sacredness of real love to cry upon this hollow mockery that was being used to ensnare the simple, honest soldier? There was only one, and she was at that moment entering the drawing room for the purpose of being presented to the general. Need I name her?

Ella, for it was she, had been upstairs busying herself with her toilet when General Grant had arrived and she now hurried forward to pay her homage to the great soldier. And then, as she caught sight of his face, she stopped suddenly and a deep crimson blush spread over her features. She looked again, and then drew back behind a nearby portière, her heart beating wildly.

Well did Ella remember where she had seen that countenance before, and as she stood there trembling the whole scene of her folly came back to her. It had happened in Kansas, just before her parents died, on one sunny May

morning. She had gone for a walk; her footsteps had led
her to the banks of a secluded lake where she often went
when she wished to be alone. Many an afternoon had Ella
dreamed idly away on this shore, but that day, for some
reason, she had felt unusually full of life and not at all like
dreaming. Obeying a thoughtless but innocent impulse, with
no intention of evil, she had taken off her clothes and
plunged thus n-k-d into the cool waters of the lake. After
she had swum around a little she began to realize the extent
of her folly and was hurriedly swimming towards the shore
when a terrific cramp had seized her lower limbs, rendering them powerless. Her first impulse, to scream for help,
was quickly checked with a deep blush, as she realized the
consequences if a man should hear her call, for near by was
an encampment of Union soldiers, none of whom she knew.
The perplexed and helpless girl was in sore straits and
was slowly sinking for the third time, when a bearded
stranger in soldier's uniform appeared on the bank and
dove into the water. To her horror he swam rapidly towards
her—but her shame was soon changed to joy when she
realized that he was purposely keeping his eyes tight shut.
With a few swift powerful strokes he reached her side, and
blushing deeply took off his blue coat, fastened it around
her, opened his eyes and swam with her to the shore. Carrying her to where she had left her clothes he stayed only
long enough to assure himself that she had completely recovered the use of her limbs, and evidently to spare her
further embarrassment, had vanished as quickly and as
mysteriously as he had appeared.

Many a night after that had Ella lain awake thinking of
the splendid features and the even more splendid conduct of
this unknown knight who wore the uniform of the Union
army. "How I love him," she would whisper to herself;

"but how he must despise me!" she would cry, and her pillow was often wet with tears of shame and mortification at her folly.

It was shortly after this episode that her parents had taken sick and passed away. Ella had come East and had given up hope of ever seeing her rescuer again. You may imagine her feelings then when, on entering the drawing room at the van der Griffs' she discovered that the stranger who had so gallantly and tactfully rescued her from a watery grave was none other than General Ulysses S. Grant.

The poor girl was torn by a tumult of contrary emotions. Suppose he should remember her face. She blushed at the thought. And besides what chance had she to win such a great man's heart in competition with these society girls like Geraldine Rhinelander who had been "abroad" and spoke French.

At that moment one of the liveried servants approached the general with a trayful of filled wine glasses. So engrossed was the soldier hero in talking to Geraldine—or, rather, in listening to her alluring chatter—that he did not at first notice what was being offered him.

"Will you have a drink of champagne wine, General?" said Mrs. van der Griff who stood near.

The general raised his head and frowned as if he did not understand.

"Come, *mon Général,*" cried Geraldine gayly, "We shall drink *à votre succès dans la guerre,*" and the flighty girl raised a glass of wine on high. Several of the guests crowded around and all were about to drink to the general's health.

"Stop," cried General Grant suddenly realizing what was being done, and something in the tone of his voice made everyone pause.

"Madam," said he, turning to Mrs. van der Griff, "Am I to understand that there is liquor in those glasses?"

"Why yes, General," said the hostess smiling uneasily. "It is just a little champagne wine."

"Madam," said the general, "It may be 'just champagne wine' to you, but 'just champagne wine' has ruined many a poor fellow and to me all alcoholic beverages are an abomination. I cannot consent, madam, to remain under your roof if they are to be served. I have never taken a drop— I have tried to stamp it out of the army, and I owe it to my soldiers to decline to be a guest at a house where wine and liquor are served."

An excited buzz of comment arose as the general delivered this ultimatum. A few there were who secretly approved his sentiments, but they were far too few in numbers and constant indulgence in alcohol had weakened their wills so that they dared not stand forth. An angry flush appeared on the face of the hostess, for in society, "good form" is more important than courage and ideals, and by his frank statement General Grant had violently violated the canons of correct social etiquette.

"Very well, Mr. Grant," she said, stressing the "Mr"— "if that's the way you feel about it——"

"Stop," cried an unexpected voice, and to the amazement of all Ella Flowers stepped forward, her teeth clenched, her eyes blazing.

"Stop," she repeated, "He is right—the liquor evil is one of the worst curses of modern civilization, and if General Grant leaves, so do I."

Mrs. van der Griff hesitated for an instant, and then suddenly forced a smile.

"Why Ella dear, of course General Grant is right," said she, for it was well known in financial circles that her husband, Mr. van de Griff, had recently borrowed heavily from Ella's uncle. "There will not be a drop of wine served to-night, and now General, shall we go to dinner? Will you be so kind as to lead the way with Miss Rhinelander?" The hostess had recovered her composure, and smiling sweetly at the guest of honor, gave orders to the servants to remove the wine glasses.

But General Grant did not hear her; he was looking at Ella Flowers. And as he gazed at the sweet beauty of her countenance he seemed to feel rising within him something which he had never felt before—something which made everything else seem petty and trivial. And as he looked into her eyes and she looked into his, he read her answer—the only answer true womanhood can make to clean, worthy manhood.

"Shall we go *à la salle-à-manger?*" sounded a voice in his ears, and Geraldine's sinuous arm was thrust through his.

General Grant took the proffered talon and gently removed it from him.

"Miss Rhinelander," he said firmly, "I am taking this young lady as my partner," and suiting the action to the word, he graciously extended his arm to Ella who took it with a pretty blush.

It was General Grant's turn to blush when the other guests, with a few exceptions, applauded his choice loudly, and made way enthusiastically as the handsome couple advanced to the brilliantly lighted dining room.

But although the hostess had provided the most costly of viands, I am afraid that the brave general did not fully appreciate them, for in his soul was the joy of a strong man who has found his mate and in his heart was the singing of the eternal song, "I love her—I love her—I love her!"

It was only too apparent to the other guests what had happened and to their credit be it said that they heartily approved his choice, for Mrs. Rhinelander and her scheming daughter Geraldine had made countless enemies with their haughtly manners, whereas the sweet simplicity of Ella Flowers had won her numerous friends. And all laughed merrily when General Grant, in his after dinner speech said "flowers" instead of "flour" when speaking of provisioning the army—a slip which caused both the general and Miss Flowers to blush furiously, greatly to the delight of the good-natured guests. "All the world loves a lover"—truer words were never penned.

After dinner, while the other men, according to the usages of best society, were filling the air of the dining room with the fumes of nicotine, the general, who did not use tobacco, excused himself—amid many sly winks from the other men —and wandered out into the conservatory.

There he found Ella.

"General," she began.

"Miss Flowers," said the strong man simply, "Call me Ulysses."

And there let us leave them.

CHAPTER XII

PROSE FOR THE DRAMA: WILLIAM VAUGHN MOODY, THEODORE DREISER, AND EUGENE O'NEILL

THE RISE OF THE PROSE DRAMA

WE CAN begin, luckily, with a revealing fact. Everyone knows of the decline of the poetic drama and the rise of the prose drama. In some quarters concern has been felt because the drama in poetry or verse is no longer within the range of the modern writer. T. S. Eliot, for one, has expended a good deal of thought on the possibilities of a revival in a new form of poetic drama, but these possibilities are not germane to a study of American prose.[1] Our fact is that prose overwhelmingly holds the field in our theatre, and we must make what we can of that.

Facts, for the curious, always raise questions, and the first question that the dominance of the prose drama provokes is, What kind of plays does the use of prose encourage? The answer to anyone acquainted with the intel-

---

[1]"The Elizabethan drama," says Eliot, "was aimed at a public which wanted *entertainment* of a crude sort, but would *stand* a good deal of poetry; our problem should be to take a form of entertainment, and subject it to the process which would leave it a form of art. Perhaps the musichall comedian is the best material." *Him,* by E. E. Cummings, although a prose play, shows that Eliot's suggestion is perhaps practical. *Him* is a transformation of the crude popular entertainment of the burlesque stage into a form of art.

lectual roots of prose is readily foreseen. The typical play of the last half of the Nineteenth Century and that portion of the Twentieth which we have lived is expository in character: this is the era of the thesis or "problem" play as molded by Ibsen, Shaw, Hauptmann, Brieux, and a host of others. Of course, there are numerous other types of plays written in our period, prose cousins of the historical, fantastic, symbolic, or farcical play composed in verse, but we are as far as we can travel from the crowning creation of the poetic dramatist in which weight of thought and force of feeling combined to make the Mystery-Drama of man's relation to the creator of the world. We have dropped from that, the domain of poetry, to the dramatic treatment of the relations of man to man, to our much vaunted "social drama," to one of the regions of prose.

THE LOSS OF IDEALITY IN STAGE SPEECH

It is on the heights of art that things are clearly seen, and we may be fairly certain that in our descent into the valley of modern drama some fundamental elements of writing have become obscured. The general adoption of prose for our plays has hidden, once again, the essential nature of art as an *as if* creation. A vital and heightened and purified imitation of life was precisely what the poetic dramatist wrought for, but the prose dramatist tends to be, as we say, naturalistic. Monsieur Jourdain learned to his astonishment that all his days he had been speaking prose. The contemporary playwright has also discovered that Monsieur Jourdain speaks prose, and he aims therefore to make his characters speak on the stage exactly as they would talk off the stage. "Fidelity to life!"

But there should be an element of ideality in stage discourse. By this I mean simply that the characters in a play should speak as they would like ideally to converse. The grain of the characters must not be falsified in the writing, but they must express their psychology better in words than they ordinarily do. The dramatist leaves their state of being unchanged, but he draws out from them their best powers of articulation.

Ideality in stage speech is produced, in short, by good writing: accuracy and, expressiveness in the choice of words, propriety of tone and rhythm for the given character, economy of phrasing, variation of speech characteristics, intensity, and so on. Speakability of the lines is a prime desideratum, but the playwright is himself composing "speech at considered leisure," and his leisure should bear more perfect fruits than actual people in the hurlyburly melodrama of existence can usually achieve. Slovenliness is the rule in our daily conversation: well-knit discourse should be at least the lowest level of stage writing.

WILLIAM VAUGHN MOODY'S SUCCESSFUL DIALOGUE

American literature can boast of greater glories than our home critics commonly admit, but its resplendencies do not in a single instance emanate from our native drama. Our best dramatist, though scarcely anyone realizes it, is William Vaughn Moody, who wrote *The Great Divide* in 1906 and *The Faith Healer* in 1909, but in a community of the playwrights of the last hundred years of Western literature he is no more than a respectable workman. In *The Great Divide* his dramatic style is marred by a sentimental vocabulary, but his prose construction is good. *The Faith Healer* surpasses the earlier play in every respect and quite entitles one to say that Moody's death in 1910 robbed our later dramatists of a potentially very worthy dean of their craft.

Moody illustrates clearly the ideal speech that is requisite to stage characters. In Act One of *The Faith Healer,* the farmer, Matthew Beeler, who has lost belief in the sermons preached in country churches and taken on instead a belief in Darwinism as popularly taught, has pinned up a colored print from a Sunday newspaper. The print depicts the god Pan surprising a mediæval palmer in the midst of a forest. To Rhoda, his wife's niece, Beeler explains the meaning of the picture to him in a speech the student should look up, if he suspects that in contending for a more ideal speech in our theatre I am pleading for "precious" or "fancy" talk. What Beeler says is perfectly consonant with what he is and with the occasion and the situation. He uses his own terms to express his thoughts and feelings, but how well he puts himself into words. His speech is racy, vivid, forceful, animated. He speaks a great deal better than in all probability his counterpart in actual life ever does.

DREISER AS A COPYIST

The dialogue of *The Faith Healer* can easily be placed in contrast with the kind of writing that Theodore Dreiser puts into his plays. Dreiser's aim is to *copy* the speech of everyday life, and one might say that he *flatly* succeeds. I am quoting from the last act of *The Hand of the Potter,* after the pervert, Isadore Berchansky, has committed suicide and several newspaper reporters begin to discuss the pathetic note Berchansky has left behind.

"ARMSBY (*Looking up*) : Tough, eh?

QUINN : You're right, it's tough. Ye never can tell about these poor divils, as (*he points to the letter*) ye can see by that. Here's the whole city runnin' him down an' he may not have been as bad as the people have been thinkin'. Life's a pretty stiff thing at times.

LEACH (*Going to the bureau and smoothing out the paper he has found, preparatory to copying it*) : Oh, I don't know about that. I wonder sometimes just how crazy some of them are. I know a doctor who has made a study of these cases at Johns Hopkins, and he isn't so sure that they deserve so much sympathy. I can't understand it myself, wanting to attack a little girl like that, especially when he might interest a grown girl. The public wouldn't feel one-fiftieth as terrible if he had tried to attack a grown one instead of this little kid. But a little girl! And to torture her! Hell, you might as well talk about having sympathy for a mad dog. What I can't understand, though, is how it comes that a man like that should be allowed to walk about the streets here in New York—not a person to touch him. And he had tried to attack another little girl two years ago. Well, why didn't they lock him up then? What's the big idea, letting a fellow like that run at large?"[2]

The other reporters reply to this in even more "long-winded" speeches, each one being in fact the mouthpiece of one or another social view of Berchansky's form of perversion, but there is no "rising to the occasion" such as Moody's people accomplish. This is prose as undistinguished as a street-corner discussion, and not a whit more buoyed up by æsthetic energy.

---

[2]From *The Hand of the Potter*, by Theodore Dreiser, and reprinted by permission of Horace Liveright, Publisher.

EUGENE O'NEILL—NATURALISM AGAIN

Eugene O'Neill, our most touted dramatist to-day, is more concentrated than Dreiser but he fails just as much to create a "memorable interval" between off-stage speaking and on-stage discourse. It is naturalism again, as you can see in this excerpt from *Desire Under the Elms*. It is the moment before Abbie and Eben go into the parlor to consummate their illicit love.

"ABBIE (*Both her arms around him—with wild passion*): I'll sing fur ye! I'll die fur ye! (*In spite of her overwhelming desire for him, there is a sincere maternal love in her manner and her voice—a horribly frank mixture of lust and mother love.*) Don't cry, Eben! I'll take yer Maw's place! I'll be everythin' she was to ye! Let me kiss ye, Eben! (*She pulls his head around. He makes a bewildered pretense of resistance. She is tender*) Don't be afeered! I'll kiss ye pure, Eben— same's if I was a Maw t' ye—an' ye kin kiss me back's if yew was my son—my boy—sayin' good-night t' me! Kiss me, Eben. (*They kiss in restrained fashion. Then suddenly wild passion overcomes her. She kisses him lustfully again and again and he flings his arms about her and returns her kisses. Suddenly, as in the bedroom, he frees himself violently and springs to his feet. He is trembling all over, in a strange state of terror. Abbie strains her arms toward him with fierce pleading.*) Don't ye leave me, Eben! Can't ye see it hain't enuf—lovin' ye like a Maw—can't ye see it's got t' be that an' more—much more—a hundred times more—fur me t' be happy—fur yew t' be happy?

EBEN (*To the presence he feels in the room*) : Maw! Maw!
What d'ye want? What air ye tellin' me?

ABBIE: She's tellin' ye t' love me. She knows I love ye an'
I'll be good t'ye. Can't ye feel it? Don't ye know? She's
tellin' ye t' love me, Eben!

EBEN: Ay-eh. I feel—mebbe she—but—I can't figger out
—why—when ye've stole her place—here in her hum
—in the parlor whar she was—

ABBIE (*Fiercely*) : She knows I love ye!"[3]

O'Neil would doubtless say that he always writes with
his eye on the theater, but that is the root trouble. The modern playwright acquires an intimate understanding of act-
ing and the various theater crafts: he grows adept at de-
vising good theatrical situations. But then he falls down
altogether in producing dramatic eloquence. In *The Hairy
Ape,* for instance, O'Neill calls for a highly convention-
alized and arbitrary stage setting, but he does not elaborate
arbitrary conventions for his dialogue: *that* is thoroughly
naturalistic and therefore out of key with the artifice of the
sets. The Hairy Ape, by the way, is no more brutal than
Caliban except in the ugly lines he grunts, but Caliban leaves
the stronger impression precisely because his lines are inspired by art.

THE ARISTOTELIAN CANON

These matters—one must mutter to oneself—were clari-
fied long ago by Aristotle. He classified the elements of the
drama in the following order of importance: Plot, Character, Thought, Diction, Melody, and Spectacle. The American drama can make no claims to greatness in the first

[3]From *Desire Under the Elms,* by Eugene O'Neill, and reprinted
by permission of Horace Liveright, Publisher.

three, so I have devoted this chapter principally to Diction as the most immediate concern. "The perfection of Diction," Aristotle remarked, "is for it to be at once clear and not mean," and this is a drastic criticism of contemporary dramatic prose in our land. For the prose of Dreiser's plays as we have noted is flatly mean, however clear it may be, and O'Neill's prose, not always as clear as it might be, is stripped and intensified meanness—without dignity or memorability or beauty. Only of Moody's prose can we say that it, although it climbs no heights, is not mean.

The drama is a literary form, but to-day it has been de-bauched by what, according to Aristotle, is its least import-ant element. The Spectacle has become supreme, the play has been theatricalized and no longer is it pleasurable to read plays. There is an art of the drama which gives itself perfectly to the reader from the printed page—so Gordon Craig maintains when he cites Shakespeare as a playwright who does not need production. And there is an art of the theater, completely nonliterary in character, which is yet to be born—the dream of Gordon Craig. But nowadays we have neither the pure drama nor pure theater, but a species of theatricalism that degrades both.

THE HAND OF THE POTTER

By Theodore Dreiser

[This is styled "a tragedy in four acts." It concerns the misfortunes of a young Jewish pervert, Isadore Berchansky, who before the play begins has served a term in the penitentiary for assaulting a young girl. Act One of *The Hand of the Potter* shows the process of his succumbing again to his perversion. He entices little Kittie Neafie, and later her mutilated body is found in a lot. The Grand Jury indicts Isadore Berchansky, and the man-hunt is on. Scene I of Act Four (here reprinted) shows the cornered man preparing to commit suicide. The following scene closes the play with the discovery of Berchansky's body.

G. B. M.]

ACT IV[4]

Scene I

A stuffy, wretchedly furnished hall bedroom on the top floor of a five-story tenement, the very appearance and atmosphere of which suggests heat, odors, poverty. Time, about four-thirty of a late August afternoon. A door, left, gives onto a stair landing, the squeaky boards of which can be heard. A small window, back center, shows chimneys, roofs, copings—a red, dry, colorless prospect.

[4]From *The Hand of the Potter,* by Theodore Dreiser, and reprinted by permission of Horace Liveright, Publisher.

*The windows are broken, patched and dirty. The wall
paper is a faded yellowish-gray, showing patches of
paper of another color underneath. The bedstead of
white iron enamel is slimsy, has peeled, and is creaky. It
is unmade and tousled, with soiled sheets, a dirty pillow
case, and a soiled and torn bedspread. A more or less dilapidated chair stands at the foot of it. On the floor, a
scrap of ragged carpet. Against the right wall, center, a
cheap bureau or chest of drawers, above which hangs a
small oblong mirror, the upper corners of which are
curved, and the glass of which is cracked. A soiled and
torn cover of some kind graces this bureau. From the ceil-
ing in the center of the room descends a one-burner gas
pipe. On the wall, over the bed, an old fly-specked poster
of a girl in red advertises a face cream.*
When the curtain rises the stage is empty. Enter ISADORE.
*He closes the door quickly, stands with his hand on the
knob, one ear to the crack above. Several copies of different evening papers are in his hands. He is haggard,
shabby, a full week's growth of beard on his face. His
suit is worn and soiled, his shoes dusty, and his hair,
which is partially concealed by a broken straw hat, is
tousled and frowzy. He looks pale, hungry, half-wild.
As he stands there his left shoulder jerks.*

ISADORE

*(Looking straight before him with a stiff, expectant
stare.)*
I thought he was followin' me. *(Pauses and listens
awhile longer, tries the key to be sure it is turned, listens
once more, then locks it again. His shoulder jerks.)* They
ain't got me yet! It's the red ones, that's it. *(He listens once
more, then goes over to the window and unfolds one of the*

papers, which reveals his picture nearly quarter-page size. Type five inches high, and plainly visible to the audience, reads: "FIND ISADORE BERCHANSKY!" *He stares at it, then speaks in a low voice.*) They're after me, all right, for fair. I ought to 'a' gone away in the first place. (*He strikes at something.*) G'wan away! Well, I don't look like that now. (*He holds up the paper and examines his picture with care, then drops it and opens a second and a third, each one revealing a large picture and blazing with type. As he does so his shoulder jerks. He studies the headlines. After each one he exclaims:* "Gee!" *then drops it. Wearily.*) I guess it ain't no use. They'll sure get me. It's the red ones. That's it. That's the trouble. They won't let me alone. (*He strikes at something.*) G'wan! This shoulder an' arm'll give me away, if nothin' else does. (*His shoulder jerks.*) It's the red ones, that's the trouble. If they'd let me alone I'd be all right, but I can't work. They won't let me. (*Stares and strikes at something.*) G'wan! It's that two thousand dollar reward makes everybody so anxious. (*His shoulder jerks.*) But I'm sick now, an' dirty, an' they don't know me. (*Pauses and reflects.*) Poor mom! How she must 'a' suffered! An' pop! (*His shoulder jerks.*) He couldn't stand it, he said. Well, I don't blame him. I can't either, much longer. G'wan! (*Strikes at something.*) I'm crazy, all right, an' I'm afraid to die. (*Pauses.*) Sneakin' around this way! (*He wipes his eyes on his sleeve. His shoulder jerks.*) If I had the nerve, I'd kill myself. I oughta. Pop said I should. I've been tryin' to do it for three days, now. G'wan! (*Strikes at something.*) I ain't right, I tell you! An' I never was! (*His shoulder jerks.*) It's the red ones, that's it. They won't let me alone. These spells keep comin' quicker an' quicker. (*His shoulder jerks and his face contorts slightly. He goes before the mirror, stares at himself, then darkens savagely.*

A weird expression passes over his face. He strikes at some-thing.) G'wan! (*He takes off his hat and coat and hangs them on a nail, then goes over to the window, picks up a pa-per and looks at it.*) Gee, what liars newspapers are! G'wan! (*Strikes at something.*) Here it says I tried to lure little girls to my room four years ago, an' I never even thought of it then. (*Strikes at something.*) I didn't have the nerve, an' I wasn't as crazy then as I am now. (*Strikes at some-thing*). An' this arrestin' men all over the country for me—they make me sick. (*He stirs irritably. His shoulder jerks.*) G'wan! (*Strikes at something.*) Nineteen they've arrested so far, an' they ain't got me yet. (*He smiles and examines a small item closely.*) If they don't get me pretty soon they'll hang some other fellow for me. That's the way they do! These fly cops! (*His lip curls, his shoulder jerks. He strikes at something. He tears off a small corner of a newspaper and writes on it, then puts it on the wall above his bed. Talks as he does it.*) G'wan! (*Strikes at something.*) An' that parole officer! (*Indignantly.*) What a liar! He says I broke my parole. I never did! G'wan! (*Strikes at something.*) He said not to come no more unless he sent for me—the damned faker. (*He pauses again, looks out the window, stares at some imaginary thing in the corner, goes over to the door and listens, then comes back to the bureau and looks at himself. His shoulder jerks. As he does so, his ex-pression changes, he loses control of his normal self and makes queer faces at his likeness in the mirror. Suddenly he crumples up the newspapers in his hand, hurls them at his image, then jumps back and seizes the one chair. As he does so he imagines he hears a noise, pauses, puts down the chair, goes over to the door and listens. There is no sound. He half-strikes at something, then straightens up. Once more his mood appears to change. He goes over to the bed and lifts one corner of the mattress, extracting from under it a considerable length of rubber gas tubing. Surveying it, and looking at the gas jet.*) It's the red ones, that's the trouble—the blacks ain't so bad. They wouldn't hurt me, nohow. What's the use, though? I'm crazy, an' they're sure to get me. I can't beat 'em. G'wan! (*Strikes at something.*) I might as well quit now. (*His shoulder jerks. He measures the distance from the gas jet to the bed to see if he has enough.*) It's no use. (*His shoulder jerks.*) I'm hungry! An' I'm gettin' thinner an' thinner all the time. (*He goes to the mirror once more and examines himself, then looks about and strikes at something.*) An' the red ones won't let me alone. G'wan! (*He stares at an invisible something.*) Why won't you let me alone? Say? G'wan! (*He strikes at something, turns and sits down on the bed. Meditatively.*) An' I wanted to live just like other people, an' be happy. I wanted a girl an' a home too, an' now look at me! (*He pauses, then wipes his eyes with the back of his hand.*) I'm not all bad. I've worked an' I've tried to be all right, too. (*Strikes.*) But they won't let me alone! They won't ever do it. G'wan! Get away, I tell you! (*Strikes.*) I ain't right. Look at 'em! Look at 'em! (*He gets up, moves away as if from pursuers; his arm jerks. Stiffening, his expression changing.*) But it's their pretty mouths an' their hair— that's it. It's the way they wear their shirtwaists an' paint their faces! I can't stand it! It's the red ones. It ain't my fault—it's theirs! I can't help myself no more. They make me do it. (*He grows savage, vigorous. His shoulder jerks.*) Well, I won't die, either. (*Throws down the tubing.*) Why should I? It ain't my fault. I ain't done nothin' much, have I? I couldn't help it, could I? I didn't make myself, did I? (*He stares sternly before him. His shoulder jerks.*) I'll tell 'em that, I will! I'll write it. (*He picks up one of the news-*

papers, tears off a small corner, fishes about in his coat for a lead pencil, and finding a small bit goes to the dresser and scribbles on the paper, pausing once as he does so to strike. Quotes) "I didn't make myself, did I? G'wan!" *(Reaches up and fastens it against the wall alongside the mirror. His shoulder jerks.)* Well, I won't quit yet, either. I'm not all in. G'wan! G'wan! *(Strikes at something.)* They ain't got me.

(He goes to the nail, takes down his hat and coat, and puts them on. As he does so, he hears a noise. He thinks some one is coming up the stairs, goes over and listens. A period of silence follows in which no noise is heard. His shoulder jerks. A newsboy's voice is heard crying.)

The Newsboy

Extro! Extro! All about Isadore Berchansky! Extro! Extro! *(The voice fades.)*

Isadore

(Listening.)

Huh! I wonder who it is now. I bet they've found somebody else. I better not go out, though. They might know me. *(His shoulder jerks. He goes back to the bed.)* G'wan! *(Strikes at something.)* It's the red ones all the time, not the blacks. They won't let me alone—always followin' me around. G'wan! *(Strikes.)* I gotta eat, though. I can't go on this way. I gotta eat or die. *(His shoulder jerks. He moves toward the door.)* I gotta get out o' New York an' get sompin to do, or I gotta quit. It ain't no use. *(Pauses.)* It's the red ones. That's it. They won't let me alone. G'wan! *(Strikes at something.)* Nothin' but a cup o' coffee an' a sandwich since Wednesday! *(He sniffs, reaches in his pocket and pulls out some change. His shoulder jerks.)*

Eighteen cents! An' I ain't got the strength to earn any more. Look at me! (*He surveys himself in the mirror. His shoulder jerks.*) It's all up with me, I guess. G'wan! (*He strikes at something.*) These papers'll fix me. They're all talkin' about my arm. (*Pauses.*) I wonder why Joe ain't answered my letter, an' Greenbaum, the stiff! (*He gulps.*) G'wan! (*He draws back his arm threateningly.*) I guess he's afraid. Well, that's the way—when you ain't got nothin'. (*He stiffens and strikes at something. His shoulder jerks.*) Gee, but it's tough, though! All the world goin' on an' happy, an' me——

(*He half sobs, then starts to pick up the gas tube. The sound of steps is heard on the stairs. Hastily he puts away the tube and papers, and straightens up, listening intently. His shoulder jerks. A knock sounds, then another.*)

A VOICE

(*Outside.*)
Mr. Abrams! Mr. Abrams! (*Isadore does not answer. The door rattles.*) You are in there? I know you're in there! Vy don't you open the door?

ISADORE

(*Stirring.*)
Wait a minute!
(*He goes to the door and opens it slightly. His shoulder jerks.*)

SAMUEL ELKAS

(*A small, dark, restless, inquisitive, ferret-like Jew, clothed in a dirty shirt, open at the neck, and rolled up at the sleeves, a pair of baggy, messy trousers, the suspenders of which are hanging down, and the leg-ends of which gather*

*in folds above his instep. He wears slippers. His hair is
tousled, his face and hands are damp and dirty.*)

Good afternoon, Mr. Abrams. So, you are not verking
yet? Hev you my rent for me?

Isadore

(*Taking off his hat and rubbing his stomach and hair.*)

I've been sick to-day. I couldn't look, very well. But I've
got a job, now, for to-morrow. (*His shoulder jerks. He
turns it away from* Elkas.) A friend o' mine is goin' to
give it to me. By to-morrow night I'll have your rent for
you.

(*He starts to strike at something, but pauses.*)

Elkas

(*With a gesture.*)

To-morrow! To-morrow! Alvays to-morrow! Vell, if
I don't get it by den, you vill haf to get out. You t'ink ve
verk to give rooms free to people? (Isadore's *shoulder
jerks.*) Vot is it with your arm? Is it hurt?

Isadore

(*Savagely.*)

No, no, no! Nothin'! (*He starts to close the door.*) I'll
get it for you to-morrow, sure. (*His shoulder jerks.*) Can't
you trust me till then? I'll pay you, sure. (*His shoulder
jerks. He pushes the door nearly to.*) I can get a dollar an'
a half. It's only a week yesterday.

(*As the two stand there speaking, a little girl of nine or
ten, dark, elfish, pretty, appears and stands behind* Elkas,
*who is evidently unaware of her presence. She peeps around
as if anxious to be neither heard nor seen. She has on a
worn blue gingham dress, sleeveless and cut low at the neck,*

which is very soiled and torn. Her legs as well as her arms are bare and dirty, and her hair is disheveled and not very clean, but she has the charm of sprightliness and curiosity.)

ELKAS

(Lifting his hands.)

Vell, vy dontcha, den? I kent, an' I need it bed enough. Ve haf to verk, too.

(He gesticulates antagonistically.)

ISADORE

(Crossly.)

Well, I'll have it for you by to-morrow, I tell you—by six o'clock. (*His shoulder jerks. He looks to one side as if to strike something.*) Don't bother me no more to-day, will you! I'll pay you then, sure.

(He pushes at the door as if to close it.)

ELKAS

(Pushing at his side of the door to hold it open.)

By six o'clock! By six o'clock! Den, if you don't pay, I lose Sunday, too! Vy not by noon?

ISADORE

All right, by noon. I'll get it to you as soon as I get it—by noon I'll send it over. (*His shoulder jerks.*) You'll get it, all right. Please don't worry me now. (*Aside.*) G'wan!

ELKAS

'*(Doubtfully, moving back. The child disappears.)*

Vell, if it vuz some von else, I vouldn't do it. Since you're sick, I'll let it go to-day as a favor to you.

(He goes out. ISADORE *closes the door, listens, then after a time looks up.)*

ISADORE

(*His shoulder jerks.*)

Yes, the pig! To-morrow I'll pay him—to-morrow—huh!
—I won't be alive to-morrow! G'wan! (*Strikes at something.*) It's the red ones, that's it. They won't let me alone.
A lot of difference it'll make by to-morrow! I might as well
quit now. I gotta. It's the red ones. I can't get away. He
saw my arm. (*Goes over to the bed.*) Gee, it's a wonder he
didn't connect me! G'wan away! (*Strikes at something.
With a frown.*) Maybe he did! (*Takes out the rubber tube,
fastens one end of it over the gas jet and carries the other
end to the head of the bed and rests it there. His shoulder
jerks. He takes off his hat and coat, then gets out the pencil
and begins feverishly to scribble on the wall at the head of
the bed. As he writes he talks.*) "Parole—officer—Gavan—
is—a—damned—liar." G'wan! (*Strikes.*) "He—told—
me—not—to—call—" G'wan! (*Strikes.*)—"any—more.
He—never—told—me—to—sign—any—papers—" (*Stops,
frowns, and stares at something.*) G'wan! (*Strikes.
Writes.*) "It's—the—red—ones—not—the—blacks. He—
told—me—he'd—send—" (*Stops and frowns.*) G'wan!—
"them — to — me—in—a—blank—envelope—" (*Pauses
and thinks. Frowns, then writes.*) Seven—is—right. Don't
—cry—" (*Strikes.*) G'wan!

(*A tap is heard at the door. Instantly he stiffens, re-
moves the tube from the gas jet, tiptoes to the bed and puts
it under, then draws a small knife from his pocket and listens. The tap is repeated. He does not answer.*)

A SOFT LOW VOICE

Mr. Ab'ams! Mr. Ab'ams!

ISADORE

(*Relaxing, and putting back the knife.*)
Yes.

The Voice

(*Softly.*)
Oh, Mr. Ab'ams! It's Hagar!

Isadore

(*Gruffly.*)
Yes? Whaddy ya want?
(*His shoulder jerks.*)

The Voice

(*Sweetly.*)
I've got sompin for you, Mr. Ab'ams. (*He opens the door and looks out. The little girl is there. She has an apple and is holding it out to him.*) Want this?

Isadore

(*Starting. His shoulder jerks.*)
Oh, it's you, is it? What made you wanta bring it to me? (*His expression changes from one of fear and doubt to one of smiling sympathy. He forgets to strike. A weird smile passes over his face.*)
Come on in. (*Takes her by the arm and pulls her in.*)

Hagar

(*Uncertainly.*)
I don't think I'd better. He'll scold if he ketches me up here. I'm not allowed.
(*Looks about as if to see if any one is coming. She laughs.*)

Isadore

(*Warmly.*)
Aw, come on. (*His shoulder jerks. His face grimaces oddly. Over his shoulder.*) G'wan!

HAGAR

(*Looking at him smiling.*)

I heard what you said. You said you ain't got no money, an' I felt sorry, so I thought I'd bring you this. (*She holds up the apple.*) Didn't you see me? I was behind papa. (*She laughs. ISADORE shakes his head. He looks at her greedily. staring at her arms and bare feet. His expression changes. He leers and smooths her arm and neck. His shoulder jerks. He shivers.*) Don't you know me?

ISADORE

(*Darkly.*)

Sure. You're Hagar Elkas, ain't you? (*She nods.*) You like me, Hagar, don't you? Somebody likes me, anyhow. (*To one side.*) G'wan!

HAGAR

(*Nodding her head and smiling.*)

Uh-huh! Who you talkin' to?

(*She looks around behind him.*)

ISADORE

Nobody! Nobody!

(*He controls an inclination to strike.*)

HAGAR

I seen you goin' out this mornin'. (*Looking at the papers on the floor.*) Wotcha doin' with all them papers—lookin' for a job?

ISADORE

(*Looking about apprehensively, then stooping to gather up the papers from the floor and stuff them in a bureau drawer. He smiles wanly.*)

That's right! You've got it! I'm lookin' for a job. (*His shoulder jerks.*) Come on up here. (*He picks her up and seats her on the bureau and begins to trifle with her hair and feel her knees. His shoulder jerks. Again his expression changes to a leer. His face contorts. He glances over her, then looks up, sees himself in the mirror. Pauses. Puts his hand to his head and begins to back away. As he does so, a noise is heard in the hall below, a voice calling "Hagar! Hagar!" A door slams. Voices sound, then die away. The voice of a newsboy in the street is heard—"Extro! Extro! Isadore Berchansky...!" Silence. ISADORE stares at HAGAR, who stares back at him in astonishment.*) Naw Naw! That's right! I'd better not do that any more! I won't! I can't! It's the red ones, that's it! They won't let me alone. (*His shoulder jerks.*) I'd better quit now before I do, though. I'm crazy all right. (*He goes to the door and listens, then returns and lifts HAGAR down and pushes her toward the door, his shoulder jerking. Roughly.*) Get out, kid! Quick! Quick! Get out, I tell you, before I do sompin! Get out! You don't know me! Can't you see? Quick! Quick! Hurry! (*His manner is very rough. He pushes her out, and as she gives him a frightened glance, slams the door, locks it, and then stands with his back to it, and stares.*) Naw! Naw! I'd better not do that no more! I better go, though, before I kill somebody else! I'm sure to! Poor little kid! (*His shoulder jerks. He goes to the bed, pulls off the coverlet and lays it along the crack at the bottom of the door, the while his shoulder jerks. He takes the newspapers out of the drawer and making twists of them, begins stuffing them into the cracks along the sides and between the window and in the keyhole. As he works he talks.*) Mom, you'll understand this. You know me. It's for the best. I couldn't help it. You'll understand. They won't let me alone. G'wan!

(*Strikes at something.*) Don't cry! I'm no good anyhow. I never was. (*His shoulder jerks.*) You know that. (*He wipes· his eyes.*) Be good to Masha. Tell her I always thought she was the best of 'em all. (*He pauses and stares at something, moves as if to strike, but subsides without doing it.*) She knows I like her. (*His shoulder jerks.*) An' pop! Poor old pop! (*He stops, picks up another bit of newspaper, writes on it and looks about for a suitable place to fasten it, finally sticking it in the mirror frame. His shoulder jerks. He stares curiously at something. Heavily.*) I guess they'll see that, all right. (*His shoulder jerks.*) G'wan! (*Strikes at something, goes over to the bed, takes out the gas tube, fastens one end over the gas jet and taking out his handkerchief stretches it by the corners and ties the tube to it. Looking over his shoulder.*) G'wan! (*Then he gets his coat, spreads it over the window with pins, and goes back to the bed, picks up the other end of the tube and stands there, his shoulder jerking from time to time. The curtain begins to descend.*) Well, I guess it's all day for me, all right. They won't let me be. G'wan! (*Strikes at something.*) I ain't all bad, an' I don't wanta die, but—oh— (*He sits down.*)

CURTAIN

DESIRE UNDER THE ELMS

By Eugene O'Neill

(The scene is the Cabot farmhouse in New England: the time is 1850. The flinty old widower, Ephraim Cabot, returns home with Abbie, aged about thirty-five, as his new bride. Whereupon two of his sons declare themselves free and set out for gold in California. The youngest son, Eben, falls in love with Abbie and she with him. The marriage of old Ephraim and Abbie is childless, but a child is born during the play—as the result of intimacy between Abbie and Eben.

The old farmer is deceived about the infant's parentage, but he in turn insinuates to Eben that Abbie has complained of his youthful attentions. Eben angrily upbraids Abbie for what he takes to be her treachery. She retorts by vowing to kill the child. Then follows Scene Three of Part Three, which is reprinted.

The play closes with the arrival of the sheriff to take Abbie and Eben into custody, leaving old Cabot to say: "God's lonesome, hain't he? God's hard an' lonesome!"

G. B. M.)

Part Three, Scene Three[5]

Just before dawn in the morning—shows the kitchen and CABOT'S *bedroom. In the kitchen, by the light of a tallow*

---

[5]From *Desire Under the Elms*, by Eugene O'Neill, and reprinted by permission of Horace Liveright, Publisher.

candle on the table, EBEN *is sitting, his chin propped on his hands, his drawn face blank and expressionless. His carpetbag is on the floor beside him. In the bedroom, dimly lighted by a small whale-oil lamp,* CABOT *lies asleep.* ABBIE *is bending over the cradle, listening, her face full of terror yet with an undercurrent of desperate triumph. Suddenly she breaks down and sobs, appears about to throw herself on her knees beside the cradle; but the old man turns restlessly, groaning in his sleep, and she controls herself, and, shrinking away from the cradle with a gesture of horror, backs swiftly toward the door in rear and goes out. A moment later she comes into the kitchen and, running to* EBEN, *flings her arms about his neck and kisses him wildly. He hardens himself, he remains unmoved and cold, he keeps his eyes straight ahead.*

ABBIE

(*Hysterically.*)
I done it, Eben! I told ye I'd do it! I've proved I love ye—better'n everythin'—so's ye can't never doubt me no more!

EBEN

(*Dully.*)
Whatever ye done, it hain't no good now.

ABBIE

(*Wildly.*)
Don't ye say that! Kiss me, Eben, won't ye? I need ye t' kiss me arter what I done! I need ye t' say ye love me!

EBEN

(*Kisses her without emotion—dully.*)
That's fur good-by. I'm a-goin' soon.

ABBIE

No! No! Ye won't go—not now!

EBEN

(*Going on with his own thought.*)
I been a-thinkin'—an' I hain't goin' t' tell Paw nothin'.
I'll leave Maw t' take vengeance on ye. If I told him, the old
skunk'd jest be stinkin' mean enuf to take it out on that
baby. (*His voice showing emotion in spite of him.*) An' I
don't want nothin' bad t' happen t' him. He hain't t' blame
fur yew. (*He adds with a certain queer pride,*) An' he looks
like me! An' by God, he's mine! An' some day I'll be a-
comin' back an' . . . !

ABBIE

(*Too absorbed in her own thoughts to listen to him—
pleadingly.*)
They's no cause fur ye t' go now—they's no sense—it's
all the same's it was—they's nothin' come b'tween us now
—arter what I done!

EBEN

(*Something in her voice arouses him. He stares at her a
bit frightenedly.*)
Ye look mad, Abbie. What did ye do?

ABBIE

I—I killed him, Eben.

EBEN

(*Amazed.*)
Ye killed him?

ABBIE

(*Dully.*)
Ay-eh.

EBEN

(*Recovering from his astonishment—savagely.*)
An' serves him right! But we got t' do somethin' quick
t' make it look 's if the old skunk's killed himself when he
was drunk. We kin prove by 'em all how drunk he got.

ABBIE

(*Wildly.*)
No! No! Not him! (*Laughing distractedly.*) But that's
what I ought t' done, hain't it? I oughter killed him instead!
Why didn't ye tell me?

EBEN

(*Appalled.*)
Instead? What d'ye mean?

ABBIE

Not him.

EBEN

(*His face grown ghastly.*)
Not—not that baby!

ABBIE

(*Dully.*)
Ay-eh!

EBEN

(*Falls to his knees as if he'd been struck—his voice trembling with horror.*)
Oh, God A'mighty! A'mighty God! Maw, whar was ye,
why didn't ye stop her?

ABBIE

(*Simply.*)

She went back t' her grave that night we fust done it, remember? I hain't felt her about since. (*A pause.* EBEN *hides his head in his hands, trembling all over as if he had the ague. She goes on dully,*) I left the piller over his little face. Then he killed himself. He stopped breathin'.

(*She begins to weep softly.*)

EBEN

(*Rage beginning to mingle with grief.*)

He looked like me. He was mine, damn ye!

ABBIE

(*Slowly and brokenly.*)

I didn't want t' do it. I hated myself fur doin' it. I loved him. He was purty—dead spit 'n' image o' yew. But I loved yew more—an' yew was goin' away—far off whar I'd never see ye agen—never kiss ye, never feel ye pressed agin me agen—an ye said ye hated me fur havin' him—ye said ye hated him an' wished he was dead—ye said if it hadn't been fur him comin' it'd be the same's afore between us.

EBEN

(*Unable to endure this, springs to his feet in a fury, threatening her, his twitching fingers seeming to reach out for her throat.*)

Ye lie! I never said—I never dreamed ye'd—I'd cut off my head afore I'd hurt his finger!

ABBIE

(*Piteously, sinking on her knees.*)

Eben, don't ye look at me like that—hatin' me—not after what I done fur ye—fur us—so's we could be happy agen—

EBEN

(*Furiously now.*)

Shut up, or I'll kill ye! I see yer game now—the same old sneakin' trick—ye're aimin' t' blame me fur the murder ye done!

ABBIE

(*Moaning—putting her hands over her ears.*)

Don't ye, Eben! Don't ye!

(*She grasps his legs.*)

EBEN

(*His mood suddenly changing to horror, shrinks away from her.*)

Don't ye tech me! Ye're pizen! How could ye—t' murder a pore little critter—Ye must've swapped yer soul t' hell! (*Suddenly raging.*) Ha! I kin see why ye done it! Not the lies ye jest told—but 'cause ye wanted t' steal agen—steal the last thin' ye'd left me—my part o' him—no, the hull o' him—ye saw he looked like me—ye knowed he was all mine—and ye couldn't b'ar it—I know ye! Ye killed him fur bein' mine! (*All this has driven him almost insane. He makes a rush past her for the door—then turns—shaking both fists at her, violently.*) But I'll take vengeance now! I'll git the Sheriff! I'll tell him everythin'! Then I'll sing "I'm off to Californi-a!" an' go—gold—Golden Gate—gold sun—fields o' gold in the west! (*This last he half shouts, half croons incoherently, suddenly breaking off passionately.*) I'm goin' fur the Sheriff t' come an' git ye! I want ye tuk away, locked up from me! I can't stand t' luk at ye! Murderer an' thief 'r not, ye still tempt me! I'll give ye up t' the Sheriff!

(*He turns and runs out, around the corner of house,*

panting and sobbing, and breaks into a swerving sprint down the road.)

ABBIE

(*Struggling to her feet, runs to the door, calling after him.*)

I love ye, Eben! I love ye! (*She stops at the door weakly, swaying, about to fall.*) I don't care what ye do—if ye'll on'y love me agen!

(*She falls limply to the floor in a faint.*)

CHAPTER XIII

PROSE FOR AUTOBIOGRAPHY:
HENRY ADAMS

WHY DOES THE AUTOBIOGRAPHER WRITE PROSE?

ACHIEVEMENT in the field of American autobiography (and biography) is almost as meager[1] as in American drama, but not long ago there appeared an outstanding work: it goes by the title of *The Education of Henry Adams*. After a few general remarks about the suitability of prose to biography and autobiography and a classification of types of autobiography, I propose to submit *The Education of Henry Adams* to the majority of those critical processes that have been outlined in one division or another of my book. By so doing, this chapter can then serve as a compact review of the principles set forth.

Why is prose the medium favorable to the biographer and autobiographer? Because the emotional tension with which we view the courses of our lives or others' lives is not strong. We may feel keenly about certain episodes even when the retrospect is long, but we cannot go on feeling poignantly or deeply about the pattern of a whole life. Our emotions wear down and leave us with a mood. A life excites our curiosity, stirs us to reflection, causes us to seek its significance. We fall into recollections, usually weaker in

---

[1] Benjamin Franklin's *Autobiography* antedates the time-span of American prose we are considering.

feeling than during the original events, and our minds govern our survey of what has been. We have the wisdom of aftersight, which makes for sobriety rather than rhapsody. Thus prose is our natural choice for autobiographical or biographical studies.

TYPES OF AUTOBIOGRAPHY

Autobiographers may be subdivided into three classes, the first of which does not flourish on our soil at all. This may be due to certain inhibiting traits in our national psychology or it may be due to inadequacies in our language or to both, but such a work as the *Confessions* of Jean-Jacques Rousseau is not within the scope of our writers. We cannot write our personal histories in the form of full and frank confessions. The second class, that of memoirs, is the most common. It consists of those reminiscences of such of our doings as we care to publish. The aim is not self-revelation in the guise of a narrative but simply a record of our memories. The third class is as rare as memoirs are common. Henry Adams, who represents it, leads me to call it impersonal autobiography, but, more properly speaking, it is reflective autobiography. The intention is to observe in retrospect the circling paths of one's existence and by pondering to discover what meaning, if any, the labyrinth has. In this form one tries to be candid in one's gaze and to puzzle out from the tangled facts remembered what one's life has been about. The attempt of Henry Adams was to be objective about his own life, and by a fine stroke he hit on the device of telling his story in the third person.

"Under the shadow of Boston State House, turning its back on the house of John Hancock, the little pas-

sage called Hancock Avenue runs, or ran, from Beacon
Street, skirting the State House grounds, to Mount Vernon Street, on the summit of Beacon Hill; and there, in
the third house below Mount Vernon Place, February
16, 1838, a child was born, and christened later by his
uncle, the minister of the First Church after the tenets
of Boston Unitarianism, as Henry Brooks Adams."

So he begins his account, impersonally, writing about
himself as though he were someone else, in a long opening
sentence that presages a long leisured book.

AN ANALYSIS OF ADAMS'S PROSE

We can see already—and this commences our review—
that Henry Adams belongs to the plain-style tradition of
English prose and not to the ornate school. But his is an
elevated plain style for which one finds such adjectives as
meditative, deliberate, somewhat involved and massive.

Our next move is to disentangle the means that produce
such adjectival effects. In terms of grammar and rhetoric
it is the predominance on a page of Adams of long loose
compound or complex sentences. To these can be attributed
the slowness of pace, the sense of involution, the massive-
ness of structure. In terms of vocabulary it is the presence
of a relatively high percentage of intellectual words that
among other effects lend the style its meditative character.

One does not expect of plain-style work that there should
be anything notable for its own sake in arrangements of
vowels and consonants. For in plain style (in Adams's
style) sound is strictly subordinate to sense: there is a fitness between them, but the sound values are too modest
to call attention to themselves.

Adams's rhythm, however, is pronounced enough to justify a brief scansion and a general remark or two upon it.

"Then came | the journey | up to London | through Birmingham | and the Black District, | another lesson, | which needed | much more | to be rightly felt. | The plunge | into darkness | lurid with flames; | the sense of unknown | horror | in this weird gloom | which then existed | nowhere else, | and never | had existed | before, | except in | volcanic | craters; | the violent | contrast | between this | dense, | smoky, | impenetrable | darkness, | and the soft | green charm | that one | glided into, | as one emerged | —the revelation | of an unknown | society | of the pit | —made a boy | uncomfortable, | though he had | no idea | that Karl Marx | was standing there | waiting for him, | and that | sooner or later | the process | of education | would have to deal | with Karl Marx | much more than with | Professor Bowen | of Harvard College | or his Satanic | freetrade majesty | John Stuart Mill. | The Black District | was a practical | education, | but it was | infinitely far | in the distance. | The boy ran away | from it, | as he ran away | from everything | he disliked." |

The paucity of typical verse feet (iambs, trochees, anapæsts, and dactyls) is noticeable at once. Just as noticeable is the plenitude of the favorite feet of prose: the various forms of four-syllabled feet and dochmiacs which give Adams's rhythm its grave heavy movement.

Ordonnance of thought, the reader should remember, is the next element of style to consider, an element that usually governs form as well. In *The Education of Henry Adams* a chronological sequence is followed, but it is almost purely a convenience. The real order is that of a meditation, and chronology is used simply as an aid to the principal object, which is learning from experience, or self-education. The author puts the sequence of his life before himself only for the sake of meditating upon the possible lessons it teaches, and the consequence is that we do not think of his book so much as a narrative of experiences as we regard it as an exposition of his thoughts about his life. Always the end, self-education, is kept in view, and the individual chapters are meditations upon the various areas of his experiences.

Cursory as is this account of the elements of Adams's style, we have learned enough to make some statements about his mental and emotional constitution. The style as behavior indicates that he was not quick or facile, either intellectually or emotionally, nor does it exhibit force or strength of mind or feeling. Adams had the mind of a doubter. His chief asset was breadth, and this was responsible for the sanity of his intellect and the humaneness of his emotions. He was a ponderer by temperament but not of an active disposition. The reader is invited to trace each one of these assertions about Adams's psychology back to those characteristics of his style that clearly signify their truth.

The world view of Henry Adams—which again it is possible to derive strictly from his form—is a fairly common one. He was a diminutive pupil in a cosmic schoolroom trying to learn his lessons on time. Such a world-conception lies between the Puritan view of life as a Sunday school presided over by a severe dominie and the ancient

Greek view of the world as a gymnasium. Adams saw the world through a mellower, broader, more humane outlook than does or did the Puritan, but he was too passive to be a good Greek. "Education by accident" is not in the creed of the spiritual gymnast.

So much, then, for an outline of a general approach to the prose of Henry Adams. But I do not intend to forego making other suggestions for review. You will find it difficult to isolate any passages in *The Education* that are so markedly emotional that they provide a good exercise in weighing: the style is too intellectualized for that purpose: but by this very token it provides copiously examples of thoughts for weighing. Here is one that should set your minds off on quite another investigation than the one we have followed in these pages. "American literature," says Adams in his preface to *The Education,* "offers scarcely one working model for high education."

Adams may be used still further for purposes of review. Is his autobiography, judged in the light of our discussions of fiction and the drama, to be called a work of literary art? Clearly, there is no *as if* basis to the book, and that being so we shall have to view it as a human document but not as, in its totality, a work of art. The appeal of *The Education of Henry Adams* is chiefly to our minds, and this fact should call up whatever conclusions have been reached about the language of ideas. We can even use his text as a reminder of the gist of our thinking about humor whenever we encounter Adams's occasional smile, quiet, unobtrusive, ironical, as he records one or another of his discoveries of his own ignorance as contrasted with his suppositions of truth.

Finally, let us (perhaps a little wiser for our efforts) return now to the definers of first principles.

Saintsbury: "As the essence of verse-metre is its identity (at least in equivalence) and recurrence, so the essence of prose-rhythm lies in variety and divergence."

Stendhal: "Style is this: to add to a given thought all the circumstances fitted to produce the whole effect that the thought ought to produce."

Buffon: "Style is the man himself."

A VISIT TO FRYSTON (1862)[2]

By Henry Adams

The year 1862 was a dark spot in Henry Adams's life,
and the education it gave was mostly one that he gladly forgot. As far as he was aware, he made no friends;.he could
hardly make enemies; yet towards the close of the year he
was flattered by an invitation from Monckton Milnes to
Fryston, and it was one of many acts of charity towards
the young that gave Milnes immortality. Milnes made it his
business to be kind. Other people criticized him for his
manner of doing it, but never imitated him. Naturally, a
dispirited, disheartened private secretary was exceedingly
grateful, and never forgot the kindness, but it was chiefly
as education that this first country visit had value. Commonly, country visits are much alike, but Monckton Milnes
was never like anybody, and his country parties served his
purpose of mixing strange elements. Fryston was one of
a class of houses that no one sought for its natural beauties,
and the winter mists of Yorkshire were rather more evident for the absence of the hostess on account of them, so
that the singular guests whom Milnes collected to enliven
his December had nothing to do but astonish each other, if
anything could astonish such men. Of the five, Adams alone
was tame; he alone added nothing to the wit or humor,
except as a listener; but they needed a listener and he was

[2]Reprinted from *The Education of Henry Adams* by permission
of and arrangement with Houghton Mifflin Company.

useful. Of the remaining four, Milnes was the oldest, and perhaps the sanest in spite of his superficial eccentricities, for Yorkshire sanity was true to a standard of its own, if not to other conventions; yet even Milnes startled a young American whose Boston and Washington mind was still fresh. He would not have been startled by the hard-drinking, horse-racing Yorkshireman, of whom he had read in books; but Milnes required a knowledge of society and literature that only himself possessed, if one were to try to keep pace with him. He had sought contact with everybody and everything that Europe could offer. He knew it all from several points of view, and chiefly as humorous.

The second of the party was also of a certain age; a quiet, well-mannered, singularly agreeable gentleman of the literary class. When Milnes showed Adams to his room to dress for dinner, he stayed a moment to say a word about this guest, whom he called Stirling of Keir. His sketch closed with the hint that Stirling was violent only on one point—hatred of Napoleon III. On that point, Adams was himself sensitive, which led him to wonder how bad the Scotch gentleman might be. The third was a man of thirty or thereabouts, whom Adams had already met at Lady Palmerston's carrying his arm in a sling. His figure and bearing were sympathetic—almost pathetic—with a certain grave and gentle charm, a pleasant smile, and an interesting story. He was Laurence Oliphant, just from Japan, where he had been wounded in the fanatics' attack on the British Legation. He seemed exceptionally sane and peculiarly suited for country houses, where every man would enjoy his company, and every woman would adore him. He had not then published "Piccadilly"; perhaps he was writing it; while, like all young men about the Foreign Office, he contributed to *The Owl*.

The fourth was a boy, or had the look of one, though in fact a year older than Adams himself. He resembled in action—and in this trait, was remotely followed, a generation later, by another famous young man, Robert Louis Stevenson—a tropical bird, high-crested, long-beaked, quick-moving, with rapid utterance and screams of humor, quite unlike any English lark or nightingale. One could hardly call him a crimson macaw among owls, and yet no ordinary contrast availed. Milnes introduced him as Mr. Algernon Swinburne. The name suggested nothing. Milnes was always unearthing new coins and trying to give them currency. He had unearthed Henry Adams who knew himself to be worthless and not current. When Milnes lingered a moment in Adams's room to add that Swinburne had written some poetry, not yet published, of really extraordinary merit, Adams only wondered what more Milnes would discover, and whether by chance he could discover merit in a private secretary. He was capable of it.

In due course this party of five men sat down to dinner with the usual club manners of ladyless dinner-tables, easy and formal at the same time. Conversation ran first to Oliphant who told his dramatic story simply, and from him the talk drifted off into other channels, until Milnes thought it time to bring Swinburne out. Then, at last, if never before, Adams acquired education. What he had sought so long, he found; but he was none the wiser; only the more astonished. For once, too, he felt at ease, for the others were no less astonished than himself, and their astonishment grew apace. For the rest of the evening Swinburne figured alone; the end of dinner made the monologue only freer, for in 1862, even when ladies were not in the house, smoking was forbidden, and guests usually smoked in the stables or the kitchen; but Monckton Milnes was a licensed libertine who let his guests smoke in Adams's bedroom, since Adams was an American-German barbarian ignorant of manners; and there after dinner all sat—or lay—till far into the night, listening to the rush of Swinburne's talk. In a long experience, before or after, no one ever approached it; yet one had heard accounts of the best talking of the time, and read accounts of talkers in all time, among the rest, of Voltaire, who seemed to approach nearest the pattern.

That Swinburne was altogether new to the three types of men-of-the-world before him; that he seemed to them quite original, wildly eccentric, astonishingly gifted, and convulsingly droll, Adams could see; but what more he was, even Milnes hardly dared say. They could not believe his incredible memory and knowledge of literature, classic, mediæval, and modern; his faculty of reciting a play of Sophocles or a play of Shakespeare, forward or backward, from end to beginning; or Dante, or Villon, or Victor Hugo. They knew not what to make of his rhetorical recitation of his own unpublished ballads—"Faustine"; the "Four Boards of the Coffin Lid"; the "Ballad of Burdens" —which he declaimed as though they were books of the Iliad. It was singular that his most appreciative listener should have been the author only of pretty verses like "We wandered by the brookside," and "She seemed to those that saw them meet"; and who never cared to write in any other tone; but Milnes took everything into his sympathies, including Americans like young Adams whose standards were stiffest of all, while Swinburne, though millions of ages far from them, united them by his humor even more than by his poetry.

The story of his first day as a member of Professor Stubbs's household was professionally clever farce, if not high comedy, in a young man who could write a Greek ode or a Provençal chanson as easily as an English quatrain.

Late at night when the symposium broke up, Stirling of Keir wanted to take with him to his chamber a copy of "Queen Rosamund," the only volume Swinburne had then published, which was on the library table, and Adams offered to light him down with his solitary bedroom candle. All the way, Stirling was ejaculating explosions of wonder, until at length, at the foot of the stairs and at the climax of his imagination, he paused, and burst out: "He's a cross between the devil and the Duke of Argyll!"

To appreciate the full merit of this description, a judicious critic should have known both, and Henry Adams knew only one—at least in person—but he understood that to a Scotchman the likeness meant something quite portentous, beyond English experience, supernatural, and what the French call *moyenâgeux,* or mediæval with a grotesque turn. That Stirling as well as Milnes should regard Swinburne as a prodigy greatly comforted Adams, who lost his balance of mind at first in trying to imagine that Swinburne was a natural product of Oxford, as muffins and pork-pies of London, at once the cause and effect of dyspepsia. The idea that one has actually met a real genius dawns slowly on a Boston mind, but it made entry at last.

Then came the sad reaction, not from Swinburne whose genius never was in doubt, but from the Boston mind which, in its uttermost flights, was never *moyenâgeux*. One felt the horror of Longfellow and Emerson, the doubts of Lowell and the humor of Holmes, at the wild Walpurgis-night of Swinburne's talk. What could a shy young private secretary do about it? Perhaps, in his good nature, Milnes thought that Swinburne might find a friend in Ster-

ling or Oliphant, but he could hardly have fancied Henry
Adams rousing in him even an interest. Adams could no
more interest Algernon Swinburne than he could interest
Encke's comet. To Swinburne he could be no more than
a worm. The quality of genius was an education almost
ultimate, for one touched there the limits of the human
mind on that side; but one could only receive; and had nothing to give—nothing even to offer.

Swinburne tested him then and there by one of his favorite tests—Victor Hugo; for to him the test of Victor Hugo
was the surest and quickest of standards. French poetry is
at best a severe exercise for foreigners; it requires extraordinary knowledge of the language and rare refinement of
ear to appreciate even the recitation of French verse; but
unless a poet has both, he lacks something of poetry. Adams
had neither. To the end of his life he never listened to a
French recitation with pleasure, or felt a sense of majesty
in French verse; but he did not care to proclaim his weakness, and he tried to evade Swinburne's vehement insistence
by parading an affection for Alfred de Musset. Swinburne
would have none of it; de Musset was unequal; he did not
sustain himself on the wing.

Adams would have given a world or two, if he owned
one, to sustain himself on the wing like de Musset, or even
like Hugo; but his education as well as his ear was at fault;
and he succumbed. Swinburne tried him again on Walter
Savage Landor. In truth the test was the same, for Swinburne admired in Landor's English the qualities that he
felt in Hugo's French; and Adams's failure was equally
gross, for, when forced to despair, he had to admit that
both Hugo and Landor bored him. Nothing more was
needed. One who could feel neither Hugo nor Landor was
lost.

The sentence was just and Adams never appealed from it. He knew his inferiority in taste as he might know it in smell. Keenly mortified by the dullness of his senses and instincts, he knew he was no companion for Swinburne; probably he could be only an annoyance; no number of centuries could ever educate him to Swinburne's level, even in technical appreciation; yet he often wondered whether there was nothing he had to offer that was worth the poet's acceptance. Certainly such mild homage as the American insect would have been only too happy to bring, had he known how, was hardly worth the acceptance of any one. Only in France is the attitude of prayer possible; in England it became absurd. Even Monckton Milnes, who felt the splendors of Hugo and Landor, was almost as helpless as an American private secretary in personal contact with them. Ten years afterwards Adams met him at the Geneva Conference, fresh from Paris, bubbling with delight at a call he had made on Hugo: "I was shown into a large room," he said, "with women and men seated in chairs against the walls, and Hugo at one end throned. No one spoke. At last Hugo raised his voice solemnly, and uttered the words: 'Quant à moi, je crois en Dieu!' Silence followed. Then a woman responded as if in deep meditation: 'Chose sublime! un Dieu qui croit en Dieu!'"

With the best of will, one could not do this in London; the actors had not the instinct of the drama; and yet even a private secretary was not wholly wanting in instinct. As soon as he reached town he hurried to Pickering's for a copy of "Queen Rosamund," and at the same time, if Swinburne was not joking, Pickering had sold seven copies. When the "Poems and Ballads" came out, and met with great success and scandal, he sought one of the first copies from Moxon. If he had sinned and doubted at all, he wholly repented and did penance before "Atalanta in Calydon," and would have offered Swinburne a solemn worship as Milnes's female offered Hugo, if it would have pleased the poet. Unfortunately it was worthless.

The three young men returned to London, and each went his own way. Adams's interest in making friends was something desperate, but "the London season," Milnes used to say, "is a season for making acquaintances and losing friends"; there was no intimate lift. Of Swinburne he saw no more till Monckton Milnes summoned his whole array of Frystonians to support him in presiding at the dinner of the Authors' Fund, when Adams found himself seated next to Swinburne, famous then, but no nearer. They never met again. Oliphant he met oftener; all the world knew and loved him; but he too disappeared in the way that all the world knows. Stirling of Keir, after one or two efforts, passed also from Adams's vision into Sir William Stirling-Maxwell. The only record of his wonderful visit to Fryston may perhaps exist still in the registers of the St. James's Club, for immediately afterwards Milnes proposed Henry Adams for membership, and unless his memory erred, the nomination was seconded by Tricoupi and endorsed by Laurence Oliphant and Evelyn Ashley. The list was a little singular for variety, but on the whole it suggested that the private secretary was getting on.

CHAPTER XIV

PROSE FOR EXPERIMENTATION: GERTRUDE STEIN

OTHER PROVINCES AND BORDER COUNTRIES OF PROSE

THE chapter on Henry Adams plaited together the various parts of the critical method advocated in this book. Equipped with the method, the student should eventually be able to travel into provinces of American literature not descanted upon in my combination of an anthology of prose specimens and a textbook of the principles of form and style. An obvious omission is prose for history. What are the requirements such prose must fill? To what extent have American historians (Francis Parkman, W. H. Prescott, John Motley, Henry Adams and others) approximated a good historical style? No great historical style has yet been written in our country. Wherein has been the failure? Or take up the subject of prose for letters. This is for Americans a veritable wilderness so far as settlers are concerned. Who are the best letter writers America can show and how do they compare with the better known correspondents in the mother literature?

Nor have I tried to do anything in those borderlands between prose and poetry, the region of the "prose poem" and of certain forms of "free verse": "hybrid prose-poetry," according to Saintsbury's terminology. These I shall leave exactly as described in *The History of English Prose*

Rhythm, adding only a conclusion by William Morrison Patterson[1] of Columbia University that seems from a totally different direction to confirm Saintsbury.

"The segregation of the phrases in VERS LIBRE, *produced by printing them on separate lines, serves chiefly as a means of keeping the focus of attention upon the* RHYTHM AS RHYTHM, *affecting thus both silent reading and oral delivery.* This 'rhythm' held before our attention is not so much the fundamental rhythmic experience, felt as prose or verse, but rather *the secondary or broader rhythmic grouping,* in which phrases, long and short, are *balanced* against each other, according to that native instinct by means of which we complacently make two and two equal five, so far as interest is concerned. . . . When once the game of literary balancing is introduced, the separate spacing of the phrases in free verse reminds us, gently but inevitably: 'This is a phrase! This is a phrase!' In spite of this fact, have we attained to anything that lifts us necessarily out of prose experience? What is achieved, as a rule, in Miss [Amy] Lowell's case, is emotional prose, emphatically phrased, excellent and moving. 'Spaced prose,' we may call it. With other writers the result is often merely unrhymed verse, with irregular length of line; or, as is frequently apparent in the writings of Edgar Lee Masters, a mosaic of bits of verse and bits of prose experience. Miss Lowell delivers her *vers libre* with much more swing and vim than one commonly hears in prose; but surely all particularly vigorous

---

[1] *The Rhythm of Prose,* by William Morrison Patterson, Columbia University. Professor Patterson studies his subject in the experimental psychological laboratory. He attacks the notion of objective rhythm and stresses subjective rhythmic experience. His remarks on acceleration or retardation of rhythm, on substitution, and on syncopation are his main contribution to the technic of the reader. I hold no brief for his book.

prose, if it is to be valued as a fit medium for vigorous thought and feeling, must also be thus delivered."

LITERATURE AS ALCHEMY AND AS CHEMISTRY

But before attempting in the final division of my book to outline certain universal standards of value for prose, I wish to say something, briefly, in behalf of the literary laboratory. The art of letters is in a way comparable to alchemy. The master of writing takes the gross substances of our vocabularies and the experiences symbolized by them and refines them into golden prose or golden poetry. But literature has its experimenting research chemists as well as its alchemists, and I am selecting Gertrude Stein as an example of the former class. The reader is entitled, so I hold, to be hostile to the impertinences of self-expression, but toward the literary laboratory *per se* he has no just reason for antagonism. He may be indifferent about it or he may be curious to examine its experiments, but only if he is unreasonably prejudiced against the new can he fly into anger. Waldo Frank, as we saw, is a mixed case, but it was specified that part of his work is legitimate laboratory research with literary devices, and indeed one could write some detailed short pieces on the effects of high verbal velocity, the possibilities of interior monologues, the value of lyrical crystallizations after studying his trials for innovations. Gertrude Stein is a clearer instance of literary experimentation, since she is more content to stay within that field than Frank and is more occupied with "pure research."

THE GODDESS OF EXPERIMENTAL WRITERS

Until lately Miss Stein has worked in the obscurity and the quiet that we associate with the hidden-from-the-public-eye activities of the laboratory specialist in the sciences. She is a member of a very intelligent American family: her brother, Leo Stein, has achieved a reputation as an æsthetician. Her training in academic psychology under William James and Munsterberg was thorough and has been followed by a long residence in Paris, where with great patience and a seeming indifference to public approval she has composed one huge document after another. A striking influence on her has been her association with post-impressionistic and cubist painters—with what effect on her efforts we shall shortly perceive. Now, by accident, she is famous and derided. In the stress of literary controversy she has even confessed to the belief that her writings may become classics for the future. But these recent wars over her work do not substantially change the picture her career makes. She remains the aloof and dignified goddess of those who wish only to devote their talents to experimenting with the properties of words.

I should say that the book to begin with in a study of Miss Stein's writing is *Three Lives,* published in 1909. It is lucidly written, but consists almost wholly of the curious exploitation of certain literary devices. Let me put before you the opening of the story in that book called "The Gentle Lena."

"Lena was patient, gentle, sweet and german. She had been a servant for four years and had liked it very well.

"Lena had been brought from Germany to Bridgepoint by a cousin and had been in the same place there for four years.

"This place Lena had found very good. There was a pleasant, unexacting mistress and her children, and they all liked Lena very well.

"There was a cook there who scolded Lena a great deal but Lena's german patience held no suffering and the good incessant woman really only scolded so for Lena's good.

"Lena's german voice when she knocked and called the family in the morning was as awakening, as soothing, and as appealing, as a delicate soft breeze in midday, summer. She stood in the hallway every morning a long time in her unexpectant and unsuffering german patience calling to the young ones to get up. She would call and wait a long time and then call again, always even, gentle, patient, while the young ones fell back often into that precious, tense, last bit of sleeping that gives a strength of joyous vigor in the young, over them that have come to the readiness of middle age, in their awakening."

GERTRUDE STEIN AND THE TIME SENSE OF LITERATURE

Wyndham Lewis thus describes the effect of the "prose-song" of Miss Stein upon himself: "It is weighted, projected, with a sibylline urge. It is mournful and monstrous, composed of dead and inanimate material. It is all fat, without nerve. Or the evident vitality that informs it is vegetable rather than animal. Its life is a low-grade, if tenacious, one." But it will do for us simply to tabulate her favorite devices. The first, quite well revealed in the quotation, is repetition. The points of stress in her sentences are very frequently words or phrases exactly repeated from the preceding sentence or sentences: they are cunningly placed so that the reader gets, when he expects something new, the full shock of the repetition. Or she "rings all the changes" on the central qualities of her theme: in this instance, the patient, gentle, sweet and german Lena. This naturally results in an almost static story structure— the very reverse of Waldo Frank's dynamics—for by repeating and repeating, Miss Stein very nearly makes her narrative stand still. In fact, her aim in *Three Lives* and other early books was not selection at all, but the utmost possible inclusiveness in her tale. She would discover how far one could go in a direction counter to the time-honored practice of fiction writers who sought variety rather than identity. The result was that it was less and less the building of a narrative that interested her and more and more the giving of the total quality of a character, usually of a very simple sort.

In later books Miss Stein developed her method to an extreme and made it grandiose. Her pieces are always beginning, always recurring, always very inclusive. She has told us that she wished first to produce a prolonged present in her writings and later she aimed to create a continuous present. In other words, Miss Stein is deliberately experimenting with our time sense, to congeal or freeze time, as it were, into a continuous present moment. As she "explains" it: "It is understood by this time that everything is the same except composition and time, composition and the time of the composition and the time in the composition."

Two sources may be named for this enormous revolution which Miss Stein has proclaimed and tried to effect. One is her association with the advanced painters of our age and the other is her acceptance of such romantic philosophers as Bergson, with their glorification of the flux of existence.

But literature is a time art, whereas painting is not. The painter has space for his medium and can take advantage of the eye's capacity for simultaneity of vision. Time as we experience it is *succession* and literature is condemned, for worse or better, to the effects that it can extract from succession. A piece of writing can never come at once and wholly in view as a painting can.

FALLACIES

We touch here a fairly persistent fallacy, the belief that words can produce the effects proper to the other arts, such as painting, sculpture, and music. But our associations with colored shapes are with all the other colored shapes in our personal history; our associations with sculptured objects are with all the other tri-dimensional objects we have known; our associations with music are auditory. Whereas our associations with words are with other words. This it is that makes it not so much illegitimate as impossible to try to do with words what the painter does with color, the sculptor with clay and marble, and the musician with sound. This is not to say that writing cannot be vividly pictorial or solidly formed or musical, but these are all subsidiary characteristics. Primarily, it must be true to the innate genius of words and their proper associations.

One might say that by definition the literary chemist tries to break down the impossible, tries, that is, to disintegrate the atomic forces of writing for the sake of knowing more about them or in pursuit of novel recombinations. Both the practitioners and the enjoyers of the art of writing can learn what not to do as well as what can be done from such attempts, and it is for that reason that I invite you to turn a speculative and inquisitive eye upon the contribution of Miss Stein to contemporary prose.

MISS FURR AND MISS SKEENE[2]

By Gertrude Stein

Helen Furr had quite a pleasant home. Mrs. Furr was quite a pleasant woman. Mr. Furr was quite a pleasant man. Helen Furr had quite a pleasant voice, a voice quite worth cultivating. She did not mind working. She worked to cultivate her voice. She did not find it gay living in the same place where she had always been living. She went to a place where some were cultivating something, voices and other things needing cultivating. She met Georgine Skeene there who was cultivating her voice which some thought was quite a pleasant one. Helen Furr and Georgine Skeene lived together then. Georgine Skeene liked travelling. Helen Furr did not care about travelling, she liked to stay in one place and be gay there. They were together then and travelled to another place and stayed there and were gay there.

They stayed there and were gay there, not very gay there, just gay there. They were both gay there, they were regularly working there both of them cultivating their voices there, they were both gay there. Georgine Skeene was gay there and she was regular, regular in being gay, regular in not being gay, regular in being a gay one who was one not being gay longer than was needed to be one being quite a

[2]From *Geography and Plays,* by Gertrude Stein, copyright, 1923, by The Four Seas Company.

gay one. They were both gay then there and working there then.

They were in a way both gay there where there were many cultivating something. They were both regular in being gay there. Helen Furr was gay there, she was gayer and gayer there and really she was just gay there, she was gayer and gayer there, that is to say she found ways of being gay there that she was using in being gay there. She was gay there, not gayer and gayer, just gay there, that is to say she was not gayer by using the things she found there that were gay things, she was gay there, always she was gay there.

They were quite regularly gay there, Helen Furr and Georgine Skeene, they were regularly gay there where they were gay. They were very regularly gay.

To be regularly gay was to do every day the gay thing that they did every day. To be regularly gay was to end every day at the same time after they had been regularly gay. They were regularly gay. They were gay every day. They ended every day in the same way, at the same time, and they had been every day regularly gay.

The voice Helen Furr was cultivating was quite a pleasant one. The voice Georgine Skeene was cultivating was, some said, a better one. The voice Helen Furr was cultivating was quite a pleasant one. The voice Georgine Skeene was cultivating was, some said, a better one. The voice Helen Furr was cultivating she cultivated and it was quite completely a pleasant enough one then, a cultivated enough one then. The voice Georgine Skeene was cultivating she did not cultivate too much. She cultivated it quite some. She cultivated and she would sometime go on cultivating it and it was not then an unpleasant one, it would not be then an unpleasant one, it would be a quite richly enough cultivated one, it would be quite richly enough to be a pleasant enough one.

They were gay where there were many cultivating something. The two were gay there, were regularly gay there. Georgine Skeene would have liked to do more travelling. They did some travelling, not very much travelling, Georgine Skeene would have liked to do more travelling, Helen Furr did not care about doing travelling, she liked to stay in a place and be gay there.

They stayed in a place and were gay there, both of them stayed there, they stayed together there, they were gay there, they were regularly gay there.

They went quite often, not very often, but they did go back to where Helen Furr had a pleasant enough home and then Georgine Skeene went to a place where her brother had quite some distinction. They both went, every few years, went visiting to where Helen Furr had quite a pleasant home. Certainly Helen Furr would not find it gay to stay, she did not find it gay, she said she would not stay, she said she did not find it gay, she said she would not stay where she did not find it gay, she said she found it gay where she did stay and she did stay there where very many were cultivating something. She did stay there. She always did find it gay there.

She went to see them where she had always been living and where she did not find it gay. She had a pleasant home there, Mrs. Furr was a pleasant enough woman, Mr. Furr was a pleasant enough man, Helen told them and they were not worrying, that she did not find it gay living where she had always been living.

Georgine Skeene and Helen Furr were living where they were both cultivating their voices and they were gay there. They visited where Helen Furr had come from and then they went to where they were living where they were then regularly living.

There were some dark and heavy men there then. There were some who were not so heavy and some who were not so dark. Helen Furr and Georgine Skeene sat regularly with them. They sat regularly with the ones who were dark and heavy. They sat regularly with the ones who were not so dark. They sat regularly with the ones that were not so heavy. They sat with them regularly, sat with some of them. They went with them regularly went with them. They were regular then, they were gay then, they were where they wanted to be then where it was gay to be then, they were regularly gay then. There were men there who were dark and heavy and they sat with them with Helen Furr and Georgine Skeene and they went with them with Miss Furr and Miss Skeene, and they went with the heavy and dark men Miss Furr and Miss Skeene went with them, and they sat with them, Miss Furr and Miss Skeene sat with them, and there were other men, some were not heavy men and they sat with Miss Furr and Miss Skeene and Miss Furr and Miss Skeene sat with them, and there were other men who were not dark men and they sat with Miss Furr and Miss Skeene and Miss Furr and Miss Skeene sat with them. Miss Furr and Miss Skeene went with them and they went with Miss Furr and Miss Skeene, some who were not heavy men, some who were not dark men. Miss Furr and Miss Skeene sat regularly, they sat with some men. Miss Furr and Miss Skeene went and there were some men with them. There were men and Miss Furr and Miss Skeene went with them, went somewhere with them, went with some of them.

Helen Furr and Georgine Skeene were regularly living where very many were living and cultivating in themselves something. Helen Furr and Georgine Skeene were living very regularly then, being very regular then in being gay then. They did then learn many ways to be gay and they were then being gay being quite regular in being gay, being gay and they were learning little things, little things in ways of being gay, they were very regular then, they were learning very many little things in ways of being gay, they were being gay and using these little things they were learning to have to be gay with regularly gay with them and they were gay the same amount they had been gay. They were quite gay, they were quite regular, they were learning little things, gay little things, they were gay inside them the same amount they had been gay, they were gay the same length of time they had been gay every day.

They were regular in being gay, they learned little things that are things in being gay, they learned many little things that are things in being gay, they were gay every day, they were regular, they were gay, they were gay the same length of time every day, they were gay, they were quite regularly gay.

Georgine Skeene went away to stay two months with her brother. Helen Furr did not go then to stay with her father and her mother. Helen Furr stayed there where they had been regularly living the two of them and she would then certainly not be lonesome, she would go on being gay. She did go on being gay. She was not any more gay but she was gay longer every day than they had been being gay when they were together being gay. She was gay then quite exactly the same way. She learned a few more little ways of being in being gay. She was quite gay and in the same way, the same way she had been gay and she was gay a little longer in the day, more of each day she was gay. She was gay longer every day than when the two of them had been being gay. She was gay quite in the way they had been gay, quite in the same way.

She was not lonesome then, she was not at all feeling any need of having Georgine Skeene. She was not astonished at this thing. She would have been a little astonished by this thing but she knew she was not astonished at anything and so she was not astonished at this thing not astonished at not feeling any need of having Georgine Skeene.

Helen Furr had quite a completely pleasant voice and it was quite well enough cultivated and she could use it and she did use it but then there was not any way of working at cultivating a completely pleasant voice when it has become a quite completely well enough cultivated one, and there was not much use in using it when one was not wanting it to be helping to make one a gay one. Helen Furr was not needing using her voice to be a gay one. She was gay then and sometimes she used her voice and she was not using it very often. It was quite completely enough cultivated and it was quite completely a pleasant one and she did not use it very often. She was then, she was quite exactly as gay as she had been, she was gay a little longer in the day than she had been.

She was gay exactly the same way. She was never tired of being gay that way. She had learned very many little ways to use in being gay. Very many were telling about using other ways in being gay. She was gay enough, she was always gay exactly the same way, she was always learning little things to use in being gay, she was telling about using other ways in being gay, she was telling about learning other ways in being gay, she would be using other ways in being gay, she would always be gay in the same way, when Georgine Skeene was there not so long each day as when Georgine Skeene was away. She would always be gay in the same way.

She came to using many ways in being gay, she came to use every way in being gay. She went on living where many were cultivating something and she was gay, she had used every way to be gay.

They did not live together then Helen Furr and Georgine Skeene, Helen Furr lived there the longer where they had been living regularly together. Then neither of them were living there any longer. Helen Furr was living somewhere else then and telling some about being gay and she was gay then and she was living quite regularly then. She was regularly gay then. She was quite regular in being gay then. She remembered all the little ways of being gay. She used all the little ways of being gay. She was quite regularly gay. She told many then the way of being gay, she taught very many then little ways they could use in being gay. She was living very well, she was gay then, she went on living then, she was regular in being gay, she always was living very well and was gay very well and was telling about little ways one could be learning to use in being gay, and later was telling them quite often, telling them again and again.

Part Five

THE FUTURE OF AMERICAN PROSE

CHAPTER XV

THE QUEST OF THE PERFECT STYLE

A PESSIMISTIC STOCK TAKING

STRONG doubts of the progress of American prose must come to anyone who spends a few weeks in critical contemplation of what prose we have so far accumulated. Where is there any indisputable advance in prose quality since the pens of Hawthorne, Thoreau, and Melville were dropped? Henry James is gone also, and has any living novelist exceeded his grasp of form? Nay, one must answer: the succession has not been maintained. Yet even these elder writers did not make exertion on the highest slopes of Olympus, and we must look downward from where they climbed to see the labors of our contemporaries.

Beyond caviling, American prose style to-day shows all the symptoms of decline: it has contracted, grown infirm, or turned wayward. Theoretically our literature is young, but in point of fact it behaves like the aged, for it has lost power and adaptability and awareness. Think of the course of American fiction: from the abounding vigor of Melville to the lassitude of James Branch Cabell, from the finesse of Henry James to the crudity of Theodore Dreiser, from the concentrated imaginative plots of Poe to the loose wandering daydreams of Sherwood Anderson. Think that it has been only nineteen years from *The Faith Healer* to the *Lazarus Laughed* of O'Neill—a steep drop from a workmanlike drama[1] to a widely praised but mawkish and clumsy attempt to "accept life." The humorists and the critics keep their craft in good condition but scarcely do anything more. As for philosophic style in the United States, it is, with the exception of Santayana, either aridly written or else a jargon.

Perhaps our view is too short. Splendid growths may even now be just beneath the surface. But one may well be distrustful of the atmosphere that American stylists must breathe and so find it warrantable to yield to pessimism. For there exists to-day, combined with a rather sweeping belittlement of what earlier American writers have performed, a general feeling of complacency about the future of American letters. It is unthinkingly assumed that in this field, as of course in all others, "we moderns" are progressing rapidly, and a great American literary renaissance lies just within the next decade. But it is possible to show cause in the next paragraph why this optimism is not salutary.

We award praise on the basis of an average standard. If we were farmers we would call any apple that was above the average of our orchard's yield an extraordinarily fine apple. And if each season our orchard progressively fell off in quality we would still continue to bestow superlatives on those individual apples that were just a little better. It is much that way with the "annual crop" of literature. The professional reviewer and the steady reader of current books demand something above the average level of excellence: this they hail as a masterpiece; but they remain oblivious of the fact that as the average sinks, so declines also the merit

[1] It was certainly not more than that.

of what they deem above the average. By this system of judgment retrogression may actually look like progression, for all one has to do is to forget past greatness and measure only from current mediocrity.

Against this complacency let us join to urge the coming of a mood of conquest. We require a Swift, a Nietzsche, to blight our easy assurances and to fire us with a gayly serious resolve to conquer the loftier slopes of prose. We need the serious introduction into our thoughts on prose of the idea of perfection. We need a norm of style. But how may we set forth on this forlorn yet tonic and inspiring quest of the perfect style?

THE USE OF ANTHOLOGIES

The first step is to acquire a wider acquaintance with the styles and forms that already exist in English literature, for the confines of American prose do not give us enough variety nor enough of the higher degrees of excellence. Eventually, we shall have to make the entire world of literature our searching grounds, but it is undertaking enough now to broaden our view from the province of American literature to the continent of English letters. Anthologies will greatly facilitate our work, and very fortunately there are two ably arranged anthologies available, the *Oxford Book of English Prose,* edited by Quiller-Couch, and *The Pageant of English Prose,* edited by R. M. Leonard. With these in our possession we can now set out in real earnest to be literary detectives—seeking, it is hardly necessary to add, to detect virtues as well as crimes.

In that rôle we shall find that short passages are not unjust to authors when we are considering style alone, but are in fact, in the majority of cases, quite adequate. They are comparable to those brief glimpses of a person that tell a trained detective so surprisingly much about that person's behavior. This is, as everyone knows, because the detective has developed the keenness of his observation and resorts to categories of physical phenomena to observe, such as facial expression, gestures, carriage, tone of voice, mannerisms, and so on. The trained reader should also have his system of categories (vocabulary, rhythm, tone, order of thought, et cetera) under which to assemble his impressions, and he should likewise have trained his keenness for observing stylistic manifestations. Nothing, then, is better practice than to look upon an anthology of prose as a procession of styles which are swiftly to be analyzed and named by the reader.

The lure of this kind of pursuit is the theme of a novelette by Henry James, *The Figure in the Carpet*, and a reading of that delectable tale of the hunt for the "buried treasure" in Hugh Vereker's literary style and form is an excellent stimulant before prospecting for "gold and gems" on one's own initiative. In the course of his story James formulates an ideal attitude for the student of style, and his novelette does indeed put the reader in the posture of George Corvick. "For the few persons, at any rate," James says, "abnormal or not, with whom my anecdote is concerned, literature was a game of skill, and skill meant courage, and courage meant honour, and honour meant passion, meant life. The stake on the table was of a different substance, and our roulette was the revolving mind, but we sat round the green board as intently as the grim gamblers at Monte Carlo." This is a serious attitude toward the technic of writing and not at all to be disparaged. It is not, however, serious enough, not comprehensive enough, for the study of values in literature, for values cannot be determined without a broader and deeper reference to life itself than James's characters care to make.

But, returning to our anthologies of English prose, here, in the words of one of the editors, R. M. Leonard, "will be found authors clad in ermine and robes of state; in the divine's sober garments, decked occasionally with the riband of a jest; in drab of formal cut; in the camel's hair of the prophet; in slashed doublet and other fantastic attire, furnished, perhaps, with the feathers and rapiers of the wits, or with cap and bells; in the workaday clothes of generation after generation; while the women may be seen in turban and ruff and farthingale or whatever may chance to be the kaleidoscopic fashion of the passing moment. The prose exemplified (in English literature) embraces history, philosophy, theology, natural and political science, fiction, essays, table talk, translations, dedications, diaries, letters, and parliamentary, pulpit and forensic oratory." No such picture could be drawn from a critical anthology, did one exist, of American prose, and it suggests one more reason for our restless feeling of dissatisfaction with the present state of American letters. American literature is incomplete. There are too many absent styles, too many missing forms. Where, for instance, is there among us a "dancing master of prose" such as Max Beerbohm? Who are our writers who correspond to Fielding and Thackeray? Where are our composers of dialogues? Or our masters of parables? Not until we fill in all the gaps will our literature cease to seem specialized, one-sided, underdeveloped. But it is precisely the mood to conquer these unfilled spaces that does not prevail in our criticism and among our writers. We converse a great deal about "new forms" while we neglect complacently the fact that we have not attained proficiency in many of the old forms. This is disastrous because the old forms stand in vital relation to the parts of a well-developed national psychology, and the only invention that is worth while is one that extends the development of that psychology.

But some would say that we are the inheritors of English literature. What the English have, we share with them: what they do now, we participate in. This would be so if American psychology had not, owing to a differing environment and history and racial intermixture, shifted so radically from its English basis. As it is, we are a different national Being on the way, so we can hope, to becoming an individuality among the nations of this planet. Ours is the task, not, indeed, of continuing to revolt like an adolescent from the mother culture, but of creating a parallel to it and eventually of surpassing it. For no one, unbiased by patriotism, would claim that English culture has been among the greatest recorded on our earth.

APOLLO AND DIONYSUS

We can stay within our subject and test this assertion. For years the most brilliant of living English literary critics, A. R. Orage, has maintained that the perfect English prose style has never been written. In order to discover the meaning of his contention it will be necessary to think of literature, not laterally in terms of breadth and variety as we have just been doing, but vertically. We must now think in terms of elevation, of ascending standards. We must try to picture the mount of Olympus, the seat of the deity of prose, Apollo.

The poets worship Dionysus, but the prosemen gaze up at the "shining one," the soothsaying god, the god of all plastic energies: they keep in mind "that measure restraint, that freedom from the wilder emotions, that philosophical calm of the sculptor-god." The quotation is from Nietzsche's *The Birth of Tragedy*. Read it, for no better account exists of the two principal forms of art expression possible to man and their roots in two kinds of energy, the Apollonian dream and the Dionysian ecstasy. The dramatic contrast between prose and poetry, between their deities, between their magic mountains of Olympus and Parnassus, inspired Nietzsche to a profound interpretation of Greek mythology. Read it, I say again, for Nietzsche will infect us with what Henry James's seekers of the figure in the carpet utterly lacked: the bold unslaked craving of those who seek in art as elsewhere for the very ground plan of reality. With this thirst aroused we can then really make advantageous use of a map of Olympus.

It befits me better to choose simpler terms for the opposition between poetry and prose than the Dionysian-Apollonian conflict and its resolution in a vision of mutual necessity. So I shall say that technically the difference is that poetry is metered, and prose, as Aristotle defined it, neither possesses meter nor is it destitute of rhythm. Psychologically, the difference is that prose presents thought and the emotion provoked by it, whereas poetry gives us the emotion first and the thought arising from it as a consequence. Figuratively, it is the singer (poetry) and the speaker (prose) that we must put in contrast.

If we dwell a little on these two figures we shall come to regard the "shackles" of verse somewhat differently from the custom of to-day. Poetry originates in a Dionysian mood, and the assumption is that were it not for certain regulations and restrictions the poet would altogether escape. He is truly a shackled or caged singer, but it is by virtue of regular metre that he intensifies and forms his songs. It is his regular metre, which inevitably is associated with music, not with thought, that gives his verse its dominant emotional quality. Now look at the substitute for the speaker, the prosist. The irregular beat of prose seems to guarantee that the writer is cool and collected. He is not dithyrambic, not wildly exuberant: he can be trusted in his Apollonian state to do very well without bars.

Furthermore: we do not expect the singer to sing from himself but to act as a medium. We are not, therefore, concerned with a singer's personality, but with the singer as artist. We are fond of saying that the singer or his counterpart, the poet, is "possessed" or "a reed shaken in the wind." But it is the reverse when we turn to the speaker or prosist, for while poetry is always someone singing, the speaker appears to us as mind (more or less) and appeals to our minds (more or less).

One last distinction, and then we may turn to the lowest slopes of Olympus. The ascent of Parnassus is to ecstasy: the ascent of Olympus is to sublimity. But we commence far down with journalism.

THE FIRST ZONE OF OLYMPUS

Journalism cannot be defined by forms, for it may be novels or plays as well as magazine articles and newspaper reports. It is not a term of reproach, but it is sometimes employed as such when the journalist pretends to be an artist. It is, however, a perplexing label to define. Certainly, the journalist has a pronounced practical bent: he writes solely for his bread and butter. Yet salability cannot be used as the true criterion, for great artists have been known to be equally practical. Nor can we debar journalism from literary value: there is good journalism, such as the prose of William James, and there is bad and debased journalism.

There is, however, one way of pinning our word down to some specific meaning, and that is to think of the reader of journalism. The newspaper man or magazinist always strictly limits his appeal. He takes his public as it is in its average state and he strikes purely at average psychology. He demands no exertion of thought above the average : he seeks to evoke no emotional responses not customarily made in the rounds of diurnal life. The middle ground of human psychology is his to exploit, but he must not trespass above it. His writings are like ordinary conversation : they pass the time pleasantly or interestingly or informatively, but they do not change or enhance or powerfully affect the makeup of the reader. Limitation of appeal to the reader by avoiding all play for the reader's latencies and by concentrating only on his actual constitution is the hallmark of journalism. Since the reader's actual constitution is largely, in fact overwhelmingly, sensational, it follows that journalism must bear heavily upon the reader's sensations of life.

This is by the way of description of the crowded lowest slope of Olympus. Now let us look up and we shall be able to make out two higher regions or belts of prose writings. They are called Prose and Scripture. As our gaze travels up through them, we shall find the throng becoming less dense until at the top there is only a sublime handful and these lived remote from our period.

THE HIGHER ZONES: PROSE AND SCRIPTURE

In order to keep the whole mountain in view I ought to present the broad distinction between Prose and Scripture before trying to isolate the cardinal virtues of Prose. Prose is human: Scripture is "superhuman" or "godlike." This is to say that Prose deals (with that appropriateness of tone which is style) with human and interhuman affairs, the relations of man to man, and Scripture deals (again with that appropriateness of tone which is style) with the relations of man to the cosmos. Prose is not trivial, not anchored to "average sense" or common nonsense: it can be intensely serious and practical; it is sweet reasonable discourse among men about their local affairs. Scripture, on the other hand, aims to treat with appropriate technic the larger issues of life: the future of man, the immortality of the soul, the obligation of man to his creator, man as a world being. In short, Prose is concerned with concrete existence, with bodies, Scripture with souls.

MINOR AND MAJOR PROSE

There are two subdivisions of each great form of prose writing: Minor Prose and Major Prose, Minor Scripture and Major Scripture. A little tilt between two English critics, Sir Arthur Quiller-Couch and Arthur Clutton-Brock, will give us the keys to Minor and Major Prose. It is Quiller-Couch's contention that Persuasion "is the first virtue of Prose, whether in narrative or argument. Defoe's art in telling of Crusoe's visits to the wreck is all bent on persuading you that it really happened and *just so;* as Burke, in pleading for conciliation with the American colonists, is bent on marshalling argument upon argument why conciliation is expedient besides being just. . . . But persuasion, whether in narrative or in argument, is a long process, insinuating, piling up proof; and Prose its medium is therefore naturally long." Clutton-Brock, however, says: "Prose of its very nature is longer than verse, and the virtues peculiar to it manifest themselves gradually . . . the cardinal virtue of prose is justice . . . justice needs inquiry, patience, and a control even of the noblest passions. . . . By justice here I do not mean justice only to particular people or ideas, but a habit of justice in all the processes of thought, a style tranquillized and a form moulded by habit. The master of prose is not cold, but he will not let any word or image inflame him with a heat irrelevant to his purpose. . . . But he has his reward, for he is trusted and convinces, as those who are at the mercy of their own eloquence do not."

So here we have Quiller-Couch asserting that the cardinal virtue of Prose is Persuasion and Clutton-Brock saying that it is Justice, and in a manner they are both right. Everyone recognizes two schools of Prose, but critics differ as to which is superior. What I say here—though it is heresy to Saintsbury—is that the aim of Minor Prose is Persuasion, the aim of Major Prose is Justice.

If I name some Minor Prose writers from English literature the reader may be set on the way to making his own application of these classifying remarks. Consider the prose of four masters, Sir Thomas Malory, Sir Thomas Browne, Daniel Defoe, and Charles Lamb, and you should be able to disengage the qualities of Minor Prose. It is rhetorical; it is based on the assumption that the reader is not on a level with the writer and seeks therefore to persuade him; it evokes a state of feeling. But you are not provoked to reflect.

American literature is not deficient in Minor Prose, as two examples will show. Washington Irving's well-known sentimental description of the English stagecoach in *The*

Sketch Book is one, and I need only to extract a few sentences from it to bathe us all in emotional associations.

"Perhaps it might be owing to the pleasing serenity that reigned in my own mind, that I fancied I saw cheerfulness in every countenance throughout the journey. A stage coach, however, carries animation always with it, and puts the world in motion as it whirls along. The horn, sounded at the entrance of a village, produces a general bustle. Some hasten forth to meet friends; some with bundles and bandboxes to secure places, and in the hurry of the moment can hardly take leave of the group that accompanies them. In the meantime the coachman has a world of small commissions to execute. Sometimes he delivers a hare or a pheasant; sometimes jerks a small parcel or newspaper to the door of a public-house; and sometimes, with knowing leer and words of sly import, hands to some housemaid an odd-shaped *billet doux* from some rustic admirer."

That may be called, if one wishes, Minor Prose Simple. Herman Melville will give us Minor Prose Grand.

"When gliding by the Bashee isles we emerged at last upon the great South Sea; were it not for other things, I could have greeted my dear Pacific with uncounted thanks, for now the long supplication of my youth was answered; that serene ocean rolled eastward from me a thousand leagues of blue.

"There is, one knows not what sweet mystery about this sea, whose gently awful stirrings seem to speak of some hidden soul beneath; like those fabled undulations of the Ephesian sod over the buried Evangelist St. John. And meet it is, that over these sea-pastures, wide-rolling watery prairies and Potters' Fields of all four continents, the waves should rise and fall, and ebb and flow unceasingly; for here, millions of mixed shades and shadows, drowned dreams, somnambulisms, reveries; all that we call lives and souls, lie dreaming, dreaming, still; tossing like slumberers in their beds; the ever-rolling waves but made so by their restlessness.

"To any meditative Magian rover, this serene Pacific, once beheld, must ever after be the sea of his adoption. It rolls the midmost waters of the world, the Indian Ocean and the Atlantic being but its arms. The same waves wash the moles of the new-built California towns, but yesterday planted by the recentest race of men, lave the faded but still gorgeous skirts of Asiatic lands, older than Abraham; while all between float milky-ways of coral isles, and low-lying, endless, unknown archipelagos, and impenetrable Japans. Thus this mysterious, divine Pacific zones the world's whole bulk about; makes all coasts one bay to it; seems the tide-beating heart of earth. Lifted by those eternal swells, you needs must own the seductive god, bowing your head to Pan."

As John Freeman says of this passage, "The words become more than words, the meaning is increased by suggestion and the excitement of the mind at the touch of so much beauty, and apprehensions come in crowds, all quickening and intensifying as they come." Such is the effect of very fine Minor Prose.

Major Prose, however, is the essence of reasonableness or justice. Here the aim is precisely to provoke reflection in the reader by passing from the particular to the general, by using the concrete only for the sake of its philosophical implications. Again I shall name four English writers and quote from two Americans within this region of Major Prose. The four writers can be Sir Thomas More, Francis Bacon, Swift (according to Orage, the greatest of all English prosists), and Matthew Arnold. The two quotations can be taken from Henry Adams and from Henry David Thoreau. Observe how each broadens the concrete matters of which he speaks, not into a pool of feeling, but into a maze of thinking, leaving us with something on which to reflect. This is Adams:

"All the steam in the world could not, like the Virgin, build Chartres.

"Yet in mechanics, whatever the mechanicians might think, both energies acted as interchangeable forces on man, and by action on man all known force may be measured. Indeed, few men of science measured force in any other way. After once admitting that a straight line was the shortest distance between two points, no serious mathematician cared to deny anything that suited his convenience, and rejected no symbol, unproved or unproveable, that helped him to accomplish work. The symbol was force, as a compass-needle or a triangle was force, as the mechanist might prove by losing it, and nothing could be gained by ignoring their value. Symbol or energy, the Virgin had acted as the greatest force the Western world ever felt, and had drawn man's activities to herself more strongly than any other power, natural or supernatural, had ever done; the historian's business was to follow the track of the energy; to find where it came from and where it went to; its complex source and shifting channels; its values, equivalents, conversions. It could scarcely be more complex than radium; it could hardly be deflected, diverted, polarized, absorbed more perplexingly than other radiant matter. Adams knew nothing about any of them, but as a mathematical problem of influence on human progress, though all were occult, all reacted on his mind, and he rather inclined to think the Virgin easiest to handle."

And this is from Thoreau's *Journal:*

"Nothing goes by luck in composition. It allows of no tricks. The best you can write will be the best you are. Every sentence is the result of a long probation. The author's character is read from title-page to end. Of this he never corrects the proofs. We read it as the essential character of a handwriting without regard to the flourishes. And so of the rest of our actions; it runs as straight as a ruled line through them all, no matter how many curvets about it. Our whole life is taxed for the least thing well done; it is its net result. How we eat, drink, sleep, and use our desultory hours, now in these indifferent days, with no eye to observe and no occasion [to] excite us, determines our authority and capacity for the time to come."

The main thing is to comprehend the principles for classifying prose writings, and perhaps enough has been given to make them clear. But some defense should be made of the decision to call the type of prose that Oliver Wendell Holmes and Laurence Sterne wrote Minor, and to call Major the type of prose done by, let us say, Coleridge and Thackeray. The reasons are psychological. Man is not the only emotional being on our planet: animals share with us the more rudimentary feelings. But man is alone the reasoning creature. Hence, it follows that the more reasonable man's discourse becomes, the more human it is. Humanity is the top note of organic life, and just as it is our criterion for ranking lower beings, namely, the extent to which they approach our powers, so it can be our criterion for ranking the expressions of man. How far do they realize our specifically human potentialities? Again, the effects of emotionalized prose are transient: the state of feeling evaporates and we are left with only a memory of it. But reasoning prose produces a more stable effect: it lasts longer. Therefore we call it Major.

THE SUMMIT OF PROSE

As I look now at the heights of Scripture I feel, I confess, more like indulging in aposiopesis than in trying to suggest qualities and works. But some slight remarks, at least, are demanded by my undertaking. The difficulty is magnified because, as Thoreau charged, "most men do not know that any nation but the Hebrews have had a Scripture," but it behooves us not to be like most men. I have said that Scripture divides into Minor and Major, and these parallel the divisions of Prose. Minor Scripture has for its object the evocation of cosmic emotion, Major Scripture for its object the evocation of cosmic understanding. Prophecy is the technical name for Minor Scripture, and it may be said to be *uttered*. Whereas Major Scripture is *delivered* and is the outcome of "an ecstasy of understanding" or a "state of reflection raised to a state of illumination."

A few examples—there could not be many chosen from English and American letters—will enable the reader to start forming more definite impressions of what Minor Scripture is. The examples are Jeremy Taylor, William Blake, John Henry Newman, Milton, and, among Americans, some parts of Whitman's prose. But far better examples can be found outside Anglo-Saxon letters. Isaiah, some of the Psalmists, St. Paul, are supreme examples of Prophecy.

The Prophet, compared to the Sage who delivers Major Scripture, is always a little insecure. The Sage speaks in his own right and depends on no authority but his own. He is Jesus of the Sermon on the Mount as compared with the Prophet, St. Paul, preaching on Mars Hill. He is Pythagoras delivering his *Golden Verses*. He is Lao-tze; he is the author of the Egyptian Book of the Dead; he is the author of the Bhagavad-Gita.

Here, certainly, on this highest plane of all, English and American literature have nothing to say, and they have, as we have seen, scarcely any representatives on the next highest plane. And this, I conceive, is the purport of Orage's dictum that the perfect English prose style is yet to be written.[2]

We descend now to the problems of contemporary American literature. What is needed is a direction toward some clear remote goal, and this the quest of the perfect style will provide. What is needed for writers and readers and critics alike is some North Star to guide by, some map by which we can find ourselves traveling, and that need the diagrammatic representation of Olympus will take care of. Introduce seriously the idea of perfection and even though we do not, as is most likely, attain it, we shall be stretching our capacities and achieving greater things than flower spontaneously in chaos. Goethe said of the scholar, "If he cannot accomplish, he shall exercise himself." This applies to American literature now. Let it inaugurate an Era of Exercise—toward the Sublime!

---

[2]The scheme for grading the dwellers on Olympus is derived from A. R. Orage's lectures on literature.

STANDARD TABLE OF METRICAL FEET

Feet of One Syllable	Of Two Syllables	Of Three	Of Four	Of Five	Of Six
Monosyllabic, —	Iamb, ˘ — Pyrrhic, ˘ ˘ Spondee, — — Trochee, — ˘	Amphibrach, ˘ — ˘ Anapæst, ˘ ˘ — Anti-Bacchic, ˘ — — Bacchic, — — ˘ Cretic, — ˘ — Dactyl, — ˘ ˘ Molossus, — — — Tribach, ˘ ˘ ˘	Antipast, ˘ — — ˘ Choriamb, — ˘ ˘ — Di—iamb, ˘ — ˘ — Dispondee, — — — — Ditrochee, — ˘ — ˘ Epitrite (four forms) ˘ — — —, — ˘ — —, — — ˘ —, — — — ˘ Ionic *a majore*, — — ˘ ˘ Ionic *a minore*, ˘ ˘ — — Pæon (four forms) — ˘ ˘ ˘, ˘ — ˘ ˘, ˘ ˘ — ˘, ˘ ˘ ˘ — Proceleusmatic, ˘ ˘ ˘ ˘	Dochmiac. Many possible combinations. The most common are two long and three short, one long and four short, three long and two short.	The "sixer" is not common.

STANDARD TABLE OF CONSONANTS

Manner of Formation	Place of Articulation →	Glottal — Throat	Guttural or Velar (Back) — Root of tongue and soft palate	Palatal (Front) — Middle of tongue and hard palate	Dental, Blade — Blade of tongue and gums. Tip of tongue raised	Dental, Blade — Blade of tongue and teeth	Dental, Point — Tip of tongue and gums back of upper teeth	Dental, Point — Tip of tongue and edge of teeth (Interdental)	Labial or Lip — Lower lip and upper teeth (Labiodental)	Labial or Lip — Both lips (Bilabial)
Stopped consonants or stops	Voiced		**g** (go)				**d** (do)			**b** (boy)
Stopped consonants or stops	Voiceless		**k** (cow)				**t** (ten)			**p** (pit)
Fricatives (Open consonants or continuants)	Voiced				**zh** (azure), **j** (jet)	**z** (zeal)		**th** (then)	**v** (vim)	
Fricatives (Open consonants or continuants)	Voiceless	**h** (him)	(wh)		**sh** (she), **ch** (chop).	**s** (so)		**th** (thin)	**f** (fine)	**wh** (why)
Nasals (Vowel-like consonants)	Voiced		**ng** (sing) or η (iŋk)				**n** (no)			**m** (me)
Liquids (Vowel-like consonants)	Voiced						**l** (lip)	**r** (red)		
Semi-vowels (Vowel-like consonants)	Voiced		(w)	**y** (yet)						**w** (we)